When the Day Breaks

RIK PINXTEN

WHEN THE DAY BREAKS

ESSAYS

IN

ANTHROPOLOGY

AND

PHILOSOPHY

PETER LANG

Frankfurt am Main · Berlin · Bern · New York · Paris · Wien

Die Deutsche Bibliothek - CIP-Einheitsaufnahme

Pinxten, Rik:

When the day breaks : essays in anthropology and philosophy /
Rik Pinxten. - Frankfurt am Main ; Berlin ; Bern ; New York ;
Paris ; Wien : Lang, 1997
    ISBN 3-631-32266-6

ISBN 3-631-32266-6
US-ISBN 0-8204-3514-7

© Peter Lang GmbH
Europäischer Verlag der Wissenschaften
Frankfurt am Main 1997
Printed in Germany 1 2   4 5 6 7

Dedicated to Etienne VERMEERSCH
my erstwhile teacher and guide,
and eternal counterpart.

ACKNOWLEDGEMENT

Some of the chapters in this book have been published before. They have been more or less thoroughly updated in the present volume, and I received permission to reuse them from the former publishers:

– Chapter 1: 'Fieldwork as a form of intercultural communication' was first published in Blommaert, J. & J. Verschueren (Eds.) *The Pragmatics of International and Intercultural Communication.* 1991, 131-144. J. Benjamins Publications kindly granted the right to reprint.

– Chapter 2: 'Observation in anthropology' is a severely updated version of 'Observation in anthropology: postitivism and subjectivism combined', published originallly in *Communication & Cognition*, 14, 1981.

– Chapter 3: 'Concepts in anthropology' appeared earlier under the title 'Anthropological concepts' in *Communication & Cognition*, 17, 1981. Communication & Cognition publishers granted me the right to reprint both papers here.

– Chapter 5: 'The learner's view of learning' (with C.R. Farrer) appeared before under the title 'On learning: a comparative view' in *Cultural Dynamics*, III, 1990, 233-251. Brill Publishers, Leiden kindly granted permission to reprint.

– Chapter 6: 'Learning from the teacher's point of view. Geometry.' first appeared under the title 'Geometry education and culture' in *Learning and Introduction*, I, 1991, 217-227. With kind permission from Elsevier Science Ltd., The Boulevard, Langford Lane, Kidlington OX5 1GB.

– Chapter 8: 'Objectivism versus Relativism' first appeared in D. Raven et al. (Eds. 1992) *Cognitive Relativism and Social Science.* New Brunswick: Transaction Publications, 1992, 181-192, under the title 'Objectivism versus relativism: what are we arguing about?'. Reprinted by permission of Transaction Publishers, Rutgers University, New Brunswick, N.Y.

Contents

Preface

A great number of people have been generous enough to give me advice, share their insights, point out for mistakes or omissions to me ore have been very helpful to me in other ways. I am grateful to all of them. I want to mention in particular Balu, Philip Erkens, Claire Farrer, Charlotte Frisbie, Sam Gill, Emily Lyle, Oswald Werner, Ingrid van Dooren, Armand Phalet, Arie de Ruijter, Jan de Wolf, Tom Claes, Karel Arnaut, Lieve Orye, Liesbeth Vandersteene, Ghislain Verstraete, David Krantz and Rita Van den Wijngaert. Both Donald T.Campbell and Joseph Needham showed me repeatedly how intellectual idiosyncracy can be a powerful tool for human understanding. I hope to have been a worthy apprentice. My acknowledgements would be utterly incomplete, though, where I fail to include the Navajo and Turkish consultants who generously shared their knowledge with me.

INTRODUCTION

Anthropology: From Interpretation
to Comparative Science

1. INTRODUCING THE PROBLEM

Anthropology is a discipline with at least two heads. Some have claimed it is (or should be) a science, stressing the links with biology, evolution or some parts linguistics. Others have given it a place in the Humanities, pointing out that interpretation and understanding of the Other is what anthropologists are specializing in. Between the two heads a waxing and waning movement has been going on for over a century now. A convincing -though partial- analysis of this movement of emphasis (and fashion) between the two heads has been published lately by Elman Service (1989). The title of his book gives away the story: *A Century of Controversy*. He demonstrates how the history of the anthropology of kinship can be understood as the history of the controversy between those who tried to emphasize the links with the natural sciences and those who drew primarily on the 'kinship' of the discipline with the Geisteswissenschaften (with a clear heritage from German philosophers such as Dilthey and Weber, and more recently the hermeneuticists). Service ironically concludes that two separate and irreducible cultures seem to persist within the anthropological pool.

The debate about anthropology's epistemological status (e.g., Geertz 1983 and 1988, Fabian 1984), and the ensuing discussion about the methods and concepts of ethnography (notably by critical or reflexive studies such as Clifford & Marcus 1986 to name the best known ones), has at least made clear that the interpretive mode is on the winning hand in the present era. The so-called 'scientific' paradigm, including the formalist approach of structuralism (see especially Lévi-Strauss 1958 and 1973), seems to be retreating as for now. Of course, the picture is more complicated than that: different synthetic views have been offered over the last decade, some of which may grow into a new and more generally accepted paradigm. I think especially of the neo-evolutionary approaches of Boyd & Richerson (1983) and Ingold (1986), each of which offers a different reconciliatory theory combining biological data and models (and hence science) with culturalist or hermeneutic (and hence interpretive) approaches. On the other hand, a new marxian-weberian synthesis with distinct durkheimian shades seems to emerge in the influential works of three major social scientific thinkers of the present time: Bourdieu (e.g., 1980), Habermas (1984) and Giddens (1984) can be cited as important works in this respect. The shift in paradigm, or as it appears to me, the shift towards a possible new paradigm, is still underway. This book will not primarily be concerned with that discussion, although some sides will be criticized and some positions with proponents in the discussion will be shared. My main focus, however, will be on the comparative nature of anthropological knowledge. Indeed, in the critique on ethnography, both on data gathering and on the writing process, the very fact that anthropology is and can only be a comparative discipline was nearly forgotten in the turmoil. I want to try and redirect the focus of attention of our scholarly community to that aspect.

The main features of my approach to comparison can be listed in the form of a little programmatic paragraph, aiming both at the status of anthropology as a discipline in the scientific concert and at the responsible use of that discipline in a postcolonial era. My program reads as follows: If anthropology is to be a science, it will be comparative. The comparative approaches of the past have been thoroughly ideologically colored and hence can not qualify. A systematic reorientation of the epistemological and the methodological tenets of anthropology is called for: the objects of our study are subjects, hence their subjectivity (their sociality, their cultural outlook) should be the focus of our descriptions. By implication these subjectivities should be the basis of comparison. The results of this kind of comparison will lay the foundation for scientific, i.e., universal and true, models and theories about humankind.

It is clear that the reflexive movement in anthropology is, apart from some futile breastbeating, leading to a sharpening awareness in scholars of their historical, cultural and ideological ties. This is a good thing, to be sure. However, the reflexive exercise does not in and of itself carry an alternative view on the discipline, nor on the subjects under study. Taken in itself, it rather leads to a vague feeling that any interpretation can eventually be equally valid as the next one (since we have no privileged foundation to be begin with, see Rosaldo 1988), or that mere glosses based on impressions of the individual ethnographer are the best we can do (Karnoouh 1981). In my opinion this is a category mistake: the critique is valuable, but it does not automatically provide an alternative. Not to take the critique seriously leads us to naive views on the Other, but not to make the distinction between critique and alternative theory has us slip into the (new) fallacy of total relativism.

My ambition in this book is to face this state of affairs by pointing to the epistemological tenets of ethnography first, and by sketching an alternative approach to comparative anthropology as a science. I will thus move away from mere and absolute relativism by indicating a solid and postcolonial foundation for knowledge in the discipline. My focus will be on knowledge as it appears in different cultures, and not on other cultural features. However, I am confident that the alternative is not limited to problems of knowledge, but can be generalized to the whole domain of anthropological research. My examples will be drawn from two cultures only (Navajo and European culture); this will allow me to reach the necessary depth for this kind of argument.

On the Epistemological Status of Anthropology

The comparative study of cultures is only possible in present-day scholarship on the basis of empirical work in different particular cultures.

In the jargon of the disciplines concerned, it is based on *ethnographies* of particular cultures. Even the correlate psychological subdiscipline of cross-cultural psychology draws to a certain extent on ethnographic field work (see LCHC 1978). Hence, the answers to the foundational questions about the scope and validity of comparative models and theories are at least codetermined by the status of ethnographic data and models. I will look at the latter in the first part of this book.

Over the last two decades a series of books have been dealing with the epistemological analysis of ethnography (or empirical social science in general). The classical distinction to be made here is that between objectivist and phenomenological approaches to ethnography. It rejoins pretty much the distinction between two 'cultures' within anthropology, proposed by Service (1989). Both approaches characterize a particular identification (or construction) of the object of study and imply the clear preference of one type of methodology over another one (see also Bourdieu 1980):

– the *objectivistic view on ethnography* conceives of the Other as an object, pretty much in the way of the natural scientific identification of an object of study. That is to say, the Other can only be studied scientifically 'from the outside', and can be measured, observed and classified as can any other object in the world (e.g., atoms, stones, etc.). The methodology that is attached to this construction of the object of research is the one we came to know in behaviorist, in structuralist and in most ecological and economical analyses of culture: the ethnographer is supposed to be an objective researcher who can keep absolute distance with regard to beliefs, feelings, motivations, goals and such like in the cultural subjects s/he examines. Even to the point that these aspects of culture are declared to be beyond the reach of a truly scientific research (Harris 1968), since they can only lead to unscientific interpretation and conjecture.

– the *subjectivistic or phenomenological view* is in many respects the opposite of the former one. It starts from the presupposition of a (high) degree of familiarity between the researcher and the object of research. That is to say, the ethnographer recognizes that the Other is a subject like the researcher, and hence s/he can be known as it were 'from the inside out', that is, through different procedures of empathy. The best known method in this approach is that of participant observation: the researcher gets adopted by the Other and gradually becomes like the Other. Ethnography then comes down to the description of experiences (of the researcher) in the position of a human being participating in the cultural life of other human beings. In this approach, feelings, motivations, goals, interpretations and meanings hold a central position in the ethnography. Some sophistication is reached in terms of the techniques of description, filming, recording, and so on, but the basic feature of the view draws on the presumed familiarity between observer and observed, which allows for the 'participation in the culture of the Other' to become the major vantage point of research (see, e.g., Mead 1970).

Over the last two decades a series of critiques have been formulated on both these exclusive positions. The critique has been so systematic and multiple that a new journal is devoted to it (Cultural Anthropology) and that the critics started what looks like an independent subdiscipline within anthropology: critical or reflexive anthropology. The critical attitude which made anthropologists scrutinize the empirical basis of their discipline attacked both the 'systems' of the objectivist approach (marxism, structuralism and behaviorism) and the particularizing phenomenological studies. Influential authors who worked in both (Geertz 1988) or in one of these approaches (Fabian 1984 as a marxian, and Bourdieu 1980 as a structuro-marxian) trace the lines of discussion. Lately, diverse types of 'postmodern' views seem to offer a haven for the tormented ethnographer. To make my position vis-à-vis this 'school' clear from the outset I claim that in one sense a lot of what is said in the present book can be labeled 'postmodernist'; on the other hand I clearly want to distance myself from at least some implications of the postmodernism movement. When I claim that multiperspectivalness should substitute for the monomanic system builder's perspective on human beings and knowledge, I follow Campbell (1977, partly published in 1989), but I find the same emphasis on plural, local or particular perspectives on things instead of the system-view in Lyotard and other French postmodernists. I share this critical attitude and I share the search for a series of parallel interpretations of reality. At the same time, however, I strongly object against absolute relativism and the common plea against rationality (instead of rationalism) which is often advocated by the postmodern thinkers. I hold the view that one should be a universalist, and a heuristic relativist at the same time (see below: Part IV, Chapter 8).

Partly in the wake of postmodernist philosophy and partly independent from it, the critical anthropologists of today are beginning to have an important impact on the discipline. To my eye the provisional result of this critical movement again seems to be twofold: a genuine critical search on the epistemological status of ethnography is finally being engaged in, and a more or less vague epistemological relativism is being forwarded as a respectful alternative stand in anthropology (against both the old 'scientific' and the naive phenomenological approaches). The first result is an important one, I think. I will go into it to some extent in the following paragraphs. The second result is a category mistake and indulges in an illusionary pretense of philosophical sophistication. Indeed, the mere reference to postmodernism or reflexivity does not render a view more dependable or even more interesting than its precursor. The lack of distinctive criteria to detect and evaluate a right, dependable or factually true alternative from a fraud or a factually mistaken description does not diminish the power of criticism in itself, but it certainly can not automatically generate true descriptions. Pointing out that a statement is biased is important, but it does not yield in itself a true or unbiased alternative. In my opinion this is exactly what is wrong in the 'uncritical' use of so-called postmodern philosophy by a lot of the critical anthropologists today: postmodern philosophers have taught us that a text can be read in a multitude of ways and that the standard or received view of a text is only one interpretation (Derrida 1976). In critical or reflexive anthropology this justifiable position is now translated in a questionable way: by the equation of a culture with a text (Geertz 1979 and dominantly in his 1988) which can be 'read' in different ways by different ethnographers, the discussion is shifting to three new foci.

First, the styles of reading and writing of ethnographers are critically assessed, which is again a justifiable aspect of the critical anthropological perspective. Different ethnographers have a different style in writing their texts and in reading work by others. These differences have impact on the thinking of the ethnographer.

Secondly, the equation is substituting the real culture by the text: a culture is a text, and hence can be approached with philological or hermeneutic methods. This obvious reduction is taken for granted in the so-called interpretive anthropological view (Geertz idem, Clifford 1986). Notwithstanding the fact that hermeneutics can be useful for the analysis and critical assessment of those aspects of culture that could be character-ized as primarily 'textual' (e.g., aspects of oral literature and of myths), it is utterly uncritical to equate culture with text. The sophisticated and critical linguistic anthropological reanalysis of myths at least demonstrates that even for this text-using sub-domain of culture, the equation of culture to text does not hold (see especially Hymes 1981). It is unlikely to hold for other domains of culture, where text and text structure are far from obvious.

Thirdly, in the wake of postmodern philosophy the critical anthropologists seem to slide towards a relativist epistemology. In his influential essay on 'Anti anti-relativism' Geertz (1984) successfully (I think) argues that all anti-relativist attitudes of social scientists have been ill-founded so far. The points he makes are well taken, but it is a logical jump (which Geertz does not make) to go from there and profess that (epistemological) relativism is a valid, let alone the only justified position left. Two problems obtain: first of all, selecting out relativism as a valid alternative is logically contradictory. Epistemological relativism as a program is paradoxical: it declares that all is relative, except for this very statement (which has to be singled out and subscribed to in order to make the point of relativism). In the second place, relativism does not allow for critical distinctions between better and worse, or right and wrong models or theories. It necessarily leads to nihilism, claiming that "everything goes". The obvious difficulties with this sort of position have been detailed to a considerable extent by philosophers and social scientists (e.g. Routley, 1989; Campbell, 1989). I will not go into them here. It suffices to say that the rhetorically attractive position of cognitive or epistemolog-ical relativism should be appraised in a restrictive way: a relativist attitude is healthy and therapeutic as heuristic attitude, but it cannot in itself constitute a perspective in ethnography as a discipline. I mean to say, it is certainly valid to entertain a relativistic heuristics in the process of building a scientific (or justifiable, or dependable) view on humankind, but this attitude in the searching procedure cannot be mistaken for the end result of the search. Not making this distinction leads inexorably to nihilism. In this book I explicitly make this distinction between relativism at the level of heuristics and of epistemology; I adopt the former one and reject the latter version. Granting this distinction, forces me to redefine the 'science' of anthropology. A first step in that direction is the new assessment of the epistemological status of ethnography in Part I. A second step is the sketching of a new comparative approach, which takes this status of ethnography into account (in the remainder of this book).

Praxis

In the wake of the critical literature on the discipline the onset of a restatement of basic concepts can be detected. Indeed, some of the authors mentioned above have been working on a different view on ethnography, which both takes into account the criticisms and captures new features of the ethnographic enterprise. Again, Bourdieu (1980) can be cited as an influential thinker in this respect. Apart from and beyond the two perspectives mentioned above (the objectivistic and the phenomenological schools), he sketched *the praxiological approach* as a third and possibly more accurate view on what social scientific (and in particular anthropological) research amounts to. Although no definitive epistemological theory of this perspective is available yet, some basic concepts can be highlighted here. The bottom line is that, in social science in general, subjects are studying other subjects. That is to say, the 'object' of research is another human being (or is reached by means of him/her) who has emotions, motivations, interpretations, taboos, and so on like the researcher. Hence, observation, interview and other ways to get information about the Other are never 'one way' procedures, but they are basically forms of interaction. Praxis. Moreover, these types of praxis are carried out in an intercultural setting. Epistemologically, we are dealing with interaction between subjects, meaning that facts or 'data' are to be appreciated as the result of such praxis, and not as a given or a 'find' as was the case in the 'one way' perspective. Making this point even more explicitly, I claim that what I call 'data' in this book are things, events, persons, and so on in a particular culture. However, these data are not knowable in any direct way to the researcher; they can only be reached through interaction and/or communication between consultant and ethnographer (be it a more passive interaction as in perception or a more active one as in communication, see below). *What I call a 'fact' in ethnography is an item of knowledge, usually expressed in a statement, which is or can be agreed upon by both the community of ethnographers and by the consultants of the culture concerned to be a true, correct or viable description of such 'cultural data'.* The first implication of such a position is that although data exist outside or independent of the ethnographer, facts do not. A further implication is that whatever will be considered 'facts' in anthropology has to pass a double test: it will be scrutinized by fellow scientists (like in any other science) and it will be subjected to the control and critical assessment of the members of the community. The first test is avoided by most subjectivist ethnographers, rendering anthropology impossible, since the basis for scientifically sophisticated comparison is lacking. I am strongly opposed to this view. It is good literature (maybe autobiography) at best, mere journalism at worst. The second test is hardly ever done in a systematic way by ethnographers. A misconception of anthropological research lies at the basis of this historical situation: ever since the start of academic anthropology the emphasis has been on the development of techniques and other methodological tools, disregarding the analysis of the epistemological status of anthropological knowledge (see also Fabian 1984). Hence, control and interpretation have come to be seen as exclusive competencies of the trained anthropologists and not of the intersubjective situation of consultant and ethnographer. (All this is worked out in some detail in Part I). The following paragraphs will offer a start of an alternative, working with the few authors whose feelings on this point are similar to mine.

Bourdieu speaks of the necessarily dialectical nature of social science knowledge building: the researcher internalizes what is perceived or offered by the Other and externalizes for interaction what has been building up in his/her head (concepts, models, terms, interpretations). Although I can agree with this general characterization, I think we can refine the discourse and delineate some further aspects of the praxis of the ethnographer:

– Ethnography is necessarily double-biased.(see Part I, Chapter 2)

- Ethnography should be an (exemplary) instance of intercultural discourse (see Part I, Chapter 1).
- Ethnography also involves the formation of concepts, models and (ultimately) theory. At this level it is important to be aware of theory- and culture-ladenness of ethnographic concepts.(see Part I, Chapter 3).

2. BUT THE PHILOSOPHERS WILL SAY ...

Philosophers are generalists. That is to say, they try to treat problems in the most global and hence most pervasive way possible, disregarding the disciplinary boundaries or the spatial and temporal particularities. In the generality and potential universality of their statements lies the power of the philosophical argument. I see three philosophical topics which have to be addressed: they have a direct bearing on the issues in the domain of comparative study of knowledge: untranslatability, comparison and (preestablished) order.

a) untranslatability

The analytic philosopher Quine (1960) attacked the old analytic-synthetic distinction by using the example of the ethnographer who, in his first field experience, comes up to the dwelling of an unknown people speaking an unknown language. Of a sudden the ethnographer perceives a rabbit running in the field. At that moment, a member of the unknown people comes up to the ethnographer, stretches one arm and says 'Gavagai'. Quine then goes on to elaborate on this scene: what does 'Gavagai' mean, and what could the ethnographer intelligently exclude from the range of meanings? It proves that the ethnographer can select no one meaning as a privileged or necessary or even probable meaning on a priori grounds. That is to say, 'Gavagai' can literally mean anything at all from 'rabbit', to 'hello' to 'go away' or what have you. There is no way to conclude from this incident that the utterance has an analytic meaning.

The only way to find out to some extent what the word(s) mean is by learning it in repeated and varied experiences where 'Gavagai' is used. There is, however, a limit to translation (and cross-cultural understanding), captured by Quine in the principle of indeterminacy of correlation:

> "There is less comparison –less sense in saying what is good translation what is bad– the farther we get away from sentences with visibly direct conditioning to non-verbal stimuli and the farther we get off home ground." (Quine 1960: 78).

That is, the philosopher sees two thresholds to translatability: one defined by the distance between word and (non-verbal) experience and one by the 'foreignness' of the language vis-à-vis the language of the researcher. Both criteria sound reasonable at first, but they loose some of their attraction when scrutinizing them more closely. Indeed, the first criterion bears the question of the 'visibility' of direct 'conditioning': is it warranted to suppose that criteria for 'visibility' would be cross-culturally uniform? How could one come to that sort of conclusion? Secondly, why is there an exclusive emphasis on conditioning, and not on other types of learning? In Campbell's grand overview of types of learning (his nested hierarchy of selectors, Campbell 1974) conditioning is but one out of a hierarchy of twelve types of learning. The second criterion is the 'foreignness' of the other language. Anthropologists and linguists know that no classification of languages is perfect: neither physical distance nor formal kinship offer sufficient ground to determine in an indisputable way the degree of 'foreignness' or kinship between two languages. But I think Quine has a point in phrasing his principle in gradual terms. I would propose to interpret his rule in the following way: there is less translatability the farther you move away from the structure of your own language. To conclude this first philosophical point I propose to follow the rule: there is a limit to translation across languages and cultures, and in that sense the general point is well made by Quine. On the other hand, in actual practice we can not determine precisely where the limit falls on the one hand, and we manage to get some cross-cultural dialogue going on the other hand. Quine's principle is an important one, but it does not have direct impact on the actual practice of intercultural communication and interaction. Important implications of these philosophical discussions feed back into anthropology as a comparative science: one of them is that we have to consider our research in the context of our own and of the foreign culture. My proposal here is to 'decolonize' our discipline thoroughly (see Chapter 9).

b) comparison

Anything can be compared to anything else. Also, comparison in itself is a trivial activity that we go into constantly. It will be clear that this is not the issue in the present book. Rather, the very issue of the book points to comparative 'study'. That is to say, I want to investigate where, when and how systematic comparison is possible. Again, the work by Quine points to the limits of the possibility of systematic comparison (cf. citation above). The remarks of the previous paragraph can be reminded here. However, this still leaves me with the questions of why and how to develop systematic comparison.

The why-question is a moot one. In a very general sense, one could answer it by pointing to the history of the West: over the centuries we have developed linguistics and anthropology to get to know the Other, the differences and similarities between the Other and us, in order to change the Other (and sometimes us). From a Christian perspective the Other had to be saved and hence converted to our belief system. From a political and economic point of view, the Other's land and resources had to be conquered and put to our use. Again, some sort of conversion of the Other to our living standards, values and cultural ways was seen as a possibly beneficial path to that end (a lot of so-called development programs can be appreciated in the same western outlook on the world, I think). Comparative research can fit in this picture nicely, because it at least promises that through a better understanding of the Other, the aforementioned 'conversions' could be reached more easily, with less effort or with more success. Another answer to the why-question is possible, though, and it is this last one that I want to subscribe to. Human beings all belong to the same biological species and have the same physiological apparatus for survival (with knowledge faculties as a part of it). Nevertheless, the variety in cultural forms, in material productions as well as spiritual, cognitive and emotional-volitional life is overwhelming.

Thousands of different languages and cultures have existed in the past and a lot of them continue to survive now. Moreover, at least in my experience, no deep form of uniformization or globalization towards something like a 'world culture' seems to take place (except at the superficial level of technological products and, to a lesser extent, material culture). The reason why I want to engage in comparative study is to try and study this pluriform human response in order to understand the different views and to 'preserve' the pluriformity. Why do I want to 'preserve' a pluriformity and not eliminate the weaker or 'less developed' cultures at the benefit of the more powerful one(s)? Two deep convictions drive me towards such a strategy: on the one hand, I want to stress that although we westerners seem to have dependable knowledge of a few things, there is no sensible and well informed person who can claim that we have full knowledge or that we will have it in the future. Not only does no one perspective (be it western or any other) have that type of knowledge, but moreover have we awoken from 19th century blatant optimism and become much more modest in our expectations about absolute knowledge. In other words, while still granting that particular experiences or results of research advance our knowledge on a specific topic, we grew up from the simplistic belief in the existence of the one sure winner. That, at least, is my interpretation of the power of scientific and other types of knowledge nowadays. On the other hand, the thousands of cultures that have been in existence (and have been adapting to be sure) for many millennia have undoubtedly shown their survival value. Even in the most reduced form of evolutionary thinking, one must grant that cultures have proved their survival value for peoples over longer stretches of time. That is to say, particular peoples have adapted to their environment by means of cultural artefacts and social behavior which are relatively specific to their tradition. The least we can say, as anthropologists, is that a huge variety of cultural forms (languages, habits, thoughts, religions, etc.) have been developed and have allowed peoples to survive successfully for millennia. Hence, it is utterly incomprehensible to me that a mentality is still taking hold and official programs are developed to eradicate all non-Western or nonindustrial views on life and culture, and to implement the presumably unique right or true way of living and thinking, i.e., the industrial culture of the West (see e.g., the UNCSTD program of 1979). All in all and not denying any success to this world view, the industrial culture of the West is only deployed for a few centuries now and did create wealth, but also pollution and inequality so far. Hence, its implementation raises at least some questions and cannot be taken to be simply obvious. Most of all, however, the ecological blindness in this type of view is appalling: on the basis of some successes (basically material and technological innovations) over a very short period of time a regional but politically dominant culture seems to move towards the deliberate elimination of all the variety which humankind has produced over the ages and which has proven to have survival value, all because of the blind belief in one's own worth. The following metaphor captures the idea nicely, I think: in a horse race of a thousand horses, we seem to bet everything on one single horse because from where we stand it would appear that at one turn in the long track this one horse may be a potential winner. We would then shoot off all other horses, because we are convinced to know the winner. Anybody will tell me this is a stupid way to bet, that the loss of all the other horses is a pity, that the one remaining horse may very well stop in its tracks or fall dead and hence cause total loss, and so on. Nevertheless, abiding with this analogy, this is what we do in terms of culture and knowledge nowadays: we are still so convinced of the superiority of the western world view that we try to eliminate all others. My reason to engage in comparative research is precisely to safeguard the riches of the variety, because I am convinced that this riches can teach us more and different ways to survive. Comparison then never can come down to reduction, but will show the use of the same apparatus of human build to reach different perspectives on the same reality.

The last question, namely that of how to compare, leads to the philosophical problem of the recognition of the importance of (preestablished) order in all cultures.

c) order

In order to begin to think and write about any culture I grant I have to presuppose one a priori which I consider to be a given for the survival of a culture: order. That is to say, I hold that any human culture implicitly or explicitly aims at the establishment and the continuation of order in one form or the other.

Granting that some notion of order is to be found in any culture does not learn me anything in an a priori way about the particular order notion which will be found in any individual culture. Or, in other words, it does not give me any clue as to the content or the specific format of the way nature, human beings or things in the universe are ordered. It only allows me to expect that the way to survive as a community in space and time is not completely at random. My task as a researcher then consists in finding out what the themes and forms of order will look like in that particular community. What general features of order can I take for granted as universal features? In fact, in order to refrain from the mere projection of my own cultural biases unto other cultures, these features have to be the strict minimum. I propose to allow the following features:

– the way a community labels, categorizes, signifies or otherwise culturalizes aspects of the universe can be understood by reference to one or more *root principles or cultural intuitions.* These intuitions can be explicit in the culture, e.g., phrased or otherwise externalized in a basic metaphor, or they can be implicit. In the latter case, a subjacent unity in behavior, beliefs, rules, material cultural items, etc. can be found to defeat apparent randomness, although no explicit reference can be pointed at which serves as a binding or unifying metaphor.

– both what is taught and the way it is taught the next generation testify about the order notion in a particular culture. Education in a community is a (variegated or uniform) way of socializing the offspring in the particular order of its culture.

These two formal characteristics are all I need to presuppose as universals for my type of comparative research.

PART I

Fieldwork

CHAPTER 1
Fieldwork as a Form of
Intercultural Communication

1. INTERACTION AND COMMUNICATION IN THE FIELD

It has often been remarked that an ethnographer leaves the field as 'another human being'. More often than not the experience of deeper cultural contact with other people has existential impact and changes the researcher in a variety of ways. An acquaintance to an Indian culture. There is wisdom in this remark, as many anthropologists can testify. But what exactly is meant here? I am convinced that the analysis of fieldwork as a particular type of interaction can help us to understand what is meant here, without romanticising the confrontation of 'otherness'. In chapter 2, I present an analysis of the structure of observation in the field. I defend the position that observation in the field is a highly particular type of interaction. In the present chapter I want to focus on another aspect of the type of intercultural interaction we call fieldwork, namely intercultural conversation. Before I go into this aspect, it is important to remind ourselves of the status of ethnography and of anthropological knowledge.

As a general stance I hold that ethnography can be understood as a particular type of intercultural communication. That is to say, anthropologists are conducting a specific type of conversation with members of another culture through fieldwork. Since anthropology, based on ethnographic studies, is a scientific or academic discipline, it is part of a system of learned representations of the world for the Westerner. Because the subject matter of anthropology is 'the other' or 'the other cultures', it follows that anthropology is the subsystem of learned representations of 'the other' or of 'other cultures' for the Westerner. It is the scientific discipline that is expected and allowed to offer Westerners a learned and therefore dependable and legitimate view on 'the other'.

Ethnography is the empirical subdiscipline of anthropology. It is primarily through ethnographic research that the anthropologist engages in concrete interactions and communications with members of other cultures. I see ethnography as the set of results of interactions and communications between other cultures and ethnographers. Hence, if my contention about the role of anthropology as a learned or legitimate system of representations is well-founded, it follows that ethnography can be seen as a learned and scientifically appropriate way for one civilisation to engage in interactions and communications with other civilisations. In other words, ethnography (as a part of a science) is the scientifically qualified form of intercultural communication. It is obvious that not all intercultural communication in which Westerners are involved takes the form of ethnographic research. This fact is irrelevant for our discussion, however: Ethnography remains the only discipline the Westerner can turn to if he/she wants to engage in this communication in a scientifically justified way.

So far I have treated ethnography as 'intercultural communication' on an abstract level. However, ethnography is an empirical science and it is obvious my claim will have to be sustained with a analysis of the empirical methods and techniques of the ethnographer. In other words, my object level question is: How and by what means does the ethnographer himself (or herself) engage in communication with members of another culture? Just a quick glance at the major handbooks shows that the answer is varied. However, if I take 'communication' literally there seems to be one technique which is both considered more and more as the main means for research by ethnographers themselves: the ethnographic interview. I will concentrate my attention on the interview in this chapter and not concern myself with other ethnographic techniques.

2. INTERVIEWING IN THE FIELD: WHAT IS HAPPENING?

Before I go into an analysis of the possible epistemological status of knowledge which is gained in an interview situation, it is important to look at the structure of this type of conversation in the field. However, the delineation of what interviews are is far from clear. In their handbook for ethnoscience fieldwork, Werner & Schoepfle (1987) start their chapter 9 'Interview as conversation' with the following definition:

"Any conversation between an ethnographer and a member of the culture being studied is an interview." (1987, 302).

In this general statement the authors propose an interesting view. If we take the statement literally, we are told that any communication event between the native people and the ethnographers can in principle be looked upon as a means to gain knowledge about 'the other'; any conversation is an interview. The implication of such a statement would thus at least be double:

(1) Anyone speaking and listening in the field is always 'doing research', in some sense or another, and (2) 'conversation': Speaking and listening is a two-way process involving in principle members of the other culture and the ethnographer in a common process. This general statement is thus a broad, but very provisional one: The interaction and total experience of fieldwork is stressed.

In a subsequent paragraph, however, this general statement is specified:

"An interview is an information-providing speech exchange in which some of the knowledge of the consultant is given to the interviewer." (1987, 302)

The specification in the second statement is typical of many of the positions one can find in the methodological literature today, and hence hear in the training courses for future ethnographers. The interesting point in these two quotes is that the general and two-way concept of 'conversation' is safeguarded to some extent in the 'speech exchange' concept of the second quote, which it, however, specified and narrowed in two ways:

(1) The conversation/speech exchange is said to be 'information providing'. That is to say, not 'any' conversation is an interview, but only the type that yields information. I will come back to this term. On the superficial level it seems to be clear or even unambiguous. Doesn't everyone speak about information and information processing these days? However, when I try to grasp the meaning of this term, particularly in the context of intercultural communication, the illusion of clarity vanished and I am confronted with a puzzle. An example from my own fieldwork will make this clear.

(2) The second specification of the initial term 'conversation' lies in the statement that knowledge is transferred from one participant to the other. However, the receiver is one and the same (i.c. the ethnographer). This point is unambiguously stated in a further section of the same chapter. The authors make it clear that a definite agreement on the 'turn order' is a good principle to conduct an interview by. That is to say, the interviewer asks the questions and the consultant provides the answers whereby *"the one-way transfer of information from consultant to ethnographer is taken for granted"* (1987; 309). Although again a rather obvious point of view is defended, I want to take issue with the way it is presented.

In his influential book, Spradley (1979) has taken a somewhat similar view on 'interview as conversation', although he focuses more on the dynamic aspects of the interview:

> "Both the ethnographer and informants are naive about the other's culture. The informant finds it extremely difficult to translate or interpret for the ethnographer. Only after months and months of language study can the ethnographer conduct wide-ranging interviews and begin to make sense out of many thing". (1979, 20)

According to Spradley, the partners in the conversation (i.e. the ethnographic interview) develop 'translation competence' over time. The important point, in my view, is that Spradley recognises that both partners develop their focus and their practical knowledge about each other, and that the conversational contacts are complex actions whereby each partner is engaged in building a model of the other. I am inclined to see this view as a more adequate point of departure in defining the status of the ethnographic interview as an instance of intercultural communication. It is clear that Spradley's comments allow, at least for the initial phase of the conversation situation between informant and ethnographer, for complex actions and interactions of both partners, implying that in the initial stage of the so-called "information-providing" function of the interviews is clearly understood to be at work both in the cognitive processing of the ethnographer and that of the informant(s). This point of view could be seen as a modification of the more structural perspective of Werner & Schoepfle (1987).

I want to elaborate on these views. A few examples from the field will indicate the direction I am taking. When working with Navajo informants, I was aware of the fact that I remained a foreigner, or to put in their terms: *ana'i* (an enemy: see chapter 7). This is the status that is bestowed on you when you enter into contact with Navajo people as a non-Navajo. Even though in the end one informant gave me the highly flattering nickname of *hataali neez* ('tall medicine man'), I still remained as much *ana'i* as I had been at the start. I had been born that way, and consequently this state of affairs could not be altered later in life. Nevertheless, in my status of 'enemy' I could learn to interact more or less appropriately, more or less open-mindedly, or more or less stupidly, the fact that Navajos called me 'medicine man' seems to indicate that I did rather well for a Westerner (unless the name was giving jokingly, of course) already. This simple name-calling is evidence of the active involvement of informants in the field interaction. I was not just asking questions of eliciting information, but rather my questions were evaluated and weighed by informants according to my acceptability as a questioner.

However, more important implications are attached to this simple example. First of all, the foreigner that I was, was not seen by the Navajo as a mere 'information gathering device', but rather as a whole person. The very fact of name-giving seems to point in this direction: I was put in a certain cultural category of persons. Whether this was done jokingly or not does not alter the type of category that was used. The Navajo did not label us in terms of speech, words or questions as we, ethnographers, sometimes like to do (an outspoken, eloquent informant is often considered 'better suited' for the research than a silent one), but as a type of cultural person. When I gained more insight into the Navajo culture, it became clear that the choice of *hataali* is significant: In the context of the 'ontic impact' of language (Whiterspoon, 1977, and see below) in the Navajo culture, the thinker-speaker as well as the shaman-vision seeker are very important figures, since they influence the powers in the world directly and creatively through their speech-thought-action. The medicine man, however, is more like a practitioner, who applies in a competent but rigid way the knowledge he got from a predecessor through the use of the standardised formulae, songs and actions he learned during apprenticeship. In a sense, although the medicine man's world is holy and has obviously ontic impact, it is less danger-laden than that of a thinker or shaman since their word has the potential of renovation and has do to with a reinterpretation of the natural order. The medicine man is basically 'restoring' the patient's order. The medicine man is basically 'restoring' the patient's relationship with the presumed natural order (see Whiterspoon, 1977; Farella, 1984).

I went into detail on this point, since this example illustrates an idea I want to bring to the fore: In the ethnographic conversation situation the partners in the interviewing structure can hold a variety of orders or status positions. It will be clear that I was in a different position to handle and receive information on my entry into the field than at the moment I was called *hataali*, not only my position, but also the type of knowledge which was transferred changed.

A very particular kind of compensation through exchange should be mentioned now. In some instances, we exchanged 'stories'. That is to say, when we were given a story by a Navajo informant we responded by giving a story of our own tradition. Thus we told about the world view of Heraclitos and about the 'allegory of the cave' in Plato's Republic. the reactions to our 'stories' were warm, enthusiastic and curious about 'those old men you told me about' (viz. Heraclitos and Plato).

If we try to neutralise our Western perspectives for a while and look at this type of exchange from a Navajo point of view, we gain deep insight into the complexity of this conversation situation. When we went up to the aged Curly Mustace we were to 'collect' a story on some of the ancestral kinship relations. At the end of this story (i.e., after some three hours) he said he wanted to give us some specific information, whereupon he started to tell another story. It was only much later that we grasped some of the meaning of his type of conversation, and overcame our initial situation of foreigner or 'ignorant child' by reacting to a story told with a story of our own tradition. In my view, we thereby shifted to another level of conversation: Instead of being a dull question machine, we got into a relationship of exchange, implying that we shared a format of conversation and understanding with the Navajo. This is the way I explain the warm and open interest for the story we were telling. It looked as if finally we were getting down to relevant conversation, where both parties were somewhat involved differently.

I will leave the characterisation of this conversational format at that for the time being. However, let me add one more argument in favor of this interpretation: Repeatedly we witnessed that newcomers in the field were given Coyote stories in response to questions. We had this experience ourselves when going up to informants we had not worked with before. As we came to know, Coyote stories are children's stories, that is, they are the format of knowledge transfer for those who know little to nothing about the culture. Telling Coyote stories to ethnographers is the Navajo way to start from scratch, one might say. Or, alternatively, it is the safest device to conduct a conversation with a person who is not knowledgeable. Depending on the learning capacities of the ethnographer you get into more fundamental knowledge later, telling a completely different type of stories. We used this insight in the field by refusing to accept Coyote stories (and thus children's knowledge) from informants and showing that we already knew more. Whenever such a refusal was voiced, informants would move to another 'level' of information.

What this type of experience taught us is that conversation is (a) culture specific and (b) dependent on the qualities of the partners. The culture specific nature is already shown in the use of stories, rather than discursive speech in conversation. If the ethnographic interview puts all emphasis on discursive answers to direct questions, it follows that the knowledge gained through this technique is likely to be truncated or biased. The conversation is dependent on the qualities of the interlocutors: Without the mutual building of some sort of respect, trust or understanding of one other through which the ethnographer is 'built up' as a capable, more or less adult and knowledgeable partner, no genuine or relevant knowledge is transferred. The ethnographer might be sent home with 'children's knowledge'. It is relevant to note that two facts seem to corroborate this interpretation: (a) The necessity in some cultures to initiate the ethnographer in puberty rites before sharing knowledge with him/her; and (b) the teaching of subsequent and ever more 'adult' or 'sacred' knowledge to ethnographers over many years (e.g., the four levels of thought of the Dogon were told to the French group around Marcel Griaule over a period of some 40 years: see Chapter 2).

In the light of all this, the one-way direction which is 'taken for granted' according to Werner & Schoepfle (1987) is rather questionable. The authors represent a highly particular point of view, which I can hardly subscribe to as the pivotal, let alone the only, perspective. Rather, their approach seems to put constraints on the conversation situation, which may eventually inhibit important avenues to field research. Field interviews are really complex processes which can be illustrated with this example: In some instances we felt we had to 'win our place' in the eyes of the informant in order to be able to formulate a question, or rather to have our question accepted as a genuine one. In this way, it happened many times that informants would deliberately not recognise our question (especially questions about the order in nature, ceremonial meanings, etc.) and give us the sort of answer a child would get (e.g., refer to a Coyote story, which is the locus for children's knowledge). We then tried to fight back, even sometimes to bluff, and say: "We already know so much, but we wanted to check this with you", or: "We were told this and that, but we want to make sure this is right and therefore we consult you", etc. This 'struggle' was settled most of the time in a silent agreement or implicit recognition on the part of the informant, who would then go on to confirm, to elaborate, or to refute the knowledge we put before him.

The important point in these examples is, in my opinion, that they show that knowledge transfer is certainly not always a one-way system. That is to say, both the questions and the answers have to be negotiated, amended, and so on. The examples I gave occurred more or less accidentally, but I am convinced that the training of ethnographers to cope with the ethnographic situation as a two-way conversation rather than a one-way information-transfer may alter the discipline profoundly.

All this should not be interpreted to mean that we do not get out to 'the other' to learn about 'the other'. This is certainly the case. I only claim that this learning process is fundamentally a two-party engagement and that the methodological and epistemological implications of this two-way conversational structure have not been clearly drawn by anthropologists.

3. CONVERSATION IN THE FIELD: WHAT IS 'INFORMATION'?

Charles Frake (1980) warned ethnographers against 'plying frames' in the field. He stressed that our method might entail an inappropriate interpretation of what we are looking for. In particular, our emphasis on the question-and-answer procedure, or on queries in the field presupposes a particular view on the other's language and knowledge system: we focus on systematic exposition about an explicit reference to the outside world. But as Frake put it:

> "People do not so much ask and answer inquiries; they propose, defend, and negotiate interpretations of what is happening" (1980, 50).

Although I agree with this modification, I would like to elaborate on it. The bulk of what is transferred in a cultural tradition is what could best be termed 'practical knowledge' (Balagangadhara, 1994; Bourdieu, 1981). That is to say: A subject acts appropriately in a cultural group mostly by using implicit knowledge, either in a ceremony or in daily activities such as eating, walking, playing, listening, learning, talking and other types of behavior. Some of this practical knowledge can be communicated explicitly. Some of it can be detected on a meta-level of theoretical or abstract knowledge, but the bulk seems to escape the type of communication that is so popular in the Western schooling system: direct transfer of information. Consider again the situation of the story-teller: He does not respond to a direct question and thus hardly offers 'information', i.e., linguistic utterances of a discursive nature. Rather, the story-teller probes the receiver of the story (his/her age, social position, knowledge ability and so on) and enters the learning situation in an attempt to learn to tell the story the best way possible and to teach the listener to listen and to tell stories in his/her turn. Thus, when we enter the field with a quest for information only, it may have been our own exclusive training in one type of 'school knowledge' that coached us to turn our research focus to that type of knowledge which is liable to be elicited through 'question-and-answer' procedures. However, we should recognise this as a cultural bias: It is important to become aware of the fact that this type of explicit knowledge will at best be only one aspect of the cultural knowledge system in any non-Western tradition. Moreover, it need not be the dominant type of knowledge, as is proclaimed in the West.

How should we investigate this 'practical knowledge'? Clearly, we must gain insight in the criteria of relevance and in the natural philosophy which are shared by the community under investigation. I think this is what Frake alludes to when he states:

> "The image of an ethnography we have in mind also includes
> lists of queries and responses but with this difference: Both the
> queries and their responses are to be discovered in the culture
> of the people being studied." (1980, 26)

That is to say, in the field we are bound to ask questions, but they should be questions which are appropriate to and stem from the culture under study. In actual fact, when dealing with 'practical knowledge', I propose that the ethnographer should learn the conversational strategies, the traditions in the use of metaphors and analogies and so on, rather than approach the knowledge system as if it were a purely cognitive and discursive system of explication.

If we can agree on these general and intuitive points, our next step is to reach more clarity on them. Can we find a model in present-day discourse or conversation analysis which will help us to grasp this intuitive view in unambiguous and non-reductionist terms? If we could find such a model, it is clear we would have a powerful means to understand what the ethnographer is doing when interviewing an informant.

When searching through the European literature on text linguistics and discourse analysis (especially see Van Dijk, 1984), I found several descriptions of interviews as question-answer procedures in the west, but I did not detect an analysis to cope with intercultural communication in the perspective outlined above. Of course, the literature is growing tremendously, so I may have overlooked some important works. But in general, I have the impression that the same basic focus on 'explicit knowledge' is present in these works.

On the other hand, some work in the American tradition of discourse analysis seems promising. In a volume, edited by Sherzer & Woodbury (1987), the 'tradition' of Hymes and Tedlock is presented and carried further. The most general assertion of this school of thought (comprising Hymes, Tedlock, Bauman and so on) is, in my opinion, that the focus on 'knowledge' is replaced by one on 'performance'. That is to say, the exclusive focus on language and thought which led to a bias of searching for explicit denotative meaning with linguists and anthropologists, is overcome. Instead, Hymes and his co-workers speak about 'performance' as the variegated set of aspects such as the voice, the social and cultural context, and the conventions of interaction in both performer and audience. This notion of performance is, in my understanding, a possible candidate to denote what I have called 'practical knowledge' before. If my interpretation is correct, we could use the structural analysis of authors such as Hymes, Bauman and Tedlock to begin to describe the performances of other cultures as particular types of discourse. The term 'discourse' would then indicate a *particular type* of performance-in-context (however, the relationship between 'performance' and 'discourse' is not altogether clear from the authors discussed here). In what sense can an ethnographic interview be characterised in terms of 'discourse'? I propose the following simple scheme: (1) The ethnographer gives a certain performance while engaging in a discourse in terms of his own culture, but directed towards "the other". The intention of the ethnographer is to constitute the other as an audience such that the other performs or is engaged in a discourse the ethnographer can recognise (decode, interpret, and so on). Then the informant's performance can be described as a response to his/her primary performance. (2) The informant can react to the interviewer's performance by putting on a performance of neglect, interpretation, negation, refusal or what have you.

Clearly some degree of mutual understanding can occur (some degree of overlap between the referents used, or some degree of sharing the same goal). But on the other hand, the informant can re-orient or alter the discourse even in a non-intended way. This complex process of mutual give-and-take, understanding-misunderstanding, acceptance-refusal, and allowance-denials the basic format of the field interview. All types of persuasion, clarification, assertion, demand, refusal and so on can be recognised at some time or other in this process, presumably in both parties. I grant that some instance of straightforward and unambiguous question-and-answer sequences may occur, but I clearly deny that this is the rule and I certainly refuse to accept that some technical procedures themselves guarantee qualitatively valuable data based on mutual understanding. In a nutshell, the ethnographic is an instance of negotiation rather than a Q-A device.

During my fieldwork I encountered the following types of reaction. When asked to discuss the meaning of some terms, an informant started teaching me ten Navajo terms a day with their simplest translation ('because that is as much as you anthropologists can take per day'). When asking another informant about the classification of terms, she said she could produce a taxonomy if I liked, 'though this type of classification had nothing to do with the native classification system'. The examples (which can be multiplied from my field notes) point to the fact that one type of conversation is taking place: The informants 'measure' the intentions or the expectations of the ethnographer and try to comply with them. The ethnographer can either accept the data he/she receives at face value, or with difficulty try to sort out continuously what is responded to or interpreted in the mind of his/her interlocutor. Whatever choice is made, it is clear that the field results will either be very naive or will have to be related to the complex two-way interaction structure of the interview.

A final example concerns the investigation of such 'deep' notions as 'religion', 'morality' and the like. Again, I will draw on material from Navajo research. Navajo religion has been termed 'magical' (Reichard, 1939), 'amoral' (Haile, 1943), 'restorative' (Whiterspoon, 1977), 'atheistic'

(Pinxten, 1981) and 'all-inclusive' (Wyman, 1983), to name just a few views. I guess it is clear from the variety of labels we have here that the authors had different meanings and different questions in mind. It is not clear, however, which of these labels (if any) would be appropriate to characterize Navajo religion. This results is all the more astonishing when we see the amount of published material on Navajo religion. The main problem here is, I contend, that we have been working too much in this one-way model of field interviews where the ethnographer is the receiver and thus the only one entitled to interpret, select, analyze etc. the material according to his/her intuitions. A similar critique has been voiced by Hymes (1981) where he states that Wyman's published versions of Blessingway (1970) are not appropriate in terms of native categories. They are truncated and shaped according to the format of a 'holy text' in the Western tradition. Here again, the ethnographer reacts as the superior receiver who can interpret -and even format- the message of the sender.

The general ideological consequences of the methodologically conscious choice between ethnographic interview as a one-way information-eliciting procedure and ethnographic interview as two-way intercultural communication are grave. In the first version, one restricts the impact and the possible control of the informant who is in fact seen as not knowledgeable about the processing of information by the ethnographer. In the second choice, the informant and the ethnographer are producing some sort of common construct together, as a result of painstaking conversation with continuous mutual control. A systematic mutual control is possible and can be built into the fieldwork procedure (cf. the so-called 'Universal Frame of Reference'-approach proposed in Pinxten et al., 1983), but somehow it does not yet seem to be that popular with ethnographers. It is clear, however, that in the conversational perspective on the ethnographic interview, the whole enterprise of the interview is altered to take on a form that is altogether irreducible to the one-way idea of an interview. Indeed, in the case of an interview as 'conversation' the two parties are involved in a difficult process of intercultural communication and knowledge construction.

CHAPTER 2
Ethnographic Observation

INTRODUCTION

In the present chapter I formulate some of the epistemological principles that may be important elements in the understanding of the possibilities and limits of observation in ethnographic fieldwork.

After a short analysis of the principles that are inherent in positivistic and in participant observational procedures respectively, I draw on personal fieldwork and ethnographic data to show that current approaches present the problem in too exclusive a way. The consciousness of active involvement and active control of the observational procedure by native informants has to grow from evidence about the way informants build preconceptions or even 'native theories' about the ethnographer and his culture.

From there, an interactional view on the observational situation in the field is developed and a minimal frame of reference to control the ethnographer's intuition and to systematically overview biases and conceptions of the informants is worked out.

1. THE EPISTEMOLOGICAL VERSUS THE METHODOLOGICAL PROBLEM

Anthropology has by now produced several good volumes on methodology: in particular the reader brought out by Naroll & Cohen (1970) and the works produced by the Peltos (e.g. Pelto & Pelto, 1978) are considered to be standard works on anthropological method. Strangely enough this does not help the discipline as such, a fact which is more and more recognized. What is happening?

Very generally speaking, methods are just the means that help the researcher in gathering knowledge. However, they do not constitute a frame or a set of criteria defining what 'knowledge' would be about. In other words, a method is a means to reach a goal in the proper way: truth, facts, theory about 'some other'. But it does not form truth criteria, factual constraints and theoretical principles in itself. What we need as much as methodology in any branch of science is epistemology.

Johannes Fabian already discussed the theoretical developments in anthropology over two decades ago. However, not much has changed to the better. He saw a continuous busying with renovations in methods and techniques (particularly the emic/etic history, the introduction of different linguistic models in ethnography, and the sophistication in comparative anthropology of Lévistraussian or Murdockain type) and concludes: "It is an approach in which methodology (the rules of correct and successful procedure) has taken the place of epistemology (reflection on the constitution of communicable knowledge)" (1971, 20). His book on coevalness and time in the description of cultures gives a systematic analysis of some epistemological issues (Fabian, 1984).

It is my opinion, shared by others, that anthropology needs a reorientation in epistemological thinking. More precisely the positivistic and classical phenomenological epistemologies should be abandoned and a creative search for a new epistemology should begin. This new epistemology should, finally, be typical and adequate for the strange synthetic breed that anthropology tends to be, and not the shabby sort of physics of the positivists or the 'mixed sort of literary criticism' of phenomenologically minded anthropologists.

One way to investigate the epistemology of 'observation in anthropology' is to point out the constraints that are inherent in the subject matter of the discipline. Since both 'subject' and 'object' of study in anthropology are human beings, *"the various categorical sources of bias and their correlatives"* could be isolated (Salamone, 1979, 53). Typically, this 'negative' or critical approach to the 'ethnographic endeavor is highlighted by Salamone' from the point of view of the ethnographer, that is, he stresses that observation is the researcher's relation to a reality which he is co-determining, (idem, 51). Although this view is correct in itself, it only gives us half the truth, I claim.

2. POSITIVISM EXCLUSIVELY

Margaret Mead gives a good insight into what is to be understood by a 'positivistically' inspired ethnographer. She clearly draws on a Boasian tradition when she describes the 'golden rule' for fieldwork:

> "This systematic understanding– his (the ethnographer's) total appreciative mass of knowledge–provides him with a living, changing, analytical system which simultaneously correctly or incorrectly files information received–a hitherto unnoted kinship image, a new design of a pot, a different cadence in a public speech–and so defines the search for information". (1970, 247)

The ideal anthropologist must consequently be like a 'recording instrument' (idem, p.248). She goes on to elaborate on the latter statement by specifying the type of 'recording instrument' that would be suitable for recording human emotions and relationships, but the general trend with this emphasis on data collecting and 'recording what is out here' is well expressed in the above sentences. The emphasis is on individual data, on the gathering of as much and as detailed information as possible, and so on. Notwithstanding the important methodological advances that were realised through this particular attention to minute details (especially in the Boasian tradition), it is odd that the epistemology of the approach was never fully discussed by its adherents. It is a non-believer like Fabian who goes into this problem. His general description of the approach is as follows:

> "The researcher attains objectivity by surrendering to a theory,
> a set of propositions chosen and interrelated according to the
> rules of a super-individual logic, and by subsuming under this
> theory those data of the external world which he can retrieve
> by means of established procedures of his craft". (1971, 23-24)

Let us analyse these statements for a moment. There are two epistemological presuppositions to what I termed a 'positivistic' stand.

First, there is a subject-object distinction between the observer and the observed. That is, the observer is looking at someone through a camera and the result is different from him and can be looked at as an object to some degree: the other is clearly 'out there', in the external world, and information stemming from him can be collected as it is retrieved. In this case the one observed is treated as if he is, at least partially, objectifiable. Knowledge about him can be gained in pretty much the same way it can be had from non-living systems: stimuli can be given and the responses can be observed and noted, differences in behaviour can be tested according to differences in environment and so on. That researchers in this paradigm do treat the other in this way is testified to in the actual methodological procedures that are worked out in this tradition: multiplicity of data is important, multiplicity of indexes counts, tests can be used to control former data, and so on (e.g. Levine, 1970, 190).

Second, the principle of universality through control and repetition holds. In the approach discussed the data and the conclusions may, in the end, be controlled by several, mutually independent researchers. That is, the report should be dependent as little as possible on personal or idiosyncratic aspects of the researcher, it should be reached in pretty much the same way a physicist reaches his results. Starting from there cross-cultural comparison can be begun, as is exemplified forcefully by Murdock's Human Relations Area Files system.

In general then, I claim at least these two main features are characteristic of the 'positivistic' stand in ethnography:

1) the subject matter of study is seen in a way that is similar to that of the natural sciences: a culture, a community, a person, a specific aspect of language or behaviour, and so on can be observed like an object, and

2) proper knowledge is gained whenever controllability and repetition of observations in guaranteed.

3. PARTICIPANT OBSERVATION: THE PHENOMENOLOGICAL APPROACH

In the general introduction to their *Handbook*, Naroll and Cohen explain the historical need for the participant observation approach as the need for holistic views of cultures. Instead of going into the field to collect mere artefacts, to count or measure people, or similar sorts of research, *"a technique has been worked out by which the researcher uses his entire experience as a record of the society"* (Cohen & Naroll, 1970, 4). In an appropriately titled section (*"Entree into the field"*) several authors give details on the what and how of participant observation. It immediately becomes clear, however, that quite different attitudes are recognized by different researchers as the core of the approach.

Middleton, the renowned African scholar, explains that he always refrained from too many direct questions and preferred to let *"avenues open up"* to him; he characterises his own behaviour as follows:

> "I tried, that is to say, to behave as would any polite and well-mannered person behave when a guest in someone else's home" (1970, 227).

On the other hand, Uchendu, the black anthropologist who worked with Navajo Indians, looks for more active involvement in relationships, stressing that:

> "where the fieldworker's goals and the interest of his community are complementary, reciprocity becomes a very effective technique for achieving rapport" (1970, p. 236).

The initiator of the actual method of participant observation was Bronislaw Malinowski. Pelto & Pelto start their exposition on participant observation with a long quotation from his *Argonauts of the Pacific* and then draw very concise, but highly insightful conclusions on the nature of the approach. Instead of quoting from Malinowski myself, I will start with the characterisation by the Peltos:

> "The anthropological fieldworker, Malinowski stressed, should totally immerse himself in the lives of the people; and that can only be done through months of residence in the local community... Part of the fieldworker's ethnographic knowledge becomes imbedded in his or her own daily routines. Many of the habits and concerns of the local people are internalised".
> (Pelto & Pelto, 1978, 68-69)

Although the Peltos go on to warn that not everybody will 'go native' to the same extent, they claim that in Malinowski's and in their own opinion participant observation is the primary and basic road to ethnographic information, eventually to be followed by more sophisticated methods and techniques in a later phase of research.

Let us try to examine what epistemological stands are presupposed in this approach. First, the subject matter that is observed is, according to this approach, complex, living, changing, and difficult to overlook. It lacks several, if not all, the features of 'being an object' that were recognized in the positivistic approach: the other cannot be looked at 'from the outside' or 'like an object', but must be understood through comparison by the observer with his own, often intimate, characteristics. All this adds up to the picture of the complexity and partial indeterminability of 'the other', very much like the ill-defined and unfinished view one builds of one's own personality.

Second, the criteria for 'good' knowledge of the other differ from the positivistic approach. Instead of testability on the side of the researcher himself, a 'recognition of equivalence' on the part of the one observed is taken into account. That is to say, the observer's knowledge is sufficient and correct provided his future behaviour elicits approval and recognition from the one observed (the observer elicits the response that he is or is not acting appropriately, and that is the final criterion of truth). In order to reach this sort of knowledge and in order to be able to decode the mere reactions of disapproval or approval on the part of the observed, the observer must 'try to become like them while all the time remaining a strict observer as well'. His attitude, like his status in the observation situation, becomes a paradoxical one: he has to become a subject like the one he is observing and he has to keep his distance and observe: he has to get involved and at the same time remain detached.

I think these two epistemological rules allow me to cover the range of the discussion that has been going on around the topic of participant observation in anthropology, especially since the publication of two works of major importance in the seventies: Devereux (1967) and Malinoswki (1976). Devereux, a psychoanalyst and anthropologist, wrote his basic book (*From anxiety to method*) with the intention of showing, that the reciprocity between observer and observed is essential in social sciences and that, consequently, the means of observation are *"disturbances, since they, too, elicit behaviour which would not have occurred otherwise"* (1967, 255). The first part of this message states that the first characteristic I highlighted is taken seriously and given a specific interpretation (interaction, mutual influence, observing and being observed). The second part looks for the methodological consequences of this research situation: given the fact that the 'object' never stops interaction, what then could be learned from the effect of the 'object' on the observation situation? All in all, Devereux's position implies a modification of the naive 'participant observation' situation that was outlined above, since it clearly stipulated that participation changes the object of research and that these changes (disturbances) may be more telling than what is actually observed by the ethnographer who feels he is 'just participating' in another culture. In my opinion, Devereux points primarily to the culture-ladeness of observation for anthropology: participating in the life of another culture implies that one's observation of that culture is modified through the reactions, restrictions, openings, etc. offered (or even imposed) by the members of that culture through the observer's presence there.

Malinowski, the founder of the participant observation approach, surprised all scholars of the field when his *A Diary in the Strict Sense of the Term* was posthumously published. The often brutal and aversive reactions towards natives he shows in this diary were felt to be 'strictly

emotional eruptions on his part' or 'embarrassing' aspects of his personality, depending on the willingness or the degree to which colleague-
anthropologists were shocked. Francis Hsu, who summarised and
analysed part of the discussion in a later paper, feels obliged to explain
away

> "such facets of the Malinowskian input through the supposi-
> tion that the latter was so deeply imbued with the Western
> patterns of affect that he and his natives completely parted
> ways in this respect" (1979, 521).

Consequently, Hsu advises anthropologists to get involved in *"the study
of the ethnographer's own culture [as] the first order of business in his or her
training"* (idem, 526).

It is in this respect that I believe Geertz makes a valid point when
he claims that the diary of Malinowski does not pose a moral or emotional problem in the first place, but a genuinely epistemological one:

> ".... if anthropological understanding does not stem, as we have
> been taught to believe, from some sort of extraordinary
> sensibility, an almost preternatural capacity to think, feel and
> perceive like a native (a word, I should hurry to say, I used here
> 'in this strict sense of the term'), then how is anthropological
> knowledge of the way natives think, feel and perceive possible."
> (Geertz, 1977, 481)

Geertz then continues to look for the 'subject matter' aspect in participant
observation, and finally dwells a bit on the criteria for knowledge
gathering in the approach. His study of the subject matter is interesting:
he claims it cannot be held by an anthropologist that he is really 'looking
at the world like a native', since such a program goes way beyond what
is actually possible for a human being stemming from another particular
culture. This statement is then supported with fragments of field
experiences. The general rephrasing that Geertz introduces goes as
follows:

> "The ethnographer does not, and in my opinion largely cannot,
> perceive what his informants perceive. What he perceives - and
> that uncertainly enough - is what they perceive 'with', or 'by
> means of', or 'through', or whatever word one may choose"
> (Geertz, 1977, 482-483).

It is in this sense that Geertz understands the 'emic' approach in ethnography, in which the ethnographer tries to look at the world through e.g. the concept of 'person' or 'self' as elicited from the natives, in order to understand the way they perceive the world and act upon it. Since no straightforward and direct method can be used to assail this task and since the only way to go about it is to be as particular and as globalistic as possible at the same time, Geertz proposes to adopt a method of participant observation in this hermeneutic sense:

> "... a continuous dialectical tacking between the most local of
> local detail and the most global of global structure in such a
> way as to bring both into view simultaneously" (idem, 491).

The 'local' of 'local' and the 'global' of 'global' can easily be read as the involvement and the 'detachment' respectively, that were mentioned in the general characterisation of the approach.

The reappraisal that is presented here by Geertz is very appealing. Yet, I am convinced he omits a basic feature of the 'subject matter' aspect and hence cannot really be followed in his further hermeneutic interpretation. This point will be elaborated in the following section.

4. WHAT IS WRONG WITH THESE APPROACHES?

In fact, both the positivistic and participant observation approaches cannot match actual field experience satisfactorily. It takes more than one argument to explain this, since both the nature of observation in general and that of ethnographic observation in particular should be scrutinised in order to make the point clearly.

a) observation is theory-and culture-laden.

Modern theorists of science make the point that observation as such does not exist: there is always 'observation in a context of theories'. For example, a mist of apparently scattered dots takes another meaning, is 'observed' altogether differently, once the structure of a double turning staircase (a double helix) is imagined (this is exactly what happened to the researchers on the 'double helix', cf. Watson, 1968 pictures). That is, observation has meaning in a context (Quine, 1960, part 4).

Research in 'empirical epistemology' (e.g. Campbell, 1979) brings us evidence on the theory-ladeness of observation in the sciences: even 'naive realist' scientists draw heavily on their tradition for models, metaphors and theories when involved in the actual procedures of empirical research. Our own analysis of the convictions of scientists themselves on these topics reveals that, although they would deny theory-ladeness most of the time and strive for 'pure' and data-directed observation, their statements and the set-up of their observation procedure often draws to a considerable extent on theoretical insights in the discipline (cf. Apostel et al., 1979). In anthropology then, where the subject matter is so complex and so similar to the observer himself, it cannot in principle be expected that the researcher will be able to avoid theory-ladeness of his observations to a greater extent than can his chemist, physicist or biologist colleagues.

Anthropology, however, has a second and similarly profound bias to work from: the culture of the ethnographer. This can best be illustrated by a story told to me by Werner (cf. Werner, 1979) about the coming together of a big crowd in Saigon at the time of the elections between Kennedy and Nixon. The crowd gathered in front of the American Embassy, where a window panel showed the figures of the election returns as they came in. The crowd was agitated and roared whenever a figure was shown. A member of the embassy personnel interviewed by a newspaper reporter declared that this crowd's interest in the election returns showed how the 'democratic principles' of the United States were catching on in Vietnam. The reporter went to members of the crowd and began to ask questions. It then turned out that not only the people gathered there were Saigon Chinese, but they were also not interested in American election procedures: they came to bet on the numbers as they came up in the window. The event is interesting, since it shows an ethnographic situation of observation in some detail: the ones observed are not or only partially known and their overt behaviour (excitement, etc.) can be interpreted in rather conflicting or at least diverging ways.

The overt behaviour in itself does not offer enough information to really base judgement on, and the symbolic or cognitive meaning in it has to be elicited in a way and by means of procedures that are complementary to the ones used in observation. In consequence, the use of photography and film can be a good auxiliary to observation (and indeed, it has proved to be such), but it cannot stand on its own in interpreting the cultural system. In the same way - and to a more dramatic extent, I would say - a basically behaviouristic analysis is inappropriate in anthropology. Harris (1964) defended such an analysis by providing the anthropological community with a behavioural theory and a system of segmentation of behaviour into meaningful units. He especially took care to avoid such dubious terms (sic) as 'purpose', 'goal', 'meaning' and the like. Bourdieu (1971, 180) already attacked this approach on the ground of its unpracticality: segmentation should be either extremely thorough (e.g. 400 units for a simple three minute act) or yield rather superficial interpretations, when used exclusively, since all symbolic and cognitive aspects of culture are banned from it (cf. e.g. Pinxten, 1976).

The analysis of the historical event and of the procedures put forward by Harris tells us that observation in the ethnographic context is 'culture-laden': selecting 'meaningful' units, interpreting chains of data perceived, defining relationships of cause-effect or means-end, are all ever so many ways of imposing a structure by the observer on the material observed. Since he is working with such difficult materials as religious behaviour, belief systems and social structures he is taught to refrain as much as possible from interpreting and imposing structure on them, since such matters are not well known to the Westerner and/or have been experienced to come in widely varying forms. He then can only draw on his most deeply rooted convictions and habits as a basis for comparison: he will invariably impose parts of his own cultural system of norms and structures on the subject perceived in order to render his behaviour intelligible, 'to make it speak for itself'. We are all warned against this tendency in textbooks and field manuals, but we will invariably slip into it when we confront particular behaviours without explicit frames (without 'theory'). A systematic account of such personal experiences by as many anthropologists as would care to do it would be a very welcome information bank for students in anthropology.

In my personal fieldwork the importance of the cultural bias became clear in several instances. In the first place it took me, working with Navajo Indians in Arizona, some weeks to convince informants (even those with whom I worked several times a week) that my approach was different from that of American colleagues: being a Belgian with a rather deep interest in philosophy and religion I kept asking questions about natural philosophy in Indian knowledge and about problems relating to the connection between religion and knowledge on particular points. For weeks my informants kept answering evasively and coming up with ever so many variations on a taxonomic or strictly ethno-linguistic approach to their cultural knowledge. I had to give in temporarily because the informants told me 'that they could answer me like they had done with other anthropologists' and 'that they were eager to work with me and were able to do it too'. In order not to loose informants I had to go along for a while. The informants, on their part, identified me with the American anthropologists they knew since I was a white man coming 'from a province in the extreme East of the USA'. After many trials I finally was accepted with my 'natural philosophical questions' as well, and was recognized as somebody talking about things that practically all American anthropologists shunned (in contrast perhaps to French colleagues). Interpreting this history of my own fieldwork (other aspects are of importance, of course, cf. below) it strikes me that while building up a relationship of confidence and individuality with the informants over a certain period I had meanwhile to cope with a role that was imposed on me and that fitted in the scheme of cultural biases to which the informants were accustomed from contact with other American anthropologists. In other words, I had to abide by the rule of bias that was laid out by researchers before me.

A particular incident with one informant is very significant here. Ken B., a Navajo interpreter who was thoroughly trained in taxonomic analysis in ethnography, was willing to work with me on the problem of part-whole relationships in Navajo language and thought. From the start he explained the idea that was imbedded in the taxonomic system of ordering items in a classification system, thus giving the information he had been taught on this way of doing ethnography. It was only after I insisted that this was not what I came for and that the problems I had run into while searching for a parallel to part and whole notions in Navajo had brought me to him, that he began all over again. This time he explained with many examples and with great insight that nothing like 'parts' and 'wholes' were to be found in Navajo, at least not at all in the sense these notions normally convey to Westerners. His troubles with the translation of words such as 'Almighty', 'Universe', 'Eternity' and so on in the Bible translation in which he was engaged (as a Pentecostal priest) had given hem clear insights into the fundamental differences on this point between Navajo and Western notions. Thus, again, he started by giving me an account of what he had learned of the anthropologist's biases in the first place, and only afterwards, and with great difficulty, switched to the 'native point of view'. I was grateful for the experience.

b) observation is interactional

Apart from these characteristics of ethnographic observation, a basic feature that may be more or less unimportant or even absent in observation in other disciplines (at least in the natural sciences) should be mentioned: ethnographic observation is basically a form of interaction between observer and observed. Devereux formulated this important insight for the first time, and Bourdieu (1980) built a theory around it. Not only is the result of fieldwork quite obviously dependent upon interaction (and the quality of interaction) with informants, but these authors claim that, given the fact that all the data you gather in the field are born from interaction and communication and that no other source of genuine information on cultural peculiarities is available to the anthropologist, interaction (and communication as 'verbal interaction') is what ethnographic analysis is all about.

Any anthropologist who truthfully analyses the actual impact of informants on the results of his fieldwork and who tries to sort out the relationships of dependence and/or interdependence that exist between ethnographer and informant will have to endorse a similar point of view. Ethnography is, to a large extent, a matter of interaction and communication rather than mere observation. Consequently, ethnographic observation (participant or not) is a procedure that must be viewed in the frame of the informant-ethnographer interaction. However, the main questions of ethnographic epistemology are not solved merely by this statement. We need to take just one further step and discuss the types of interaction on which ethnographers can focus in their fieldwork. I see two main avenues here.

First, interaction is important for the ethnographer from his point of view: that is to say, the ethnographer emphasises his input in the interactional process and considers this part to be of sole or main interest. He can do so because he believes that only his part of process can be controlled or known; it is considered utterly impossible to have a full grasp on the informant's input into the observational interaction process. Along these lines of thought, there are still two possible approaches: the ethnographer can either believe in the controllability of the interaction process (on his part) or he can claim that intuitive grasp and more or less boundless *einfühlen* is what matters most. The latter position can be advocated in different ways: 'emphatic involvement' (Mead, 1970, 248) or, indeed, in Fabian's negative characterisation:

> "ethnography looses objectivity to the extent that it counter-
> acts communicative exchange and permits 'analytical' formali-
> zations to reveal over a discursive interpretative stance"
> (Fabian, 1979, 1).

The former position, where the ethnographer believes in this control over the interaction with informants, can take different forms as well. A well known and rather strong form of control would be the use of the 'Notes and queries' system to approach the ethnographic situation. A weaker form is exemplified by Uchendu's work with Navajos, where he deliberately and expressly chose to 'push' communication by exchanging information of a significant nature with informants: *"reciprocity becomes a very effective technique for achieving rapport"* (1970, 236). However, all possibilities are not exhausted with these two views on the ethnographic interaction situation.

Second, interaction is important for ethnographer and consultant alike, from both points of view. It is odd that little has been said about the actual involvement and genuine interest on the part of the one observed - the informant - in ethnographic literature. It always appeared as if the informant was not really interested in the interaction and ethnographers have mainly stressed their own interest and, consequently, their own impact when dealing with the ethnographic situation. Nevertheless, it seems worthwhile to re-examine the situation from a genuine interaction point of view: two parties are involved and both have interest and show means and powers of control to some extent. Negotiation of questions, aims and means of research is what often happens (Pinxten, 1993).

Again, it is possible to distinguish between two 'dimensions' of interaction here: the relationship between the two parties can either build on intuition (non-control) or explicitness and control. Both dimensions can be distinguished by both parties, leading to the possibility of no less than four types of interaction: both parties interact on intuitive grounds only; both parties have control (use 'analytical' tools) in their observation; either one of the parties controls while the other one works intuitively (two possibilities). I will not examine all four, but will be satisfied just to elaborate on the more unusual ones.

It is clear that the 'intuitive', 'participant observing' or 'non-analytically bound' approach of the ethnographer is well known in ethnographic literature (stemming from the tradition that was started by Malinowski), while the 'control' or 'analytical tool' using ethnographer may be recognized either as a behaviourist (cf. Harris, 1964) or as an ethnoscientist (Werner & Schoepfle, 1987). However, the statements on the part of the one observed may seem a bit odd. It is precisely my point that they need to be taken seriously, since evidence on their validity can be gathered easily.

Dogon ethnography offers a beautiful example. Griaule and Dieterlen worked for more than thirty years with the Dogon and gradually came to know and record a huge system of symbolic knowledge. (Whether all of their work is good and valid ethnography is not at issue here). Dogon knowledge and symbolism is neatly divided into four 'levels' of abstraction and secrecy: common sense notions gradually get integrated in a highly abstract system of symbols (Griaule & Dieterlen, 1965, Introduction). Fewer and fewer Dogon are knowledgeable the higher one goes in the system of levels. An important point now is that throughout the thirty years of work with the Griaule crew, Dogon elders managed to systematically hide from them those levels of thought that they were not supposed to be upto at any particular moment and to consciously and deliberately unveil a next higher level of knowledge when the ethnographers were deemed able and trustworthy enough to get this type of 'higher' information. This is absolutely remarkable. The fact that the Dogon thus controlled the information that was given and published should remind us all how tremendously dependent we are on the people we work with. In the case of the Dogon they seem to have guided the ethnographers, maybe not in their actual selection of perceptual impulses, but most certainly in their identification and interpretation of meaningful observations. This is an example of how the 'ones observed' do have an impact on the procedure of ethnographic observation (and fieldwork in general). What is presupposed by the Dogon is a certain amount of information, built up gradually for sure, in the personality and the culture of the ethnographer. It is with this information at hand that they allow the white man to gradually 'observe more and more' of the cultural system.

A second and somewhat different example of impact of the native's part is given by the Navajos. This situation probably obtains with a series of cultures, but my illustration draws on my own fieldwork, and is hence restricted to the Navajo case. It is my point that Navajos developed something like a 'native anthropology' within their cultural knowledge system and that they will necessarily approach the observer with certain a prioris that draw from this system of knowledge. Consequently, the observer is controlled by the expectations and knowledge the natives have, supplementary to his own biases.

Navajos have a dual ceremonial system. One part of it concerns the good and orderly way of the world of Navajos: it is to be found in the "backbone of Navajo mythology", Blessingway (Wyman, 1970), and the more than thirty particular ceremonies that are tagged into it. The other part is called 'Enemyway' (or Squaw Dance or War Dance, Haile, 1945). The latter does not deal with the natural order in the Navajo world as such, but rather serves as a means to rid Navajos (warriors in the first place) of the influences of other tribes, Mexicans and Whites. In their general work on Navajo culture, Kluckhohn and Leighton (1946, 124-139) deal with the different tribes and races that Navajos know about and how they relate to 'The People' (the Navajo, that is). Each foreign people is considered to have its peculiarities and its history. In the War Dance ceremony this emphasis on knowing the other, i.e. the enemy, is stressed even more: the patient or subject of a ceremony has to gather things that belong to the enemy he has met or clashed with. In practice these things are called *"the scalp' although they can actually consist of a lock of hair, a corner of an enemy's coat or dress"* or whatever (Haile, 1945, 8). It is believed that contact with non-Navajos has a bad effect upon Navajos and that this effect can be cured by an Enemyway ceremony. Actually, it is believed that the patient is haunted by the ghost of the enemy and: *"The War dance therefore has no other purpose than to make war upon and kill the ghost of an enemy"* (Haile, 1945, 7).

The main thing about this ceremony, with regard to the problem of the present chapter, is that Navajos clearly show an active involvement in the process of observation that is carried through by the ethnographer: that is to say, they meet and inform the ethnographer according to their preestablished view about his culture. It is fairly obvious that the interaction between observer and the one observed will be different when the latter (or both parties) joins in the interactions with specific aims to control the information gathered (as is explicitly said by medicine men (e.g. Symposium, 1977; Werner, 1979), to allow the observer in daily practices but not in ceremonial life (e.g. Werner, idem) and so on.

The importance of such 'threshold' maneuvers for Navajos is illustrated by two further events in my own fieldwork. After lengthy and often delicate and personal interviews with Frank Harvey, my main informant, I asked whether I was still *'ana'i'* for him (enemy, non-Navajo, potentially dangerous human being). Without any hesitation he answered with great emphasis, "Of course you are". If anything, this event shows that whites remain whites and are to be approached as such without so much as blurring the boundaries between them and The People. In actuality, the 'white' code of greeting (shaking hands) and talking (facing the white man) was continued throughout all our meeting, whereas Navajos were invariably treated in the traditional Navajo way (touching each other's fingers instead of shaking hands, looking away while talking to somebody). On another occasion, we talked about the phenomenon of Enemyway. Frank Harvey mentioned that all the different tribes the Navajo know (Utes, Paiutes, Hopis, Pueblos, Apaches, Zunis, Whites and Mexicans) had their specific characteristics and history

for the Navajos, while the Blacks did not. Consequently, 'it is impossible
to perform an Enemyway concerning contact with Blacks, because we do
not know their history and their ways.' This information shows the
earnestness that is invested in the building and using of a perspective on
'the other' by Navajos.

I am aware that this example of Navajo involvement with white
culture and society may be specific to them. Maybe their form of
ethnocentrism led them to be 'on their marks' where contact with other
cultures is concerned: *"others can only cause illness and misery"* (Haile,
1945) and should be studied carefully to do away with their bad effects,
whereas these same 'others' can never be 'enough Navajo' (since they
were not born Navajo) to be able to know enough about the 'Navajo
way' in order to abuse this knowledge and become a witch for Navajos.
Probably this ethnocentrism greatly helps them to stay alert for the type
of interactions the 'other' (i.c., the observer) is allowed to build with
Navajos, but the example clearly shows that the 'ones observed' need not
be passive, receptive or naive in the observational situation. I think it is
reasonable to presuppose that involvement, control and a sort of 'filter'
mechanism are always present to some extent in the party that 'is being
observed' by an ethnographer. To accept this conclusion is to accept a
thoroughly altered view of observational procedure: not only does the
ethnographer come to the field with his own cultural biases but he may
also have to consider the native cultural biases in 'the one observed' with
regard to Westerners, ethnography and ethnographers and what 'observation' should amount to. A final example illustrates my point in a rather
dramatic way.

Due to the delicacy and sophistication of his Navajo knowledge
only older men could get in touch with the thinker-sage Curly Mustache,
and ask him about his insights. The interest I displayed for Navajo natural
philosophical questions was generally disregarded in the beginning of my
stay on the reservation, but through a peculiar event that involved Curly
Mustache a shift in status (for me) and permission to ask the 'thinker's
questions' came about. Frank Harvey happened to go up to Curly
Mustache with me to feel him out on some questions. When later Curly
Mustache died, the general acceptability of my questions on natural
philosophy was enhanced for several older people, precisely because of

my 'sharing' of mutual respect for the old sage and of acquaintance with
him. It was as if 'I had been involved' in a different way with Navajo
thought and therefore was now allowed to ask these questions to other
people. The same applies, mutatis mutandis, for contacts with Frank
Harvey himself: in the beginning he treated me like 'just another cowboy-
anthropologist' (immediately jumping to a specific type of answer,
refusing to speak about witchcraft, etc.) but his attitude changed as mutual
understanding and confidence grew. I had to convince him of the
usefulness of my project and had to persuade him that the study did not
imply any harmful after-effects for his people. Again, part of the
knowledge of Westerners that Navajos share is presented as severe limits
to involvement on their part:

> "Well, years back, there used to be white people who came in
> without permission from Window Rock (administrative
> capital), to do prospections which were illegal...because of these
> facts, people here got some funny feelings about this kind of
> foreigners. But, nowadays, some of the anthropologists are
> living with the Navajo people, at their home, and not at the
> school or the trading post. That is all right". (Harvey, 1979,
> 148).

In a general way I characterise the field situation as one of 'double
biasedness', where both ethnographer and informant co-determine
through their presuppositions the status of ethnographic knowledge.

5. SUBJECTIVISM AND POSITIVISM COMBINED

> "Space is both natural (physical environment) and man-made-
> house-forms, market areas, playgrounds, shops and other places
> of work - the dimensional properties of spatial relations".
> (Chapple & Spicer, 1979, 10)

This statement, made by two leading anthropologists in the Newsletter
of the American Anthropologist, and intended to be 'advise' for young
fieldworkers, provides a good entry to my conclusions. Let me sum up
what has been found in the foregoing analysis and then come to the initial

steps of the phrasing of an alternative view on the epistemology of ethnographic observation.

The positivistic approach states that field observation is based on two fundamental epistemological principles: a) the possibility of 'objectifying' the other, and b) controllability and repeatability of the observational procedure. On the other hand, the phenomenological view holds that the principles are: a) mutual identification of observer and observed, or 'becoming' the other in the process of observing him or her, and b) recognition of equivalence of the observer by the one observed. These pairs of criteria are not altogether in opposition to one another, but they do exclude each other in fieldwork practice.

In my analysis of the observation situation in my own fieldwork I stressed two principles that are found as only secondary aspects in the other approaches outlined: a) observation is theory- and culture-laden, and b) observation is interaction. The second principle is incompatible with the positivistic outlook, since 'interaction with an object' is an awkward expression. The positivistic fieldworker is wary of the impact of the other in his work (cf. Harris's, 1964, opposition to the 'uncontrollable' aspects of goal, meaning, etc., and his conviction that 'the other' cannot be depended upon since he may tell lies). In the 'phenomenological' view interaction may be incorporated (cf. Fabian). In my own field experience I had to recognise the impact of interaction and communication as very basic, indeed determining the results to a great extent. In addition, I am inclined to conclude from the relatively unsuccessful work I was told about by informants that in those cases a lack of or a miscomprehension of interaction was a fundamental element in the explanation of failure. Finally, the theory-and-culture-ladeness of observation is not recognized by either approach. It is not incompatible with a positivistic or scientific approach to anthropology however (cf. similar discussions in general philosophy of science fired off by Kuhn, 1962), while it is excluded by 'phenomenologists'. The latter take it for granted that their intuitive or *einfühlende* approach to 'the other' will eventually get them to understand and identify the one observed; thus there is no place for the relativism implied by the principle of theory-and culture-ladeness. One way to cope with the problem is presented in the pessimistic outlook of Karnoouh (cf. 1981): he states that genuine understanding of the other is impossible because of what I called the 'culture-ladeness' of observation. Consequently, untranslatability is maximal and should simply be acknowledged, according to this author. On the other hand, those authors who do believe that something valuable and indeed genuine can be known in a 'phenomenological' approach disregard culture-ladeness altogether (e.g. Fabian, 1979). I claim that since the problem is a real one and the impact of theory- and culture-ladeness can be demonstrated clearly (cf. section 4 above), a different solution should be mapped out. In this way the rationale of 'positivism and subjectivism combined' takes shape.

On the one hand the subject-subject relation is important in fieldwork, and interaction seems to be an intrinsic feature of the fieldwork endeavor. These two principles warrant some sort of 'participant' or 'phenomenological' approach. On the other hand, the fieldworker is trapped in a situation where his own biases and those of his consultants have a serious impact on the quality and value of his observations. Therefore, some sort of positivistic attitude is called for. What is needed, then, is a device to control the interaction between both parties to some extent. Moreover, the control should be such that the fieldwork can be modified, redirected or deepened whenever need be, that is to say, whenever the highly personal and strictly accidental changes in attention and insight that happen are recognized and worked into the field results. The conclusion should be, in my opinion, that a device is needed that would render both ethnographer and consultant conscious of the ways in which they are biased. As indicated in the analysis of Dogon and Navajo ethnographic studies I claim that the control should work for both parties since both have (no doubt somewhat different) biases which they bring into the observational interaction.

The conscious explicitation of biases (or knowledge that accompanies observation of 'the other') is a first step, I think. Thus, the preconceptions of the Navajo should be taken seriously: it is with these biases in mind that the Navajo enters and indeed organises future interactions with ethnographers. The informant may alter his insights slightly during and after each confrontation, but the basic outlook is likely to stay invariant. The system of questions and presuppositions that is available to the ethnographer in such manuals as the 'Notes and Queries' does constitute a rather similar device, although its sophistication will probably be higher in view of many modifications by competent fieldworkers. Still, the cultural biases of such manuals can hardly be overestimated, as is apparent from 'native' criticisms of the anthropological approaches (e.g. Owusu's criticism of the British tradition in anthropology, 1978). What is needed, then, is a device that would go beyond these manuals to such an extent that it a) allows for a less culture-specific view of what is seen and discussed in interaction with other cultures and b) creates a sufficiently general meeting ground for mutual observation and interaction for both parties, so that both can use it to match their own conceptions and to enter into further exploration of the other. Such a device can be the result of and is also used as a means of negotiation in the field.

This approach has been worked out to some extent by different and relatively independent scholars in recent years. I will call the approach the 'frame of reference' or 'intercultural metaframe' outlook, since in all the examples we now have of it some sort of intermediate frame is introduced to organise the interaction and communication between informant and ethnographer. The best known example is a perceptual naming test that has been used extensively both in ethnographic studies and in cross-cultural comparisons, namely the Munsell card of color chips. It was the great imaginative power of Berlin & Kay (1969) that led to its widespread use to measure and compare color naming in some 98 different languages. The procedure is clear: the Munsell card comprises a presentation of all possible physiological differentiations in color of which humans are capable (as shown in more than one hundred years of color research). Ethnographers go to particular cultures and ask the natives to indicate (by pointing to the color map) which of their color words would match what areas of the card. The authors found languages which distinguished between two, three and ultimately eleven basic categories of color. The mixture of epistemological stands hold here: the positivistic aspect is recognized in the strictly scientific (indeed physiological) phrasing of the frame of reference (i.e., the Munsell card), and the subjectivistic aspect resides in the culture-specific identification of meaningful areas of color by the informant and in the more or less rigid way 'labeling' or 'referring' is interpreted in the fieldwork. The latter was interpreted in a rather narrow way by the authors of this study (cf. also Conklin's critique, 1973) through the very exclusive use of ostension in the field situation. Still, one can imagine that - even with color differentiation - more symbolic and social references can be allowed in the identification of categories within this frame. This goes beyond the scope of the Berlin & Kay study, however. The more generalised prototype approach of Kay led recently to a theory of categories to be used in semantics and in cognitive anthropology (Lakoff, 1986; Holland & Quinn, 1988).

Similar studies were done with another perceptual test battery: the collection of visual illusions that was developed by Campbell, Segall and Herskovits (1966) was used in comparative studies in different cultures. The research resulted in the conclusion that illusions tend to be culture-laden, since different cultural knowledge systems tend to have different ways of coping with the problems that are expressed in the visual illusion battery (Campbell, 1968). Although this study is very specific, its general perspective is very much akin to the frame of reference outlook I advocate.

Another major domain of anthropological study is kinship; Good-enough (1970) offered a general overview and a theoretical reappraisal of the age-old study of kinship. In the main chapter of his book (Chapter 4, dealing with the theoretical problems of emic-etic, distinctions) he goes on to define an approach that is pretty similar to the one advocated here, but restricted to kinship studies: anthropologists have come to a point in kinship studies where they can work from a general frame of kin notions and test and specify these in actual fieldwork. In practice, Goodenough proposed to work with a set of 'basic features' and apply them through detailed and culture-specific empirical work in cultures all over the world. Again, the positivistic element (the frame of 'kin features' that the ethnographer and the informant can use to build a common ground for mutual understanding) is largely complemented by detailed, idiosyncratic, particular and otherwise non-systematised information that grows in the interpersonal relation of actual fieldwork. the latter aspect clusters around the frame of reference notions which are the aspect of the ethnographic enterprise that is typical of the present outlook.

Finally, time, space or any other social, cultural or cognitive categories can be researched on in similar ways. Bernabé (1974 & 1980) and Pinxten (1975 & 1983) have been working on explicit frames of reference for temporal and spatial analysis respectively. In both cases time or space are understood in the broadest possible sense, including physical, perceptual, actional, social, symbolic and what have you aspects. again, in both cases the authors have sought to develop a scientific frame that would be general enough to allow for all possible divergent identifications and to be useful in field negotiation. The frame of reference approach they present falls within the epistemological outlook outlined in this section. It can be used for analysis of cultural knowledge systems in any community. The same principles can be mentioned as typical features of both frames of reference: a highly general and strictly scientific set of concepts (distinctions, meaningful criteria for temporal or spatial behaviour) is worked out and serves as a control for the intuition or biases of ethnographer and informant. This has a profoundly hermeneutic touch to it. The frame serves to elicit and engage communication, interpretation, refusal, and identification on any relevant notion in as wide and varied a way as is imaginable in the cultural knowledge system of the informant.

The principles that are fundamental in the 'frame of reference' approach to ethnographic observation, can be summarised in the following way.

– First, the one observed is not really constituted in the fieldwork observation, and certainly cannot be 'objectified' in any direct way. Instead, aspects of his ways of organising the world gradually emerge from an essentially interactional process. The one observed is supposedly similar to the observer himself (at least to some degree), but this preconception cannot be taken up in the actual mapping out of the subject matter of the field experience. Instead, the mediating instrument of research, i.e. of communication and interaction, is rendered explicit in the frame.

– Second, truth is not a meaningless notion in this approach, but it is a greatly ramified one. It is not reached according to principles which the observer alone (but not the one observed), can handle. Instead, truth (or some degree of rightness: Goodman, 1989) is reached from the moment both informant and ethnographer agree about the result of research. This result then relates to the mediating device (frame of reference) in the sense that it is the modification of the frame (to whatever extent: vast alteration or minor modification) that is deemed satisfactory and understandable (communicable) by both interacting parties. The result is to a large extent a common construct engaging both parties and involving biases of both. The impact of power in field relationships is not explicitly dealt with here (but see chapter 1). It deserves a separate analysis, linking my view with Bourdieu's (1971 & 1980).

I hope to have drawn more exact lines between the two classical approaches and the 'new approach', because I have been searching for the epistemological principles that underlay these three outlooks in anthropology. The important questions about the nature and limits of anthropological observation have hardly been treated in the discipline and a start as inconclusive and general as the one presented here should thus have some reason for existence. I do believe that a major shift in anthropology was brought about by Malinowski's search for a specifically ethnographic method, and everybody knows that (aside from very rare exceptions) the field experience is a tremendously powerful and irreplacable means for the exploration of both the other culture and the discipline of ethnography itself. However, I believe that the modification that is introduced by the frame of reference approach, which combines some of the advantages of the positivistic or scientific outlook on ethnography with the basic and forceful aspects of the Malinowskian approach, is a necessary step for ethnography. This discussion cannot be decided on mere grounds of methodology (as has been tried in the past). It should be won or lost on the basis of epistemological choices: what do we want to study and what can we study with some degree of earnestness? I hope the present chapter has shown at least one way to open this discussion.

Note

I am very much indebted to my wife, Ingrid van Dooren, who not only was an irreplaceable help for me in the fieldwork trips we undertook, but also urged me to reconsider the strange phenomenon of 'native anthropology' that Enemyway seemed to constitute for the Navajo Indians. I am very grateful to my friend Jean Bernabé who discussed many of the topics in this chapter at considerable length and was never bored with me when I started the discussion all over again on subsequent occasions. Finally, the Navajo Indians have given me the tremendous opportunity to work and live with them, I feel their teaching has been very important for my life and my work. I hope the present chapter does them justice and may help fellow anthropologists to really integrate the view of the informant as much as possible in the outlook they adopt on anthropology as such.

CHAPTER 3
Anthropological Concepts

1. THE EPISTEMOLOGICAL STATUS OF ANTHROPOLOGICAL CONCEPTS AND PROCEDURES

Ever since Kuhn's (1962) forceful analysis of the social components in scientific development, representatives of different disciplines have been progressively granting leeway to this type of research. it is now comfortable and even a bit "à la mode" to point to the social constraints or the political pressures that favoured one rather than the other development in a discipline. As far as I know, however, very little genuine and encompassing epistemological analysis of anthropological concepts and procedures has been carried through. I propose to introduce a few basic epistemological questions, combining some highlights in the Kuhnian approach with some more traditional problems. In this way, I hope to reach the rational proposed by Campbell (1989): to combine the social study of a science with the analysis of traditional epistemological problems.

a) theory-ladenness of anthropological concepts.

In the preceding chapter on observation in anthropology, I emphasised the impact of the ethnographer's biases on the knowledge elicited. One of the most tenacious and often overlooked set of biases could be called, from the standpoint of an epistemologists, the theory or paradigm the ethnographer is working with. In the beginning of this century, anthropologists tended to think that a culture could be 'collected' in some sense or other. The 'Boasian' program emphasised that, in a world of disappearing cultures, it was most important to send out ethnographers to all cultures 'on the verge of disappearing', in order to collect material culture, lexicons and pictures (Mead, 1976). The objects, pictures, texts and other items gathered this way were then placed in a museum for anthropological collections. Anthropologists managed to develop this habit to such an extent that numerous peoples in Africa and in the Americas abhor of this type of researchers, since "they render a living people into a museum piece" (personal communication on the Navajo reservation).

The point that interests me in this chapter is the mental disposition, hidden in this conception of 'the other' which subsequently led to a standardisation of outlooks for fieldwork, a unification of concepts and cultural features and even a standardisation of questions to be asked by the ethnographer, regardless of the field s/he was entering. The latter statement refers to the tradition of manuals for ethnography, exemplified in a grand way by the British *Notes and Queries*. The idea prevailed that 'the other' had no individuality of any importance. Identical methods thus could be used to 'collect data' on Eskimo culture, on Hindu ways or on Bantu tradition. All one had to do was follow the book of questions and quasi-automatically one would end up with a detailed ethnography about the people one happened to visit. Even the added emphasis on participant observation did not really blend this procedure, since after the fact series of ethnographic monographs which resulted from this approach, tend to resemble one another to a formidable extent. The 'thingification of culture' (Fishman, 1979) that is implicit in this approach is a good example of the theory-ladenness of concepts and facts in this particular tradition in anthropology: instead of the culture a mere collection of objects is the result of research.

It is enlightening to mention a well known credo of Victor Turner in the light of the foregoing paragraph. Turner makes it a point to stress that social reality should be seen primarily as a form of 'becoming' rather than one of 'being' (cf. e.g. Turner, 1969, and Keyes in Turner, 1978, 243). This epistemological emphasis is irreconcilable with the one advocated in the Boasian tradition mentioned above. Furthermore, it is not surprising that a genuine interest in the processual aspects of a culture was absent from the 'museum' tradition in anthropology (cf. also Fabian's critique below), whereas the dynamic or processual view of Turner has a very elaborate, multiperspectival and more or less opaque way of dealing with 'objects' in another culture. The confrontation of these two traditions, working from very different theories about culture, 'the other', and so on, shows the importance of the epistemological topic of theory-ladenness for anthropology. I illustrate this emphasis on theory-ladenness with the analysis of structuralist anthropology.

Structuralist anthropology emphasised the fundamental status and the all-pervading nature of binary organisation of cultural material. As early as his *Anthropologie structurale* of 1958, Lévi-Strauss felt the need to stress the all importance of 'dualist organisations' against possible criticism by inserting (alongside papers which explained or exemplified its role in specific domains of culture), the famous paper 'en hommage' to J.P.B. de Josselin de Jong, in this major exposition of the doctrine. The particular focus on binary or dualistic organisation in any given culture follows more or less automatically from the phonological methods and concepts Lévi-Strauss gathered from Jakobson's courses. The dualistic organisation of all cultural phenomena is not so much a result of research or even a heuristic device to start investigating things: it is a fundamental given that is only 'reproduced' by the researcher. Lévi-Strauss states:

> "It concerns an original logic, the direct expression of the structure of the mind... and not a passive product of environmental action on an amorphous conscience" (1962, 130).

A similar opinion is to be found in other texts by him, claiming a neurophysiological status for the dualistic organisation on the one hand (*Le totémisme aujourd'hui*) or a definitely universal basis of thinking (*La pensée sauvage*), and watering down the position to a mere methodological tool of detection and description in the Second *Structural Anthropology* (1973). In Lévi-Strauss's structural anthropology, the dualistic interpretation of cultural phenomena is always the preferred way to approach culture. Consequently, one will not be surprised to find a certain more or less schematic description in terms of oppositional pairs of aspects of culture of very diverse peoples. Whether the dualisms are given in the data or in the methods of analysis, they surely are what the anthropologist should be looking for. In other words, they belong to the outlook or the system of biases the researcher takes with him when entering the field.

One of the dramatic results of this sort of approach has been highlighted by Fabian (1984). He locates the impact of the ahistorical approach in the image of 'the other'. The simple effect of structuralist theories on our knowledge about culture studies is that (since structuralism focuses exclusively on synchronic structural characteristics) these cultures do not seem to have any history of their own. The 'objects' of research appear to be described 'totally and as a system' in terms of purely structural relationships. The image one gets of these cultures while reading these structuralist papers or books is one of totally static and ahistorical societies. The particular feature of anti-historicism or ahistoricisim (cf. Lévi-Strauss, 1958, Chapter I), which is inherent in structuralism is thus projected on the subjects studied. Attempts to 'dynamize' structuralism are meant to overcome this deficiency (e.g. Laughlin & d'Aquili, 1974).

This is a typical, though somewhat synthetic, illustration of the fallacies of theory-ladenness in anthropological thought.

b) contextuality of anthropological concepts

By 'contextuality' of anthropological concepts, I mean to focus on the social, political, cultural and historical aspects which influence fieldwork and thus will in some way affect the ethnographic result. Since both the ethnographer and the 'native subjects' are culture bearers in a different culture, the impact of the contextual aspects on the results of the encounter cannot be overlooked. Unfortunately, in keeping with the pretension of anthropology as a science (and thus of the decontextualised status of anthropological knowledge) this focus has been neglected to a considerable degree. I point to some examples in order to make the problem stand out clearly.

Fabian (1984) analyses the way in which 'coevalness' (and thus history) has been either neglected in or altogether denied to other cultures over the last hundred years. The emphasis on static and timeless description which is eminent in the physical sciences (cf. Prigogine, 1981; Prigogine & Stengers, 1979) was taken up in the social sciences as well in a glorious strive to be seen as 'scientific'. Consider the immediate political context in which fieldwork is done and which is, more often than not, not rejected by ethnographers. Owusu (1978 is one of the first 'native' anthropologists to have drawn attention to this point. In his devastating critique on ethnography of Africa, he focuses on the work of the one scholarly example every anthropologist is taught about during his studies: Evans-Pritchard's work on the Nuer. Owusu analyses the results of Evans-Pritchard's study in the light of the political context at the time of research of both the ethnographer and the Nuer. It appears that Evans-Pritchard entered the field a few years after the English military administration carried out a bloody 'pacification' of the Nuer. This fact, which is never mentioned by Evans-Pritchard and has consequently been forgotten by most people, adds a tremendous amount of potentially vital information for the evaluation of Evans-Pritchard's work. Owusu stresses that the clear and very short-term memory of bloody suppression of a people by the compatriots of the ethnographer who comes to study them, must certainly have had a strong impact on the fieldwork. Undoubtedly, the ethnographer starts out as a representative of the oppressors to begin with since he will have the authorisation to do his fieldwork from the administration who directly or indirectly was part of the pacification procedure. The data which Evans-Pritchard gathered from the Nuer were more probably than not filtered or otherwise coloured by the memory of the dramatic events the people had just endured.

This point is well taken. Every ethnographer knows that some aspects in his of her field have to do with power relations between different groups, of which he may be a representative by his mere colour or nationality. Moreover, Talal Asad (1974) mentions in his valuable reader on the subject of anthropology and colonialism that it is only after the Second World War and because of the loss of colonial territories that any thorough consciousness of the role and impact of colonial situations on the status of anthropological data is seen to be growing within the discipline (esp. 12-13). A unique forerunner in this regard is Tax (1945). Even then, a considerable amount of anthropologists keep denying this plain fact by boosting about the 'scientific' status of anthropology. In the light of the growing consciousness of the contextuality of scientific knowledge in general this opinion seems to be becoming more and more untenable (cf. below sub c).

A recent example of the growing consciousness of the contextuality of ethnographic work can be seen in the growing literature of epistemology of anthropology. A specific and forceful example of a detailed aspect of this trend should be recognised in the emphasis on self-reflexivity of anthropology as a means to avoid naive and (with regard to 'the other') obnoxious research (Ruby, 1982). To get a clear view of the degrees of naivety or harmful unconcernedness in the ethnographer I advocate the system of five epistemological windows that Werner (1981) worked out. He lists five steps of growing ever more epistemologically (and in my view politically) conscious in the process of doing ethnography:

–*the ethnological window*: the ethnographer claims it is important to gather as much data as possible (and gradually more and more) about any cultural form or product of the culture he studies. The claim is that through more knowledge one will automatically get better knowledge and learn about the cultural knowledge system of the other;

–*the stereo vision window*: one tries to have a view of the culture of the ethnographer and of the culture of the native people. This combination of views will secure more insight. Kluckhohn advocated this view on anthropology;

–*the first diachronic epistemological window*: the ethnographer has become weary of his of her intuition. In the field a diary is kept and when writing up a report the fieldnotes and the diary are continuously consulted and analysed. Mead has initiated this step.

–*the second diachronic epistemological window*: the anthropologist does not really trust his capacity of functioning as a mere 'tape recorder' of the culture in his fieldwork. The fieldnotes and even the transcriptions of a former period are constantly rechecked. In this case the ethnographer clearly begins to recognise the importance of biases and of contextuality in the actual field activities. In checking the old transcriptions he will have to seek advice with informants and colleagues.

–*the systematic distortion hypothesis:* the ethnographer becomes conscious of the 'datedness' and full contextuality of his data gathering procedures. He will now check any insight he thinks he has on the spot and compare it with former and later readings of the data. Roy D'Andrade focuses on this strategy. The idea is that personal and contextual biases sneak into the data and that some form of intersubjectivity can only be guaranteed when comparing and cross-checking in different times and different contexts.

In this five window system, one sees a growing epistemological consciousness and an increasing search to counter different forms of naivety and biasedness by variation of dependence on contextual aspects.

c) culture-ladenness of anthropological knowledge.

This section deals with a notion of 'culture' that is common among cognitive anthropologists. It details on the natural philosophy, the habits and rules which are incorporated by a community and are necessary and sufficient to act appropriately within that community (cf. Goodenough, 1970).

In the ethnographic study of science studies have been done which focus heavily on this dimension: Latour & Woolgar (1979) have done thorough fieldwork in a famous American laboratory, while Knorr (1981) reports on similar work by her own. Apostel et al. (1979) conducted a first empirical study on the epistemological positions of scientists as observers in Ghent, while Pinxten (1980) did a similar analysis for Prigogine's works. All these studies are pioneering studies. They thus have the drawbacks and the advantages of any novel enterprise. They are sketchy and unbalanced, but daring. Along the road a distinguished scholar in psychology and philosophy joined the group and proposed to think through some of the propositions and statements offered. Campbell (1979) elaborates on the initial concepts and proposes to describe scientific groups in terms of 'tribal' rules and behaviours. This proposition closes the circle and heaves the discussion back into an epistemological discourse: science is produced by groups of people with their world view and convictions and, consequently, scientific knowledge may be analysable in terms of categories which are normally uses for 'other' peoples. The cesure between 'us' and 'them' is abolished and a genuine analysis of the cultural nature of any type of knowledge (and of differentiation between types) can finally begin.

One of the most intriguing and at the same time unavoidable insights gained from this type of analysis is that science is indeed based on a cultural knowledge system. When the rules of this particular system, its emphases and preferences, will be substantially known, we will be able to compare and eventually contrast scientific knowledge in specific instances with e.g. Bantu or Navajo knowledge. We do not know whether the difference will be found along an opposition between 'theoretic thinking' and 'bricolage' (Lévi-Strauss, 1962b), but the present data seem to point to as much analogical, contextual and pragmatic (or 'opportunistic') reasoning in science as in any cultural knowledge system we know of (Knorr, 1981; Atra, 1990).

At this level then, the particular emphases of particular cultures can be revealed and discussed. Some of this has already been hinted at in previous studies, but a general and clear-cut discussion has never happened. The works of Horton (1967; 1991) on African thought and of Needham (1965) on Chinese science come to mind as excellent treatises on differences in cultural knowledge systems. Once we will be courageous and modest enough to recognise the culture-ladenness of science (and of anthropology), we will be able to delineate the epistemological status of scientific concepts and theories in a more realistic way.

Let me offer just one example of what the consciousness of culture-ladenness of anthropological knowledge can lead to. The example concerns a basic problem in anthropology, namely the question of translatability. In his beautiful book on ethnopoetics Hymes (1981) devotes a complete introductory chapter to this topic. Traditional anthropology aims at giving a report that is understandable to the western reader. In this attempt the use of native poetry is normally subject to a set of conditions which are dictated by the cultural principles of the anthropologist and which often violate the rules of the culture reported on. Hymes points to the habit of the anthropologist to delete parts of the poem, forge the word order and more or less neglect the literal expressions found to come to a polished, beautiful sounding and smooth verse that can be appreciated by the reader (i.e. the Westerner). Typically, repetitions, meaningless interjections and the like are deleted in translation so that some of the flavour of the poem we (Westerners) recognize can still be appreciated. The product that is thus offered is very different from the original, but the rules of knowledge treatment (through repetition, etc.) of 'the other' are so much different from ours that we feel justified to 'overrule' them and adapt some of it to suit our rules. This is a clear 'violation' of facts, but the 'scientific' flavour that is ascribed to the exposition is deemed enough of a warrant to allow for such alterations. This is a typical instance in anthropology of the phenomenon of culture-ladenness: we superimpose our rules and define treating knowledge on theirs.

d) the construction of the anthropological object.

The characteristics which are ascribed to the object of study in any scientific discipline are often left implicit and even unconscious by the members of that discipline (Rubinstein, 1984). Bourdieu has the merit to have classified the implicit 'epistemologies' of anthropologists. He distinguishes between three different approaches, depending on the differential ways to deal with the 'object' of research (1980):

– the *phenomenological approach*: this epistemology is apparent in the disciplinary trend in anthropology which emphasises participant observation as a genuine method to elicit data. The presupposition here is that 'the other' is like oneself. There is a great deal of familiarity with the 'object' of study which is given, because 'the other' is a subject as well. Therefore by empathically trying to become like 'the other' (living among them, acting and talking like them, etc.) one will gain a view from the inside. At the limit one can report on the culture and thought of 'the other' because one has sufficiently grown to be like him.

– the *positivistic approach*: this epistemology is found in such schools of anthropology as behaviourism and structuralism. In this case, the object of study is felt to be outside of the observer and unfamiliar to him. 'The other' is objectified as much as possible, following a tradition in physical-ist thought.

– the *praxeological approach*: this epistemology is elaborated by Bourdieu and some other contemporary scholars (Fabian, 1971 & 1979; Pinxten, 1977; Pinxten et al., 1983). It aims at combining the objectivistic and the subjectivistic approach: the external knowledge of "the other" is internal-ised by the researcher and the introspective knowledge of the researcher is externalised onto the subject of research at the same time. The dialectic between both movements allows for a full understanding of the cultural phenomenon. In this case the 'object of research' is visualised as the communication and interaction processes between self and 'the other', and material culture, language, social organisation and so on are ever so much external forms or artefacts of the processes themselves. As a consequence, the researcher should be hesitant to believe his eyes when rounding up facts and should always and profoundly seek confirmation and critique through the medium of 'the other'. No objective features can be taken for granted, and the introspective insights of participant observation are nothing but one-sided hints.

I adopt the latter, praxeological view on anthropological work. Since 'the other' is a subject as well and since interaction and communica-tion between subjects has the delicate status and the multiperspectival character we have learned to ascribe to them in our own social interac-tion, the status of anthropological knowledge is dependent on all peculiar modifications and hazards we recognize in forms of human interaction. This need not necessarily lead us into a limitless relativism but it should warn us and make us weary of easy and straightforward methodologies to conduct research.

Having determined what are, in my opinion, the epistemological issues to be conscious of as an anthropologists, I now go on and screen what the anthropologists have so far come up with to fill in the picture of 'man the knower'.

I am conscious that there is an implicit paradox in this strategy. How can you first criticise former anthropological work because it did not meet the right epistemological standards and then go on to use some of its results to amend epistemology itself? The answer is that, because any serious epistemological question involves a certain amount of circularity, you can only build up a discipline by making explicit its epistemology which is then founded partly in the results of the discipline, which are then evaluated again by means of possibly more refined epistemological statements, and so on. The relationship between epistemology and the discipline (e.g. anthropology) is by necessity a dynamic one, and even, as will be shown later on, dialectic one (cf. also Rubinstein, 1984).

2. AN ANTHROPOLOGIST EXAMINES SOME EPISTEMOLOGICAL CONCEPTS

a) untranslatability and incommensurability

Quine (1960) is recognised to have formulated a basic critique in semantics. Starting from the fantasy-ethnographer he explains the impossibility of translation and meaning through estrangement in the ethnographic context. Notwithstanding his convincing arguments, his view has not been shared by everybody in semantics and anthropology. The disciplinary boundaries prohibit knowledge of the philosopher's work by many linguistics and anthropologists. Quine's general idea is that any translation implies an in principle impossibility to determine meaning on an a priori basis. One can only learn about the meaning of an expression through painstaking trial and error runs. Even when competence in the foreign system of linguistic and cognitive codes is acquired some number of untranslatable message will remain.

On the conceptual level, a similar emphasis on the incommensurability of theories and concepts has been developed by the tradition following Kuhn (1962).

Both philosophical theories stress that a certain form of relativism cannot be avoided. I subscribe to this position in principle, although I strongly object to the pessimism and defaitism that often go with it. The following makes clear the reasons and arguments for this objection. I have the conviction that the study of ethnographic context and anthropological theories offers important modifications on the foregoing epistemological positions. I propose to examine a bold statement: both universalism and relativism hold.

After a fruitless debate between universalists (mostly linguists) and relativists (both linguists and ethnographers) in the 60's and 70's, the conviction is growing fast that both positions have some truth, provided they are allowed to speak about particular phenomena.

The fundamental 'tools for thought' of any new-born human being are his body and his environment. Any new-born has essentially the same means of motion, perception and manipulation at his disposal, although his environment may offer very different materials to move, perceive or manipulate. The conviction is growing that the first conceptualisations of all human beings will be of the same rough and qualitative nature as Piaget (1970) found in Genevan children. The motoric and sensorial system of the child allow for a very imprecise, prelinguistic and prelogical organisation of experience. This organisation will to some extent depend on the forms and manipulatory qualities of the material (e.g. plants cannot be categorised in many different ways, because they more or less dictate their category to the human perceiver by their very qualities, see Kay, 1979; Atran, 1990). On the other hand, this organisation will be heavily dependent on the qualities of the human body and the human perception and action apparatus. The latter aspect must explain why universal categories can be found: e.g. spatial differentiations in very diverging cultures and languages seem to have a universal basic category of 'neighbourhood' (in terms of reachability) and 'overlapping' in common (cf. Pinxten, 1976; Pinxten et al., 1983). There is no spatial knowledge imaginable without these genetically and logically basic differentiations, and the actual structure of the human body can account for their universality: an infant will first divide his environment in function of what can be reached or grasped versus what is literally "out of reach", and he will have to learn depth through 'hide and seek- procedures and through 'coverage' of space by his own body. In colour differentiation the actual discrimination potential of the human eye is the physiological (and not e.g. the physical characteristics of light diffraction nor the aesthetic qualities of different colours) basis from which man's differentiation of the colour spectrum can be studied (Berlin & Kay, 1969; Kay, 1979). However, once the human being is a grownup his system of differentiations will be seen to diverge from that of practically anybody else. Most certainly the system of differentiation will be different from one cultural or linguistic community to the next one. It is at the level of further sophistication and of greater refinement in knowledge that the researcher will detect marked differences and will start to speak about cultural relativism and untranslatability, the obvious mechanism seems to be that the child is socially and culturally integrated throughout his rearing period and that he learns progressively to incorporate the particular outlook that is historical in his community as a more detailed and more sophisticated alternative to his first, rough and sensori-motor differentiations. The full-blown knowledge system of another culture thus appears at first sight to be radically different from the Western one (cf. Whorf's interpretation, 1956), while the difference might really reside only in the sophistication which developed diverging forms of a basically universal primary bias of experience.

Thus, the emphasis on 'natural kinds' (Quine, 1969) or the focus on the compelling aspect of 'entitativity' of things and categories (Campbell, 1973) of the philosophers can be reconciled in a specific interpretation with the relativism of these same philosophers (Quine, 1960; Campbell, 1989).

On top of this there are ideological aspects of translation: Translation is not only limited and cognitively hazardous as Quine and others contend. t is also an ideological endeavour. On the Fourth Russell Tribunal (Rotterdam 1981) the primary demand of Indian representatives, was that something should be done to stop the activities of the Summer School of Linguistics. This training center for missionaries is held responsible for the uniformed and deficient reporting on many Indian languages and cultures. The technical and so-called 'value-free' shield with which linguists are equipped in this type of school keeps them from becoming conscious of the abortive and altering character of their reports on the language and culture they study, and of the Bible translations they implement.

The problem is a difficult one, since the process of translation is only superficially understood (Steiner, 1973). A few examples will make clear what is meant here with the 'ideological' aspects of translation. Witherspoon (1977) devotes a good deal of his beautiful book to the concept of language as it is understood by the Navajos. Language is not only a system to express thoughts, but is itself seen to be formative vis-à-vis thought and reality: it is the system of externalisation and thus of realisation of concepts, which in themselves can modify the world of the speaker and his environment. In other words speaking directly transforms reality. By denying this aspect the Navajo knowledge is abused and will become potentially dangerous. A far-reaching example in this same context is the reporting on the religious system of the Navajos. When examining the religious system of a people, anthropologists tend to look for unities and forms that have some referent in their own tradition: thus, 'God(s)', 'spirits' and the like are searched for. The same has happened in the study of Navajos: the medicine man has been characterised as the possessor of magical, spiritual, theistic and other powers, depending on the intuition of the anthropologist at work. A recent analysis of the usability of all of the Judeo-christian categories in the Navajo context revealed that they cannot be matched here (Garisson, 1975; Pinxten, 1981). The best way to characterise the 'object of reverence' of the Navajo religious practices turns out to be the Navajo tradition itself. Since the cognitive-symbolic representation is not readily recognised as the 'Holy of Holy' in the Western conceptualisation this focus was never come up with by anthropologists. The inability to grasp this perspective and the subsequent series of 'imposed recognitions' (Gods, spirits, etc.) is a clear instance of ideological impact on the part of the anthropologists.

A more subtle mechanism is pointed out by Rothenberg (1972). In his attempt at 'total translation' he stresses that endless and meaningless repetition, nonsensical interjections, tones of expression and so on are ever so much genuine and meaning carrying aspects of a native American poem: they are never found in the English translation, where the exclusive focus will be on so-called meaningful syllables, rhymes and syntactic rhythm. The deletion of the native material corrupts the whole sense of time and atmosphere expressed, and renders the translation inadequate and even untruthful. It is this tradition of translation-as-corruption which produced the expression in one of Hymes's consultants and which serves as a title to his book: *In vain I tried to tell you* (1981). Hymes comments:

"In vain I tried to tell you" indeed, when editing censors structure (1981, 7).
I second this statement.

Both forgoing aspects of anthropological results add modifications
to the relativistic positions outlined by philosphers: the knower is bound
to be subjected to the epistemological limits of translatability and
commensurability, but these limits are less forbidding or exclusive in
practice than they appear in Quine's philosophical hypotheses.

b) culture-specific metaphors and concepts

Campbell (1964 & 1989) sums up the results of several years of
cross-cultural psychological work on visual illusions. It appeared that
different cultures tend to generate different illusions. The explanation
brought forward to cope with this fact is tentative: it looks as if the
environment and its processed form in a particular culture co-determine
the way the members of a cultural community perceive. The human
subject corrects his perception according to the rule the cultural tradition
(in a particular environment) dictates and thus falls prey to the visual
illusion which is especially suited for this 'correction'. For example, the
'carpentered' environment of the Westerner thus generates a high
vulnerability for the Muller-Lyer illusion, but not so with the Bantu forest
context. The point made by Campbell and his collaborators is: different
cultures have different ways of directing and shaping perception and thus
will have different perspectives in their world view. In its generality this
point has never been refuted, as far as I know, although discussions have
been engaged as to the explanation and the range of this cultural bias (cf.
above sub 2a). Much work remains to be done in order to have an
overview of the full impact of such cultural constraints on perception.

On the level of language use, the construction and use on
metaphors and the culture-specific use of cultural concepts in the
development of rigorous and dependable knowledge, some important
research has been done. Elkana (1981) and Horton (1991) offer useful
overviews.

A few examples will make clear what is meant here. By the end of the 19th century, a theory was developed in physics which characterised light as a wavelike phenomenon. The reference was clearly to motion in a substance like water, which is seen to progress in the form of waves. In other words, the metaphor used to start building a theory of light was drawn from common sense knowledge of water (though, of course, the theory transcended common sense). The idea of 'substance' and of a world consisting of such substances to begin with seems to be a prerequisite in order to understand this line of reasoning. When looking at the Navajo way of featuring light, one finds that both the word used and the conceptualisation of light brings it in close relationship with cornpollen (stem *dinidiin* in both cases). Both aspects of nature indeed have in common, in the perspective of Navajos, that they express and are to some extent the basic sources and means of life-giving power: the pollen is used in many ceremonies because of this feature and the sunbeam is considered to be the main source of power and strength for everything growing on earth. Thus, their metaphorical closeness is substantiated through their similarity of function in the world. it is thus both logical and culturally accepted to think of light when thinking of pollen for a Navajo, because they have analogical functions in a system that is basically characterised by the continuous process of procreation and survival. This dynamic and ultimately crucial relationship between things in the world points to forces and processes rather than substances. The metaphorical and conceptual processing of this bias will yield the view speaking of cycles of processes rather than categories of objects.

In a similar way the Westerner will tend to describe a phenomenon or situation by pointing out the features or attributes of them (and by phrasing them in a predicate system): something *is* so and so, because it *has* such and such properties. This dominance of the categories 'to be' and 'to have' is so obvious in our tradition that we tend to forget that they are merely representing one perspective on nature and man. We tend to conjecture (implicitly) at once that this categorisation rests on and is justified by some direct relationship of correspondence between it and the phenomena in the outside world. Navajos, on the other hand (and many other peoples as well), have different categories and a different set of premises when speaking about the nature of the world: they will invariably speak about processes and changes, events and transformations as the 'basic material' of nature (cf. Witherspoon, 1977; Pinxten et al.,1983). Their conceptualisations will start from there and yield a markedly different picture of the world. The huge amount of aspectival nuances one finds in the languages is an expression of this difference in perspective (Young & Morgan, 1980).

The epistemological relevance of these data is obvious. Instead of focusing all attention on the set of concepts and metaphors (or prescientific world view) which complies with the atomistic ontology of the ancient Greeks, one has to investigate the usefulness and truthfulness of other prescientific world views (cf. Prigogine, 1969; who pleads for the end of atomism). The epistemologists should get rid of their biases and blindness vis-à-vis non-western cultural knowledge forms and seek to apply the same rules and criteria of trustworthiness and relevance to them, which they reserved for western outlooks until now. The world view of the Navajos enables them to cope with the world in a certain way, and the system of the Bantu gives them control over their environment in another specific way (Horton, 1991).

c) on the boundaries of the domain of knowledge.

Similar remarks hold for the scope and boundaries of the domain of knowledge of the epistemologist, as have been stated in the previous section.

On the basis of the foregoing discussion I want to plead for the adoption of some insights from other cultures in our world view and scientific knowledge. Notably, parapsychological phenomena cannot be explained or accepted in science, because they cannot be described in terms that are justifiable to the scientist today. The forces the parapsychologists speak about are deemed fictive, because the known physical channels, the accepted and measurable types of energy in our sciences cannot describe or explain these forces and energies. They cannot be controlled and subjected to the agreed upon tests and therefore they belong to the world of fantasy and fraud. In Navajo medicine practice (as in those of other peoples) the person is always treated as a whole of physical, psychological and social aspects. If a person falls ill, he will be cured as a totality by means of a series of practices and chants including the use of herbs, the purification of body and mind, suggestion and the inducement of trance, and so on. If a person is acting irremediably against his own people he will be convinced of his unworthiness, eventually to commit suicide. the intertwinement of aspects and behaviours of both the accepted (psychological-sociological) and the parapsychological type is too opaque that one is left with the definite feeling that the sharp distinction between both is primarily a matter of cultural choice or bias. There is, in other words, no clear-cut distinction between the status of their knowledge and ours in my opinion. To speak with Elkana (1981): no 'Great Divide' between them and us can be defended.

Coming back to epistemology in the strict sense, I have to state very clearly that all this does not make me an ally of the famous adagio 'anything goes' (Feyerabend, 1968). The relativist (or nihilist, according to Campbell, 1979) is wrong when he assumes that, since some temporary interpretation about truth and relevance has to go, we thus are allowed to accept anything. My general contention is that other cultural knowledge systems have strict norms to determine what is true and what is false, what procedures can be followed to get to the truth, and what criteria of success are withheld to evaluate the result. Chinese have been known to apply a strict logic in this respect (Needham, 1965) and my own experience with Navajos leads me to condemn the nihilist position just as forcefully. A difference with the western and scientific tradition (restricting science to our communities) lies primarily in the premises and in the ways to use knowledge. Finally, it seems to lie in the definition of the object of study and of the domain of analysis. An example of a much more mundane sort will make this clear. Conklin (1981) produced a marvelous and scholarly first class work about the geographical knowledge of the Ifugao. What he did was to make an ethnographic study of the social, cultural and economic life of that people and select important data on religion, rituals, ownership of land, use of land, and so on. Using these informations in the way the Ifugao do, Conklin went on to visualize and conceive of the geographical neighbourhood in terms of these social, economic, religious, etc., differentiations. He then began drawing maps, using the highly sophisticated means of map drawing that western geographers have developed over the last centuries. However, the criteria to partition land, and the principles to organise space were those of the Ifugao. We thus get a map of the population patterns in terms of the kinship and ritual alliances between people, and a map of the plateau system in terms of social organisation and seasonal labor, and so on. In other words, we get an Ifugao geography, an instance of anthropology of science or better: anthropologised science. We can easily see that a lot of what we are doing as scientists is exactly of this nature: we use criteria which are economical or political or any other non-scientific flavour and 'deify' them as real, true or scientific in the discipline we are working in (e.g. the fashion of using economic models in psychology or biology feeds on an ideological premise rather than a scientific or ontological one). We narrow down the scope of analysis by defining the subject matter in this way and a lot of the discussions about the disciplinary or 'proper' thing to do in fact focus on cultural preconceptions about the object of study. We adhere to one and just one perspective on nature when doing research; it should be worthwhile – although heretic when you look at it – to change perspectives as much as possible and to seek to compare knowledge from different perspectives. The development of geography 'from the point of view of the Ifugao' (Conklin, 1981) is one such example, the development of geometry from the perspective of the Navajo (Pinxten et al., 1987) is another one. The discipline of ethnomathematics (Ascher, 1991) gives a more synthetic scope. The consciousness that science feeds on culture at the very basic level of conceptualisation may well allow for more initiatives in this realm.

PART II

COMPARISON

CHAPTER 4

The Comparative Study of Culture

INTRODUCTION

This chapter focuses on the concept of 'root principles' or 'cultural intuitions' in a culture and its role in the development of a new and intercultural perspective on comparison. Here, as in the rest of the book, both notions are used as synonyms.

1. THE PROBLEM OF COMPARISON.

A multitude of scholarly works exist which in one way or the other deals with comparative analysis. Some useful overviews offering ample examples of the models and theories of the past are e.g., Holy (1987) in anthropology and Whaling (1984) in religious studies. I will not go into this literature in any depth. Rather, I will be satisfied to mention the main trends in anthropology and religious studies only and to evaluate the presuppositions in these domains. It will then become clear what is missing for an adequate approach.

In his critical overview of anthropological comparative theories Mark Hobart (1987) distinguishes satirically but appropriately between different eras: *stone age science* refers to the comparative method of Radcliffe-Brown (and can be extended to that of Kroeber as well, I think). Radcliffe-Brown looked for 'social facts' which *"are held to have essences discernible independent of observers and frames of reference"* (Hobart, 1987, 23). Diverging cultures would then be compared on the basis of these essences, and regularities (or even 'laws' in a natural science fashion) would be induced from as much empirical data as might possibly be got. Hobart criticizes this view as outdated and *"even at the time of its proposal ... an unlikely fossil..."* (o.c., p.24). Probably the most forceful and most prolific school in anthropology was the one founded by Boas and continued by Kroeber, Benedict and Mead. They were aligned to the British structural functionalists to the extent that they too sought to describe structural and functional aspects of cultures first and foremost in an empiricist perspective: one described what could be seen, heard and experienced directly by the trained ethnographer. In the second place, one then tried to recognize a pattern or presumably underlying regularity which could explain the continuity and unity of an apparent pluriformity and variety. Hence, patterns or structures within and between cultures were induced from variegated empirical data. Kearney summarizes this outlook as the aim *"to define the underlying 'pattern', 'configuration', 'basic personality','ethos', or 'world view' of a society."* (Kearney, 1984, 23). He thus lists all the main terms used by this school of thought. His conclusion is that all of these terms and concepts have in common that they refer to mental processes, which lands them   in the category of idealist approaches. Whether or not 'idealism' is an important feature is beside the issue, I think, since fundamental epistemological critique (see chapter 1) and related methodological questions have historically shown to be more relevant to discontinue this approach.

The second period goes under the title of *steam age science* and deals with structuralism. In my view classical comparatists can be situated here too (genre M. Eliade and J. Campbell). Hobart rightly states that empiricism is replaced by rationalism in Lévi-Strauss's work in that innate structures of the mind give the ultimate legitimation of the model in structuralism. It thus led to theories which are not falsifiable anymore (because of the postulates) and which project a universal structure in the 'mind' of man (and hence of culture) which is next to irrelevant for the description and explanation of cultural reality (see especially the extensive critique in Bourdieu, 1980). In a nutshell, one might say that the postulated structure in this type of comparison is at the same time the result of the research, while no way is left open empirically to check, question or even modify the 'theory'.

In what might then be called *computer age science* (the title is mine, not Hobart's) the problem is identified in the following way: *"So, we are comparing, not facts or the world, but descriptions or discourses."* (Hobart, 1987, 32). In this era the focus is on two questions, according to Hobart: the relationship between our descriptions and the indigenous ones, and the quality of our translations. He then goes into some philosophical discussions (Quine, Wittgenstein and Hollis mainly) which I will skip for the moment (see Pinxten 1994 & and Pinxten & Balagangadhara 1989).

In the comparative study of religion the situation is more complicated still: a multitude of approaches has been developed by generations of scholars. Whaling (1984) distinguishes no less than six different schools: phenomeno-logy, depth psychology (of the Jungian type), social and structural anthropology, sociology, history of religion and theology. In all of these a distinct comparative outlook has been developed. Since the latter is labeled in a variety of ways (from 'science of religion' to 'comparative religion') I propose to stay with the more explicit title used so far: the comparative study of religion. Within that field the same phases could be distinguished as in anthropology (see Hobart's view above). The bulk of material we have so far is to be found in the 'steam age science' and some of it in a later phase (see especially Whaling, 1984b and King, 1984). The phenomenological tradition (best known through the works of Van der Leeuw and Eliade) aimed at the development of typologies or classifications of religious aspects. The classification is reached by means of a fundamentally subjective analysis of religious experiences: through epochs the religious experience is isolated away from a context of judgement and seen as a phenomenon in itself, as it were. Then, through the method of eidetic vision, the presupposed essence of the religious phenomenon is grasped in an intuitive way: the researcher reaches this essence through *einfühlung* (or empathy) rather than by means of observation, experiment or another more objective method. These two procedures are typical for the phenomenological approach and the results of their application to the religious experience are held to be universally valid by the proponents. Several critiques have been voiced: e.g., the analysis is purely subjective and ahistorical. The former critique is generally not considered to be valid by the proponents, since they hold (on a priori grounds, that is) that the religious experience is given to all humans. Hence, the analysis of this experience should be accessible to all human beings. The latter objection (i.e., the lack of an historical dimension) has been taken seriously by later phenomenologists who tried to build a synthesis between historical and phenomenological approaches (e.g., Eliade, Puech, Bottéro, and so on). However, the standing criticism of subjectivism, and hence of euro-centrism in the phenomenological approach to religion, is one that has gained more and more power over the last decade, I think. Notably non-western speakers have been pointing out profound differences between the Mediterranean religions and other traditions (see Whaling, 1984c), as well as the explicit refusal to use the term of 'religion' to denote their own tradition (e.g., in North American Indian traditions–Gill, 1987; Frisbie, 1987- or in Hindu traditions–Balagangadhara, 1994). At the least these criticisms seem to show that the subjective findings of the phenomenologist can not readily be universalized. Starting from a very different inspiration the famous Harvard theologian W.C. Smith proposed in his *Meaning and End of Religion* (1964) that the very notion of religion has been used in a multitude of ways even within western history and hence can not be held to secure a solid basis for a 'universal theology'. Smith adds arguments to the criticism from within the tradition, where non-westerners attack it from without.

The psychologistic (Jung and Campbell) and the sociologistic (Wach) reductionism both share the basic critical characteristics of the structural anthropological views of Lévi-Strauss: in the former case the psychological archetypes and in the latter (vague) sociocultural contexts must function as the universal basis on which the religious experience can be founded or to which it can be reduced. Again, apart from the dubit-ability of these foundations in themselves, they serve to underscore a supposedly universal phenomenon of religious experience. When we take the non-western critics seriously, these theories must be stripped of the universality pretensions. In general, the critiques on the 'steam age science' anthropologies can be repeated here.

Both King (1984) and Whaling (1984b) show convincingly that the classical histories of religion dealt to a very large extent with the history of written cultures and even with those of the Mediterranean area alone. Moreover, those historical approaches which dealt with non-western religions used categories and descriptive models which were taken from the former area studies with minor or no modification at all. In recent years, and partly under the influence of the 'global history' paradigm (in Wallerstein and others), systematic expositions of non-western religious traditions find their place in the literature. Most often Chinese, Indian, Japanese and other non-western scholars try to go into systematic comparisons between their own tradition and a western religion. Again it is striking that the scholarly categories of the West still seem to dominate the approach. The net result of this dominance is that the chances are that the non-western tradition keeps being described in and hence partly reduced to the western experience of the world. The decolonization of the sciences seems far from realized in these instances.

The theological theories have been and still are exclusive in a variety of ways: they tend to start all description and analysis from the perspective of one or the other religion (most of all one or the other church) and hence 'place' other traditions in terms that are clearly and unalterably defined. The very terms and concepts, the nature and the limits of religious experience and practice are defined in revelation or in holy texts. These approaches teach us more about the theological view on others than about the others themselves.

Let me try to recapitulate what has been said so far. The oldest type of comparison (here nicknamed the 'stone age' version) is occasionally still practiced by scholars, but seems to be abandoned in most centers in the world now. Comparison in these studies comes down to the development through induction of categories which are deemed to be universal. The induction is naive in that theory-ladenness nor culture-ladenness of terms and concepts in science are even thought of. Hence, most of these studies produced artefacts of analysis which were uncritically proclaimed universal essences. In most cases the lack of foundation of the categories or universals of this type of comparison has been attacked adequately by the structuralists in their attempts to at least define a nonrandom basis for universality of traits or categories. The early historical studies of religion are of the same type.

The second order comparisons fail to meet the standards of genuine comparisons because they either reduce the non-western phenomena to predefined subjective, or to otherwise particularistic, categories which prestructure and hence corrupt the phenomena under study. Indeed, the comparative researcher in this paradigm projects an a priori and hence universal mental pattern (be it a structure or an archetype) into all and any living culture and then goes on to describe observable features as particulars to be deduced from the general and universal given. In other words, the rationalistic artefact serves to identify, describe and eventually classify and interpret a disturbing variety of observable facts in a priori and hence uniform categories. The categories are beyond the control of the user and can only be reached properly by means of the intuitions of the researcher. The subjective element (i.e., the intuition of the researcher) has an enormous impact in this approach: it dictates the categories to be compared and the rules of comparison. The same critiques can be formulated vis-à-vis the phenomenological approach to religion: some of the critique is endorsed explicitly in its straightforward subjectivism. However, granting that one starts in a subjective perspective does not make the comparison any more objective. Or, in the terms that are dear to anthropologists and comparative religion scholars alike, it does not make the research results any less eurocentric. Since the basis of comparison is defined in one cultural tradition only (most if not all the time the European tradition) comparison then consists in describing the 'others' in such a way that they fit into the a priori categories.

Finally, the 'computer age' type of comparison is a recent and still fragile growth. I want to try and explore what its characteristics should be and how we can conceive of a systematic deployment of such a comparative study. The 'mistakes' of the former types of comparison should enable us to reach a more genuine and less parochial study of culture and religion. This will certainly mean that I cannot compare isolated 'facts' or data (as was believed in the 'stone age') nor that I should compare non-western culture with a frame of reference that is exclusively western (as was believed somehow or other in the 'steam age'). With Hobart I claim that we can get beyond a naive position by realizing that what we compare are in actual fact different discourses or cultural knowledge domains, rather than isolated 'facts'. The discourses are at least two in comparative research: the researcher's and the subject's. Therefore, one of the problems in this age of comparative studies is to gain clarity about the relationship between these two discourses and about the range and character of translation between both.

2. 'ROOT PRINCIPLE' OR 'CULTURAL INTUITION' AND COMPARISON

The concept of 'root principle' is a simple one. It is based on the image or metaphor of the root of a plant: one single root hidden from the eye in the soil feeds and sustains the plant above ground level. It feeds stems, leafs, flowers, fruit in any amount and of different sizes. It is obvious that a layman cannot predict the size, color or form of the plant by simply looking at the root, but the image at least conveys the idea that a more or less variegated set of plant aspects can be understood to belong together or to form one unity once it is understood that the variety has the same unique root. Looking at it from another perspective, a chaotic and abundant mass of plant material can be 'sorted out' and properly perceived and understood once one finds the root(s). Without stretching it too far this image is used here in a metaphorical sense with regard to cultures and cultural material: what appears at first sight to be varied, chaotic, unconnected or utterly disparate in a culture can, upon closer examination, be recognized to be unified or closely linked because of a common root principle. A somewhat similar argument holds for the synonymous term of cultural intuitions: they express the non-discursive or immediate notions which are underlying the level of rational discourse. The image of some sort of root or foundation obtains here too.

Two important remarks should be made at the outset: any cultural community can have one or more root principles, which can be made explicit (e.g., in language metaphors, in symbols, in art work) or not. Secondly, any root principle the anthropologist can detect should be characteristic for and set in the terms of a particular cultural community. In other words, the strictly inductive regularities of the Boasian perspective, and the rationalistic universal structures of Lévi-Strauss as well as the universalist subjectivism of the phenomenologists of religion are different from the 'root' image used here. The semantic notion of 'presupposition' bears some resemblance but is clearly more formal and poorer than 'root principle'.

a) the concept of 'root principle' or 'cultural intuition'.

The social scientist must be fully aware of the theory- and culture-ladenness and of the interactional nature of research. (cf. the Introduction of Chapter 3). A fortiori, this awareness has to be kept up when engaging in the comparison of data or models, each of which is reached within the research situation of a doubly biased interaction (see Chapter 2). Looking at the study of other cultures in this perspective can only yield an attitude of respect for any culture since it stands for a fully developed autonomous perspective on the world and should be studied accordingly. It is in this context of respect that I want to introduce the concept of 'root principle' as a tool for description and for comparative research. An example from the western subculture of scientific research will make clear what is meant.

Dwelling on insights and distinctions which have been around for a while in both cognitive and cultural anthropology I defended elsewhere (Pinxten, 1987) the point of view that a body of scientific knowledge in particular (and a cultural outlook in general) does not exist in the void. In the jargon of the philosopher we say that particular and seemingly discrete elements of knowledge at the 'object level' (i.e., the level of discourse, observations and concepts) are linked with one another at a deeper or 'meta-level' of understanding. It is the latter which I call the level of 'cultural intuitions' or 'root principles'. Insights at this level have a precognitive status and are immediate in the experience of the knower. Drawing on distinctions from within anthropology, I demonstrated how and why a scientist like Prigogine can be called revolutionary (in contradistinction to most of his contemporaries): he concerns himself with the object level discussion of his science (thermodynamics) and with the 'philosophical' presuppositions in it such as the concepts of time, change, etc. The latter are most often considered to be 'mere' metaphysics and not to lie in the proper domain of the scientist. Rather, they are considered to be given, or cultural, or even religious in nature; they do explain the apparent unity in the scientific view on nature, but they remain implicit and 'prescientific' for the researcher. Prigogine concerns himself both with these deeper insights and with science proper (see e.g. Prigogine & Stengers, 1984). It is good to focus on one element of his perspective to clarify the point I try to make here: he is actively interested in the way temporality (as irreversible or reversible processes) is shaped in the culture of the scientist. Prigogine finds that 'time as history' is not represented in our natural scientific view of the world, that is at the level of theories and models of physics or chemistry. He then goes on to offer alternative models and algorithms in order to introduce a more genuine notion of time (namely irreversible time) into the scientific theory (this is basically through his theory of dissipative structures). I am using this case only as an example to illustrate my point on 'root principles': scientific knowledge along with any other type of knowledge is based on, and is to a large extent unified by deeper and vaguer insights .

Chinese naturalists conceived of the world as an organismic system which is governed by the Yin-Yang mechanism; this complex of two fundamental forces or operations in the universe alternate in dominance and define in their particular combinations the state of things at any one moment. The explicit philosophical treatment of Yin-Yang dates at least from the third century before Christ, but its use as deep category for thought can not be dated. The Chinese notions of order, cosmos, law and so on can only be understood properly against the background of this fundamental couple. (For all this see Needham, 1965, Vol. II, especially 232-244 and 272-278). Yin represents coldness, female-ness and a series of natural or symbolic features, whereas Yang stands for heat, maleness and so on. The two exist in a dynamic unity (symbolized by a circular movement) which in turn characterizes each and every particular phenomenon or event in the universe. It is this mechanism or dynamic unity that I identify as a basic 'root principle' for the Chinese tradition. Measures of truth or falsehood, coherence or contradiction do not apply at this level. However, the 'root principle' of the Yin-Yang unity is presupposed in the Chinese notions of law, of cosmos, etc., as is well illustrated in Needham's magnificent work (o.c.).

In a similar way I identify 'action habitat' as a crucial 'root principle' for the Navajo tradition (my own fieldwork). Navajos live in a universe which is likened to and experienced as a home: everything (including human beings) is interrelated with everything else and all things exist inside the encompassing cosmos. Time is seen first and foremost as the growth of the universe or as the deployment and spending of forces within it. Powers or forces are manipulated in intricate ceremonies which serve primarily to restore a presupposed equilibrium within the cosmos, which is time and again disturbed by human beings who are ill-defined and hence disturbing creatures by birth. Again, the notion of 'action habitat' is only hinted at in explicit references or in the ceremonial knowledge. However, it is the notion that best captures the various aspects of explicit or overt cultural knowledge Navajos display.

Finally, in the western tradition I can point to a similar level of 'root principles' in different domains. I will use the example of cosmology again to conform with the above examples. European views on the universe share at the least the 'God's Eye View' and a type of atomism: from the Ancient Greeks on we hold the view that we look at the cosmos as it were 'from the outside', that is from the position God took as creator and beholder of the cosmos in the older views. Combined with this perspective Westerners think of the cosmos as a whole which can be decomposed in its part (earth and sun being two of these parts, both in the medieval and in the modern view). These 'cultural intuitions' (God's Eye View, and atomism) again can not be tested on their truth or falsity; they are presupposed in the cosmologies proper (see especially Koyré, 1957).

These examples should suffice to illustrate what is meant by the term 'root principle'. I can now proceed to try and formulate a more binding circumscription of the term.

A 'root principle' or 'cultural intuition' can, but ought not to be made explicit in a cultural community. It does not serve the role of an axiom in the real sense, because the more particular statements are not actually deduced from it. Instead, a 'root principle' seems to serve in analogy with the way presuppositions or maybe postulates do for the organization of knowledge in a particular community. In a very general way each community lives in a particular environment and in a specific cultural tradition. No human being or group starts completely anew, but all of them are embedded in a cultural past. In that past or tradition a particular sensitivity has grown within the community which rears and guides individuals and groups in their choices and tastes. This sensitivity takes form in one or more 'root principles' which are explicitly or subliminally active as a basic perspective on life and the world (ideology, cosmology), or as a feeling about which way of approaching a problem is right and which way will 'cause trouble' or is out of step with tradition (morality, knowledge). It is these perspectives, feelings, insights in 'rightness' or traditionhood and so on, which I want to capture under these technical terms. Whenever the anthropologist gets an answer like: 'we do it because that is our way' or 'that is our tradition' or 'that is ours and not ... (the white man's way, the enemy's way)', I suspect s/he stumbles on a culture specific 'root principle'. That is to say, these vague and apparently evasive answers indicate that a question is asked about a 'root principle'. Most of the time, it is unspeakable or implicit or subconscious, but nevertheless it guides the choices, the behavior and the cognitive categories at the conscious or explicit level. The social scientist or philosopher can try to project or detect 'root principles', in so far as they appear as the presupposed or hidden aspects of a culture that explain, combine or otherwise make more meaningful the elements of conscious or explicit behavior in that culture, which appear as unrelated or disparate or random without them.

This short characterization makes clear that a culture cannot be reduced to its 'root principle': there may be more than one and the relationship between (overt) culture and root is not a deductive one. On the other hand, it leaves open whether a culture can be seen as a system (in the way several American colleagues seem to imply, e.g., Geertz, 1973) or a superstructure rather than as a partially integrated conglomerate of styles, habits and what have you. When I use the term 'root principle' I do presuppose that human beings in a cultural community have, because of their make up and because of the perceived or presumed uniformity or order (at least to some degree of detail) of the world they live in and teach the following generations about, a series of common problems to deal with. The make up of human beings thus universally entails that the human body divides space in at least two magnitudes: the space we are IN and the space we can manipulate (i.e., of objects); in a similar way time is divided for the human species in lived temporality and time beyond us (in past or future, sometimes also in the present as with transcendental time); and so on. On the basis of these mere features of the human being a series of domains for cultural rooting can be delineated. This universal make up of human beings does not preclude culturally relative ways of structuring the world in more detail, but it does allow us to delineate a series of domains which will be culturalised. For each of these domains separately, or for subsets of them in unison (depending on the particular culture), a root principle will be found in any concrete culture. I will not sum them up in an exhaustive list (which is a task beyond my power), but a hint at some of them can be illuminating: the cosmos as an englobing presence, temporality (ancestry, birth, death, etc..), space, self (against others, body, nature, etc..), nature versus culture, order or regularity, and so on.

b) the use of cultural intuitions or root principles in comparison.

It is obvious from the foregoing paragraphs that the superficial comparison of items of (explicit or overt) culture is wrongheaded according to me. Any particular instance of behavior, any isolated thought, or any religious practice can only be studied properly against its own cultural background. The mere counting of similarities and differences in external form (see e.g. Nordenskiöld, 1938) can at most be relevant for neighboring and intensely interacting groups, but should be feared to yield undependable knowledge otherwise. As a general stand I hold that the two older types of comparison (termed 'stone age' and 'steam age' science by Hobart) offer deeply colonial or ideological rather than scientific models and theories of culture and humankind. Why is that so?

In the case of the configurationalists (Boas, Kroeber, and so on) both description and comparison are carried out in the categories of the researcher: s/he describes cultural phenomena on the basis of (external) observation, or of subjective participation in the culture and the language. All this is scientifically honorable, but discussions over the past decades have shown that this approach does not offer any guarantee against contradictory reporting or against heavily biased description. Comparison then consists in the point to point comparison of particular descriptions on the basis of the interpretation of similarity and differences in the mind of the anthropologist. Boas anticipated this sort of criticism, it appears to me, when he wrote the famous introduction to the Handbook of American Indian Languages (Boas, 1911). He makes his own (linguistic) presuppositions as explicit and systematic as possible in the list of 'grammatical categories' he offers. Although the list is not to be understood as (a priori) universals of language, they serve the same purpose as universalia do. Even with the critical and highly informed mind of Boas a certain amount of eurocentrism could not be avoided: thus, Boas has to recur to a presumably universal structure of the mind to begin the very work of comparison. He says:

> "When we consider for a moment what this implies, it will be recognized that in each language only a part of the complete concept that we have in mind is expressed, and that each language has a peculiar tendency to select this or that aspect of the mental image which is conveyed by the expression of the thought ." (Boas, 1911, 39)

What do I propose instead as both a scientifically justified and a postcolonial way of comparing? I point out the procedure first and analyse its philosophical implications afterwards. I take self or ethnic identity as an example here. Any genuine comparison should at least include the following steps, I think:

– the preliminary identification –on a provisional basis to be sure– of the 'root principle' on a topic or domain in the culture under study. E.g., what is the underlying and unifying view ('the root') for the identification of oneself (as a unity) and of the others, as it can be induced from learning processes and from common knowledge in a group?

– in a second step more thorough ethnographic description of particular, explicit and concrete language and behavior concerning the selected topic is engaged in: what do they say about themselves and about others? How do they treat others in comparison with the behavior towards their own folk? It is clear the description will not blindly follow the 'root principle' identified. Insights from the empirical work will always feed back into the provisional formulation and hence amend and modify the identification of the 'root principle' focused on. Right up to this level the research remains within the domain of one particular culture. Both steps have to be gone through for every single culture one wants to include in the comparison.

– in a third step the researcher engages in the comparison of two or more cultures on the basis of the foregoing steps. This implies that their 'root principles' should be compared to any degree possible before the researcher can think of comparing any detailed aspect of the cultures involved. Only then and within this frame of interpretation/comparison the concrete, explicit or particular models or theories from each culture should be compared to the extent possible with correlate or similar ones in the other culture(s). It will be clear that 'the extent possible' will be determined or limited by the 'root principles' of each culture under comparison. Indeed, no two 'facts' or 'data' can be compared as such in any sensible way, I claim. Rather, any aspect of a particular culture must be understood in the frame of that culture, meaning first and foremost in the frame of its 'root principle(s)'.

– finally, on the basis of such comparisons universal features can be made explicit. These characteristics will be *universal a posteriori* if they are anything. That is to say, their universality will have to be argued for on the basis of their function and meaning in the particular cultures under research. They will be universals which come out of detailed and scrupulous empirical work, and not projections which are based on presupposedly general characteristics of mankind or culture according to the theory of the researcher.

The philosophical or theoretical tenets of this view on comparison are many:

(a) this approach is a sort of inductivism. I clearly subscribe to the general perspective of the Boasians (and hence turn against structuralism) in that I claim that comparison has to be set up on the basis of intense empirical work. However, I differ from the Boasians on several points: in the first place, the insights of the researcher have no 'untouchable' status, based on their resulting from 'scientific' observation and interviewing. This was a serious form of naivety in the older theories (where the researcher's biases were used to describe the other or where the researcher's insights were declared superior to those of the subject of study). In the era of critical anthropology this type of simpleminded attitude is surpassed. In the second place, there is difference with the Boasians in that questions, concepts, cultural attitudes, and material products in my approach have to be dealt with in the ethnography of each culture in terms of that culture. Grand systematic schemes or structures which are either proposed on a priori grounds (as is the case in Lévi-Strauss's structuralism) or on the basis of induction within the framework of the culture of the researcher (as is the case in Kroeber and Boas) are rejected. As mentioned before, I think that both former approaches show a colonial feature on this point, i.e., by totally disregarding the perspective of the culture of the Other (their 'root principles') and comparing cultural phenomena in the terms of the researcher's culture only. With this second difference I become an ally of the type of comparative researchers whom one finds nowadays in Geertz' paper on local knowledge (1983) or Parkin's work on the anthropology of evil (1983).

(b) (potential) universality and apriorism are unlocked from one another. Features are not declared universal because of the demands of the theory, but because the (highly culturally colored) facts show them to be so. At the theoretical or epistemological level my point of view is similar along this criterion to that of Shaner (and Yuasa, in Shaner et al., 1989) who claims that an evolutionary approach and a comparative perspective on knowledge and culture should be combined rather than opposed to each other. To the best of my knowledge, I can not say whether other inductivist comparatists (like Geertz and Parkin) share this point of view. A net result of this unlocking of apriorism and universalism is that the attitude of projecting categories from one's own tradition of thinking onto others, which is in fact what structuralists and phenomenologists have been doing, does not yield universals (or necessarily true statements), but merely consists in universalizing (or declaring universal) one's own categories. Hence, it is a clearly ideological move in the guise of science.

(c) regional versus global comparison. When comparative anthropological research looks for universals a posteriori, which would result from intercultural interaction, the type of research will differ from what has been done before. I do not follow Holy (1987) when he claims that global comparisons are to be avoided and hence regional comparisons will be the order of the day for anthropology. Following my principles of critical anthropological analysis, I claim that comparison will depend on deep ethnographic work in each culture concerned, describing that culture in terms of *its* 'root principles'. It follows that any individual researcher will be able to compare only two or three cultures: his/her own and the culture(s) s/he worked with in a very intense way, systematically allowing critique and control on the ethnography by the autochthones. But this limited comparison (limited in terms of number of cultures) can be repeated for any number of times, with specialists and consultants from other cultures. Hence, the grand systematic comparison by one individual scholar (type Lévi-Strauss or Eliade) or a small group (type HRAF) is considered by me to be naive and ideological rather than scientific, but global comparisons in themselves are not condemned or disqualified, as they are in Holy. They just become much more difficult and hence maybe more unlikely in terms of the old tools and habits of research which are still popular in anthropology. The difficulty is primarily one of organization, and concerns the way to get proper ethnographers together in a framework that is neutral and vast enough to allow genuine negotiation and interaction. However, present-day information processing equipment already allows to carry out great and subtle simulations of complex material. There is no reason to doubt that comparative simulation, which abides with the sophisticated philosophical criteria outlined above, is possible.

(d) universalism and relativism revisited. Elsewhere (Pinxten, 1976) I defended that the mere opposition between universalism and (cultural) relativism is simplistic. Like most dichotomies, the present one falls apart upon closer examination. A third position becomes feasible, once we cut ourselves loose from the fascination for the simple dichotomy. The third position is to be found under different names, I think. Entitativity is one of them (Campbell, 1973): aspects of the world have a certain degree of entitativity, meaning that they can be perceived and thought of in different ways only to a certain degree. Those aspects with a high degree of entitativity (e.g., plants, animals and other instances of matter) as it were force themselves upon the human observer and thinker. They will be found in only slightly different identifications in many cultures (the plant classifications are a good example), but the way they are further integrated in larger, eventually symbolic categories is not determined by the features of the first level entities. So, a woman is seen as a separate being in all cultures, but can belong with fires and other dangerous things in a category separate from a man (Lakoff, 1986). A second aspect of such an approach to the dichotomy is that the human apparatus for perception and knowledge has both universal and relative features: all human beings have stereoscopic vision, and all have a similar neuronal make up; moreover, all are erect bipeds allowing for a unique hand-eye manipulation of the world for knowledge build up.

These remarks and pieces of analysis must suffice to make clear what the tenets are of the type of comparison I advocate. The extensive examples of the second part of this book may allow the reader to check the usefulness and workability of this perspective.

CHAPTER 5
The Learner's View on Learning
(with Claire K. Farrer)

1. THE PROBLEM

In this chapter, that resulted from a joint, Western teaching experience with Navajo and Apache topics,[1] we focus exclusively on the culturally embedded learning process from the perspective of the learner, whether Apache, Navajo, or Western. Teaching techniques and principles are only marginally relevant in our present effort to elucidate some of the culturally salient differences in perceptions concerning learning. Secondly, we believe there are differences between the ways in which Western children learn as compared with children from the Navajo or Apache worlds and that these differences are predicated on primary cultural presuppositions.

A dichotomy, Them and Us, immediately arises by our literal juxtaposition of Apache and Navajo with Western learners. It is good to keep in mind that we are aware that few dichotomies can be sustained upon closer examination. Nevertheless, dichotomizing can be fruitful to bring out differences and formulate questions. Therefore, the dichotomy in this chapter has a heuristic value, rather than an epistemological one: it will help us highlight differences, but it will have to be overcome to draw an adequate representation of either of the two parts of the dichotomy.

We are first led to questions of similarity and difference, or comparison and contrast, between Them and Us in respect to aspects of learning processes – e.g., consistency, logical operators (inclusion, exclusion, etc.), paradox, and so on – whether we refer to learning or thinking in their, or our, tradition. It is our belief that the use and format of these aspects of the learning processes differ on several points between Them and Us. Our concern is with the whys and hows of the differences. We begin our discussion with paradox and its differential meanings between Them and Us. The preliminary identification of a cultural intuition of Navajo and Apache (my first step in comparative analysis) states that they see knowledge transfer as person - and context - bound and hence are not bothered by the need to avoid paradoxes as the westerner is. Therefore our first focus will be on the role of paradox.

We use the concept of paradox in its most common sense:

> "A statement or proposition which on the face of it seems self-contradictory, absurd, or at variance with common sense, though, on investigation or when explained, it may prove to be well-founded (or, according to some, though it is essentially true)" (Oxford Dictionary, 1984, 2072).

The notion of a paradox flows throughout Western academic discourse. Nonetheless, our understanding of Western schooling tradition is that paradoxes are problematic and are to be avoided; the occurrence of a paradox is not permitted, if one is to think and operate logically. It is not altogether clear whether this norm (i.e., to avoid or dissolve paradoxes) did or does hold for practical knowledge in the West. Indeed, we often tend to live with 'two conflicting standards', or we can be taught to follow conflicting interpretations in our daily lives (e.g., both homeopathy and allopathy in medical treatment). Nevertheless, proper reasoning (as it is learned in and outside of school for several generations now) does not permit paradoxes: we do not 'really' know or we did not learn something 'adequately' if we end up with two conflicting opinions about it. Paradox forces the Westerner to choose between two possibilities, for, if paradox exists, then we assume that one of the premises is incorrect. We choose one premise and discard the other. Logically, this process is captured in the principle of the 'excluded third' (or excluded middle): a statement is either true or false, but it cannot be both at the same time.

An illustration of this normative emphasis can be found in developmental psychology and in the theory of schizophrenia by the Bateson-Watzlawick group. A citation from Bateson illustrates that schizophrenia is learned behavior and has to do with norms and values of right and wrong:

> "The organism is then faced with the dilemma of either being wrong in the primary context or of being right for the wrong reasons or in the wrong way. This is the so-called double bind. We are investigating the hypothesis that schizophrenic communication is learned and becomes habitual as a result of continual traumata of this kind. That is all there is to it." (Bateson, 1972, 245).

Of course, Bateson is rightly remembered, in part, for his contribution to the production of schizophrenia in Western culture as being due to a double bind - to a paradox that the person cannot resolve. To be faced with paradoxes that cannot be resolved is to produce schizophrenics in Western cultures. In addition, the standard view on logical reasoning in the West is *"The assumption that no contradiction is true, and hence that the reasoning that results in the contradiction is fallacious."* (Priest, 1987, 30).

In his book devoted to the analysis of contradictions and paradoxes, Priest (1987) attacks classical logic on this point and aims at preparing the ground for the acceptance of some contradictions as 'true'. He is, however, very conscious of the uncommonness of such a program; in his own words *"[It] is outrageous, at least at the spirit of contemporary philosophy"* (idem, 7). One of the main reasons why contradictions are unacceptable in proper reasoning, according to the Westerner, is that the law of non-contradiction *"has traditionally been endorsed as a priori unassailable"* (idem, 259). The concurring consistency is considered to be 'normal'. To these extralogical criteria for proper reasoning Priest adds a last, in our minds a clearly sociocultural, explanation : *"the sheer weight of orthodoxy"* (idem, 259 footnote). Of course, the general stance toward contradiction or paradox is a norm in Western thinking rather than a factual given. We maintain that, in learning, it is a guiding norm for present-day Westerners and serves powerfully to organize not only how we think but also what is appropriate for thought.

A correlate in Western learning processes is that absolute, context- and person-independent, truth (in the exclusive sense) is a major principle guiding the development of thinking and learning (see the developmental studies of Piaget, especially his 1937 work). The explanation or justification for this status of paradox is that ultimate truth is, by definition, universal and unchangeable. Change is excluded under most circumstances, since there is a major shift in Western thinking when one 'truth' replaces another (cf. Kuhn's (1962) notions of paradigm shifts). If change does occur in the knowledge base, the former 'truth' is dropped as incorrect, incomplete, insufficient, predicated on a revised – or newly revealed – epistemological base.

In order not to oversimplify the picture we must mention an important addendum here: although it can be said that absolute or ultimate truth is the guiding principle, it is also the case that such truth can not be reached at all times. The learner often settles for less. The long standing tradition of rhetoric distinguishes between two types of argumentation in the history of the West, corresponding to two concurrent views on truths. Some truths are absolute or universal, and hence do not allow for change or modification: the theological convictions as well as scientific truths (both a priori and factual) have this status. Other beliefs are held or attained on the basis of persuasion, of shared values and interpretations, and the like. The difference is, however, not fundamental when looked at from the point of view of the learner or knower; indeed, the learner is persuaded to share a certain view on matters through appeal to soundness, evidence, or necessary truth of these beliefs. (See Perelman & Olbrechts-Tyteca, 1957, and later rhetoricians on these matters). So, from the perspective of the learner, the guiding role of absolute truth is the vehicle by means of which s/he can be won over to a certain view. Differences in opinion, in the Western mode, are viewed as handicaps of perspective which are either false in nature or the result of a lack of soundness, intelligence or information; differences are not seen as a positive value. One either has/knows truth or does not.

The emphasis on norm and on the context of absolute truth leads us to a further clarification on the use of paradoxes. Paradoxes seem to be important for the Westerner first and foremost in what is often called theoretical knowledge. That is to say, the Westerner does not feel bothered by them to the same extent when they are in operation in practical knowledge: although homeopathy and allopathy can not be used at the same time, they will often be used at separate times by the same patient; similarly, although vegetarian and omnivorous diets are mutually exclusive in the mind of the Westerner, in practice they are allowed to alternate in the food habits of many people. This acceptance of contradiction in practices is in sharp contrast with the norm that disallows contradiction in pure or theoretical knowledge. It is this theoretical type of knowledge, which is clearly separate from the often denigrated practical knowledge, that is taught in schools, and what is held by scientists and philosophers to be the real or higher sort of thinking. The learner is believed to get a better grasp on the world by developing a cognitive map or world view, that is by building a theoretical knowledge frame about the world. In this knowledge frame, true statements have to be absolutely true, irrespective of time, space, person or situation. An important instrumental feature for the learner of this knowledge is the discursiveness of this knowledge: everything that can be known in such an absolutely true way can be expressed in explicit statements that describe and explain the state of the world. In the tradition of the West, this implies that there is one unique way that reality is and one unique way in which it should be rendered in the language of the learner. This emphasis on discursiveness and on the importance of at least some theoretical knowledge for everybody in this society is clearly illustrated by the tremendous expansion of literacy (through schooling for everyone) and of vulgarization of scientific and philosophical work for the layman in all media. Neither of these phenomena can be found in the other cultures we have under consideration. Within the broad cultural context of learning in the West, the status and use of paradoxes plays a normative role in that the expected unique rendering of absolutely true statements about reality forces the Western learner to avoid paradoxes or to solve conflicting versions of reality by recourse to a higher authority or a redefinition of premises.

Our observations of the Navajo and Apache lead us to conclude that this situation in regard to paradox does not obtain. With both groups, different and apparently conflicting 'truths' or opinions can be maintained in harmony with each other. For example, one can follow the Medicine Man's/Woman's view and the Whiteman's view or the Peyote Way all simultaneously and even though portions of one may well contradict portions of another. The conflict is one of non-fit only to Western perceptions, not to those of the Apache or Navajo; indeed, for most Navajo and Apache there is no conflict. Rather one can choose opinion A at moment t1 and opinion B at moment t2; or one can select the perspective of person X in a certain situation and that of person Y in another, but perhaps analogous, situation. For the Apache and Navajo, the value of an opinion is always attached to, or related to, a person and a situation rather than being person- and context-independent. This does not preclude 'logical reasoning', to be sure; rather, it substitutes an emphasis on absoluteness for one on contextuality, or a stress on temporal and spatial universality for one on change. The premises differ, not the structure of reasoning.

The explanation, or justification, for this stance is that one must always be prepared for constant change and have the ability to adapt to it. If differences or conflicts are recognized (as is, for example, the case in witchcraft accusations), they are explained in terms of the difference of persons or circumstances, or as differences in the way in which one was taught/learned or views the situation. Thus, their perception of what Westerners call paradox is that the differences are not in conflict but have a positive value and are intrinsic to reality.[2] In fact, reality will be held by Navajos and Apaches to be changes, processes and differences, rather than objects or image-like phenomena. The Apache and Navajo correlate for absolute truth can be conceived of as being those tenets or beliefs that are differentially distributed throughout the universe. Human beings acquire only aspects or parts of this truth through the medium each of them uses. Thus a seer can have insights from his or her angle and translate them in a poetic vision to a larger audience; a medicine wo/man can manipulate forces in the world in a primarily nonverbal ritual act and evoke or express aspects of absolute truth in that way. In general, it is held that higher knowledge is inaccessible to the layman other than through ritual, visionary, and other nondiscursive means in the hand of the so-called holy men (i.e., thinkers, ritual specialists, speakers, seers, etc.). The transfer of knowledge of this kind is through a different medium than is the case for the Westerner. The characteristics of the medium differ: no discursiveness obtains, and thus no necessity arises for a normative use of paradox. This ends the ethnographic detailing of the notion and the use of paradox in the cultures under study.

It is clear that, although marked differences between Navajo-Apache and Western attitudes and opinions have been highlighted, a dichotomy between them can only be defended on some points (e.g., absolute versus contextual truth) and not on others (e.g., logical versus alogical reasoning). Thus, we reiterate that our posing of the paradox or dichotomy is for heuristic purposes only.

Turning to a consideration of a linked phenomenon, consistency, we again observe significant differences between Westerners, on the one hand, and Navajos and Apaches on the other. In the West there is a high value placed on consistency; it is a structural characteristic of knowledge and hence of the process of learning. It is a norm for the learner. Consistency leads to a dominant preference for an unique, and presumably correct, view. Just one.[3]

The authoritative character of an uniquely true rendering, including facts within a consistent theory, is sustained by a specific use of data, written sources (texts), and the like. They have authority over individual and person-bound opinions by virtue of their consistency and within a perspective that sees them accepted as valid, valuable, true, or right on the basis of the received belief. We Westerners accept that this truth may well be modified, or discarded, at some future time, but for the moment it is canon until there is a revolutionary shift based on new data, new truths, new facts, or increased understanding where prior there had been only a partial understanding. Again, we refer to the work of developmental psychologists: in his description of the development of thought in Western children, Piaget (1937) indicates how each age has its own world view which is supplanted at a later period by the new, more structured and better informed view of the next phase. This type of development process holds for common sense reasoning, according to Piaget. In learning, the focus on the unique interpretation of others (in texts and data) is implemented by giving them the imprimatur of authority.

By contrast, Apache and Navajo authorities are always multiple and are dependent upon the interacting persons, the time, the place, the effect, the event, and the topic in any one instance. Hence, authority cannot be used automatically as a coercive force in learning beyond that instance. And consistency cannot be justified by recourse to authority. (Quite obviously, we here challenge the universality of e.g. Piaget's theories and vision.) For Apaches and Navajos, there are a series of truths, none based on literary texts but many based upon the spoken and remembered word. That word, in its multiplicity of possible realizations, is intrinsically flexible and ready to respond to changes in persons, events, effects, or topics. Its consistency, to stretch the term, is its variability. Before exploring these topics in any more depth, we need to explain our own analytic apparatus for approaching the topics.

2. THE ANALYTIC TOOLS

It is the conviction of both authors of this chapter that a culture (or a particular aspect of it) can be approached both respectfully and adequately by describing it in terms of its root metaphor and/or root principles. One author works with the notion of root metaphor (Farrer 1981, 1991a & 1991b). The term 'root metaphor' refers to the result of a sense-making process whereby disparate items are likened to each other through recourse to a rationale, or organizing, principle that is stated, and believed, to underlie the entirety of the culture; the metaphoric move is made with the purpose of defining or otherwise indicating similarities between the items and their consonance with the most basic structural organization possible in that culture.

Metaphors are usually thought of in terms of literary moves and linguistic forms (as in poetry or with prose symbolism), but they exist beyond the limits of the linguistic medium as well. They can be found in nonverbal artefacts; they can be visual or actional, or they can be mental. (See Hatcher, 1974 for the Navajo, or Farrer 1991a & 1991b for the Apache, or Fernandez, 1974 for a general statement of metaphoric moves in expressive culture).

A root metaphor serves to organize aspects of culture in general into a harmonious and readily understood whole in the same way that a linguistic metaphor serves to illuminate a poorly understood or new aspect of an item or thought by reference to another, generally well-known, one. The word 'basic' is key here in that in order for an understanding to be a root metaphor, it must organize the entirety of a culture for the society or societies forming it. For Mescalero Apaches, the root metaphor may be rendered by '⊕', in its plastic manifestation, or by recourse to stating that the root metaphor consists of the number four, sound/silence, balance/harmony, and circularity. When Apaches indicate the fundamental principle of orderliness in their culture, they refer to this root metaphor. When they express the way of tradition, the way the world is in the eyes of the people, they use this root metaphor. They use it as well in their everyday lives as when they predicate formal speeches on its principles or when they salt food in accordance with its mandates. A culture has only one root metaphor, although it may have many corollaries of it and manifestations of it; similarly, it may have many key symbols that radiate from it. While basic to thought, structuring, action, and belief, root metaphors are not necessarily readily apparent.

A very deep distinction in the Western view on the world is that between the subject (or knower) and the object. Anything in the world, including the self of the knower can be objectified: i.e., it can be looked upon as if from the standpoint of the outsider. This general structure of the relationship between a human being and his/her world is a candidate for the position of 'root metaphor' in the West, we think. Although we do not deal with it in any great detail here, we are cognizant that this stance also produces the dualistic perception so characteristic of Western thinking and organization.

The other author works preferably with the notion of root principle or cultural intuition (see Chapter 4). Within the general structure of objectification hinted at in the former paragraph, with its inherent duality, we find the so-called 'God's Eye View' as a common trope, or root principle in Western cosmological thinking. From ancient times on, the Westerner has built cosmology by conceiving of the cosmos as a whole that can be grasped, seen or thought of, as if it were one unified object. This view draws on a conception of a God-Creator who is situated *outside* of the universe, eventually holding it together or contemplating it from His unique perspective as Creator. When the Western layman or scientist conceives of the universe as a closed or a bounded unit, s/he mentally adopts the position of the God-Creator, who is the only one to be able to look upon the universe in this way, thus allowing the scientist or layman to approach that which is, in our Western conception, the view of God. The likening of God and human being in the observation and knowledge development process is consonant with the Western root metaphor that holds there is an essential dualistic organization of reality and structure such that insider and outsider or viewer and viewed or God and people or Them and Us constitute basic and proper organizational principles for apprehending the universe and our places within it. Thus, we maintain, the Western root metaphor is one of dualism.

We hold the hypothesis that since culture is transfered from one generation to the next by means of one or more types of learning, the root principles will (tacitly or explicitly) be illustrated in learning.

Root metaphors and root principles are linked to each other in our minds. The relationship between them can best be expressed by means of a comparison: a metaphor relates to a root principle or intuition in a particular culture in the way a Gestalt relates to the particular act or process that yield the particular Gestalt. A root metaphor provides the means by which both extended, or secondary, metaphors and Gestalts are expressed, while the root principle is the foundation from which a Gestalt develops. A root principle is a given for members of the culture; it is culture specific. In order to clarify our terms, we here resort to a few examples of root principles in the cultures under discussion.

a) examples of learning

(1) When Jan enters the school in Ghent, Belgium his life is altered in a variety of ways: he will now remain inside of the building for the rest of the day and only leave it to go home at twilight; he will sit most of the time at his desk and face the front of the classroom like all other children with him; he will set his brain to work and read, write and calculate for several hours, occasionally stopping for half an hour to run around and

yell in the interior playground; he will subordinate himself to the authority of the man or the woman who stands in front of the classroom and who teaches what is to be known and how to acquire that knowledge in a quick and correct way. Whenever Jan does not understand, he can ask questions of the teacher and sometimes also of his co-students. Sometimes Jan has to learn series of numbers or words by heart, sometimes he can go out with the teacher and his classmates to check something he learned in the field. Most of the time, though, the things Jan learned in previous lessons matter more for what he is learning at the next moment than what he can see or hear in the outside world. On some occasions the teacher brings in some of the outside world: for example, a lizard may be studied and discussed in the classroom while it is sitting in a glass container. When the bell rings, the lessons are over and Jan can go home again. When you ask Jan why he goes to school, he says he learns things there in order to be able to live in the real world when he is an adult.[4]

Any child who enters a Western primary school is given roughly the same curriculum as the next one. All knowledge is collected in teaching guides and children's school books, which are meant to be used on a national and even an international scale: indeed, what is considered true and valid for one learner has this status for all possible learners in the Western tradition. By the same token, all this uniform knowledge can be taught by any teacher chosen at random. He or she has to qualify in terms of diplomas (on the basis of uniform requirements about knowledge and skill), but the role of teacher is not linked in any way to kinship ties, cultural background, or other more personal characteristics any individual might have. Indeed, it is considered highly inappropriate to call attention to any such characteristics. Learning could be summarized in terms of three partners as follows: there are individual minds (the learners), mediators (the teachers) and the objective knowledge about the universe (the curriculum, most of all in the form of texts). Learning is bringing elements (including structures, models, etc.) from the third partner into the mind of the first partner. The third partner 'exists' in the same way for all individuals and is independent of any characteristic of the two other partners.

(2) When working with *Dàghaashch'ilii* (or Curly Mustache, hereafter D) on the Navajo Reservation, one of us (R.P.) was told the following story

relating to learning: when D was young he had been watching a spider construct its web for several hours. He was still able in his old age to relate exactly how the spider went about the work. The story took him close to an hour to relate and contained many details about the actual process of construction.

In the same way, Navajo children can be seen sitting next to their mother or aunts on the reservation and watching the older women weave a blanket. No questions are asked; the child just sits and looks intently at what is happening. After a series of sessions of watching, the child can 'suddenly' set up a small loom and start to weave a sashbelt or a small rug. Again, questions are seldom expected and hardly ever asked.

When one of us studied the Navajo school situation, with the goal of developing a curriculum for geometry teaching (see Pinxten et al., 1987), several white teachers complained to us that Navajo children are silent and apparently inactive in the classroom. One striking remark of teachers was that children never asked questions in the classroom, the absence of which was often interpreted as a lack of interest or of zeal.

When we decided to work on a geometry curriculum, we laid heavy focus on perception and visual exploration of phenomena in the environment (e.g., the hooghan, the rodeo ground, etc.), which were visited and experienced outside of the school. In the classroom the perceptions were discussed and then the invitation was made to the children to rebuild or reconstruct (on a smaller scale) what had been seen. The enthusiasm was great, but most striking to us was the high level of precision and the beauty of what the children constructed as replicas. In this case learning could be characterized as follows: each individual is confronted with reality and has to build his/her own interpretation of it. Reality exists around the individual and in him/her. Learning is manipulating the real phenomenon with all the risks (of disturbance, disruption, etc.) attached to it.

In the above examples and in other instances, we witnessed that children and adults were learners in a variety of ways, and that teachers had different qualifications and statuses with respect to both the learner and the subject matter. For instance, we came to understand that only those adults who were both old and knowledgeable enough qualified to learn from D. Any Navajo of less than say 60 years of age, who moreover did not have sufficient background knowledge about the tradition, could not approach D. to learn from him. The knowledge D. extended in the stories he told were meant to be heard by the old and knowledgeable members of the Navajo people. This rule is not an idiosyncracy of D., but it is generally applied and respected by all. Transferring knowledge to those who can not cope with it in an adequate way is dangerous and will lead to abuse of knowledge and danger for the whole community, according to the Navajo. Similarly, children are not told to learn by heart or imitate as such, but they are expected to grasp meaning and to reach insight by their own effort. Only in this way will the knowledge they gather be appropriate for them and hence beneficial for the people as a whole.

(3) The other of us (C.F.) has had similar experiences in her work with the Mescalero Apache (Farrer, 1991b). The research that led to a year's stay at Mescalero concerned the educational process of Apache children and specifically trying to devise ways to make Anglo-dominated schools more relevant to Apache children in order to motivate them to stay on in school. The very problem itself was one that was peculiar to Native Americans in that mainstream culture parents believe themselves to be in a superior position vis-à-vis their children and therefore able to command them to remain in school, at least through the early teenage years. Apache parents do not see themselves as having such control over the lives of other individuals, even their own children. While Apachean parents may grieve that their children are not staying in school long enough to allow them to be competitive in mainstream American markets or job venues, they do not perceive themselves to have the power or authority to demand that children remain in a place the latter find to be irrelevant; nor does Apachean culture support the notion that one may command another. Rather, the expectation is that those who follow do so by being convinced of the logic of so doing or they are motivated by a desire to acquire information held by another. The root principle is that each person, beyond babyhood and prior to senility, is not only capable of making valid decisions but also to do so; further, those decisions are not subject to ratification by outside others.

In a school situation, then, children must be engaged. All too often, the engagement is stifled, albeit unwittingly, by Anglo teachers or those Indian teachers trained by, and committed to, the Anglo model. This model means that the teacher, as authority figure, demands attention and respect, both of which are demonstrated by sitting quietly with eyes-front attention.[5] For Apache children, already well socialized into their culture, this proper way of attention paying, there is an immediate problem. The proper way to pay attention is first to be circumspect and quiet; this is demonstrated by lowering one's eyes for to establish direct eye-to-eye contact is to make a statement that the learner is on a par with the teacher. Secondly, Apache children indicate their willingness to be instructed by coming close to the one who has the knowledge or skill to be acquired; thus, especially in kindergarten and first grade, Apache children try to get next to the teacher. Such behavior often makes teachers uncomfortable; they describe the action as the children 'crowding' them or not giving them 'breathing room'. When the teacher then sends the children back to their seats, the children feel both rebuffed and conflicted: how is one to learn if not permitted to be close to the teacher in order to observe as closely as possible? Teachers expect to instruct verbally; Apache children expect to be taught by demonstration and their own close observation. Anglo teachers expect questions and answers in order to assess the level of knowledge of their charges; Apache children would not presume to question an adult and will speak of their knowledge only when they feel they have fully acquired all the necessary components of a skill or body of information. Here there is a clash of several root principles, but essentially it comes down to the fact that Westerners expect respect and attention to be accorded in particular ways as do Apaches it is deleterious to children in that the particular ways are not similar, let alone isomorphic.

Similarly, when she was herself being instructed in things Apachean, CF found that questions were not allowed. Each questioning attempt was answered by the demand that she 'pay attention', with the presumption that by being quiet, observing, and thinking, the desired knowledge would be made abundantly manifest as indeed it was. After having absorbed information through paying attention, she could be corrected when she made an incorrect assumption or reached an illogical conclusion; also, after having paid proper attention, she was included in discussions of esoterica based on the body of knowledge she had been trying to learn. In this manner, her knowledge base could be increased without direct instruction. In sum, she was treated as though she were an Apache learner, rather than an Anglo one. And that meant that the Apachean root principle that proper learning only being achieved by careful and close observation had to be followed rather than the Western principle that relies upon questioning frames for the transfer of information. (For further discussion, see Farrer, 1991a.) It will be clear from these examples that the root metaphor is exclusively structural and has to do with the expression of structural features, and the root principles deal with the procedures and structures.

b) the dimensions of learning

When we look at the examples given in the previous section, we begin to see that very different ways of learning are emphasized in the Navajo-Apache and in the Western traditions. Different procedures for learning, therefore, are inculcated and developed in the learner. Again, no dichotomy will do the job, but rather we propose that different values obtain on a set of bipolar dimensions which can be identified in both traditions:

(1) The Apache-Navajo place more emphasis on qualitative ordering and aesthetic aspects and less on quantification and universal statements or conclusions from ancient times; they do not emphasize universal truth at the cost of particular experiences.

Concomitantly, learning takes place at the speed, and in the terms, of the individual's insights. One will only learn what one understands, and the limit of understanding is only the limit of one's learning ability and volume. In Western schools the emphasis on quantification and universal truth yields techniques of rote learning rather than learning by insight. The learner will often 'take in' information that is said to be important without understanding it; the mere possession of this information (and testing of that possession) is considered to be proof of knowledge. We can not say that the particular and different types of knowledge in these cultures causes or induces the different learning strategies, but we claim that there is a correlation between knowledge characterization and learning strategies.

(2) The Apache-Navajo learners stress detail and orthopraxy, with less concern for sharing exactly the same contents (or orthodoxy). The Western learners are led by orthodoxy and attend less to differences in practice; they emphasize general features at the cost of details. An implication of this difference is that for Apache-Navajo learners the constant awareness of the contextuality of knowledge guides the learner in choices between relevant and irrelevant meaning or information. In the Western frame, relevance can be purely decontextualized or even formal at the extreme limit (see Sperber and Wilson, 1987). Hence, the Western learner learns to reason in a purely abstract, psychologically unreal world (see the discussion on 'new math' teaching in this respect, in Freudenthal, 1970). This kind of decontextualisation can only be done because there is a belief, for Western learners and teachers alike, that decontextualized thinking trains the mind and that 'coming down to concrete instances' is always possible. Apache and Navajo learners are wary of decontextualized learning and hold that contextual details matter at least as much as general features. A different *balance* between abstract and concrete seems to obtain. Both, of course, practice concrete and abstract reasoning. The essential differences are between decontextualising as an ideal vs. contextualised knowledge that always brings abstract and concrete together and the resulting balance between abstract and concrete examples during the learning process.

(3) Apache and Navajo learners depend heavily on personal experience and on person-ladenness of knowledge. The interpersonal learning situation is both discrete and unique, while the personality of the teacher is an integral part of every particular learning process. In the Western case the emphasis for the learner is more on authority and less on experience; hence, texts are used extensively as substitutes for personal experience. In correlation with these features, knowledge is considered to be preferably, or optimally, of a decontextualized kind. The personality of the teacher in the interpersonal learning situation is secondary: any qualified teacher will do, eventually even a machine, as can be seen in programmed instruction. From the point of view of the learner an even more pro-

nounced view on the importance of the personality of the latter in Navajo education can be mentioned. The program of the Dine Philosophy of Learning (DPL, Navajo Community College at Tsaile, Arizona 1989) offers a very convincing example:

> "For Navajos, education has an overriding purpose, which is to produce a desired material, mental, and spiritual condition (*hozho*), where one may live in harmony with others in society and in nature." (1989, 4).

Learning thus aims at the further development of a type of personality, according to tradition: the explicit aim of DPL is to reorganize the curriculum in detail of concepts and methods of teaching *"along the lines laid down in the creation narrative."* (idem, 6). A more literal statement of a choice for contextual and person-bound knowledge is hard to imagine.

(4) In the Apache and Navajo learner all knowledge gathering is a process of negotiation and interpretation, within the appropriate context for knowledge transmission. In the interpersonal learning situation, the knowledge given by the teacher is not mere data, but also the process of transfer is one of negotiation, interaction, and so on with other interpersonal aspects, which turns this knowledge into the personal reconstruction by the learner of the 'traditional' interpretation of the teacher. Thus, we have the basis for differing interpretations of the same event or differing understandings of the same process. In the Western case, any knowledge transfer focuses more on the data, or elements as such; the act of interpretation consists mainly in the integration of these bits and pieces into the uniform frame or theory or into the hierarchical organization of knowledge that is deemed to be closest to the truth, irrespective of the personal features of the teacher.

There are a correspondingly divergent set of procedures for learning among Western learners. Very generally, we see more emphasis on perception and exploration for the Apache and Navajo learner; for the Western learner, we perceive more emphasis on the verbal transfer of knowledge, with the consequent reliance on written reports of verbal behavior, i.e., on texts. When the learner reaches a right or 'true' view (that is, one that overlaps or is congruent with the objectified representation in his/her mind), then the end of the learning process is reached. The learner is engaged in a dialogue between his/her own (partial) representation and the objectified representational system, not directly with reality itself. Only so-called creative thinkers challenge the correctness or truth of the objectified version and hence create new concepts and models which go beyond the received view on things. This is possible for the Western learner or thinker precisely because reality is intuited to be 'out there'.

If our analysis is a valid description of learning processes, then it is clear that both the status of knowledge and of knowledge acquisition differs markedly in the Apache-Navajo and in the Western traditions. In the objectified, Western representation of reality, the 'house of knowledge' stands on its own throughout history: learners and teachers transfer all building blocks and ties across generations, and the mere objectification of the global map of knowledge implies its continuation as a historical phenomenon. Later generations can add to it, eventually change parts of it or even redefine the foundations of it. In the Navajo and Apache cases the learner is always manipulating reality itself in the learning process: every individual act of understanding or learning changes reality itself, not any objectified version of it. As a consequence, the learner's insights or knowledge do not have a detached, objectified or spatio-temporally decontextualized status; they are an intimate and inalienable part of reality. Any future reality will be different from any former one by the very act of learning itself. Hence, mythical or ancestral representations of reality are as present as the result of any individual involved in a learning process. Ancestral knowledge is just one more element of present reality, not an objectified, distanced, inert position of wisdom or truth. Two important consequences follow from this status of learning. Firstly, any individual learner's insights, or aspects of knowledge, exert power on -or better in- reality. Any particular item of anyone's knowledge is therefore a part of that person's power. Any transfer of knowledge is, by consequence, a giving away and so a loss, of power. Secondly, history is not an attribute or vehicle of an objectified representation of knowledge about reality. If we would like to identify a correlate to the Western notion of history in the Apache and Navajo cases, we would have to render it as something like 'the process of what is constantly in the making'- a phrase that is not only infelicitous in English but also a concept that is likely to cause cognitive disjunction for Westerners.

The consequences of our present interpretation of the differences between Apache-Navajo and Western views on learning and knowledge are considerable. History can only be used as a justifying and power-laden reference in the West, because history is attached to the objectified version of reality, irrespective of any 'true' reality if, indeed, there is such a thing (see Berkhofer, 1971). There is a presupposition of privileged correspondence between objectified rendering and reality itself. This, again, leads to discussions of the power impact of knowledge in terms of the indirect relationship between objectified knowledge and reality, not of the individual learner in his/her relationship to reality, as for Apaches and Navajos. In the Apache and Navajo case the learner's power impact on reality is direct and history does not enter the picture. Reality existed now as it did in the past and does in the future; actions and beliefs now impinge on reality, whatever its temporal setting. Since objectification in the West makes primary use of texts as solid, dependable and unchanging renderings of the objectified version of reality, the power struggle in the Western culture often takes the form of rhetorics with textual arguments or of whose history qualifies for the term 'history' and which history is 'correct'. The Navajos and Apaches argument refers to reality itself with the learner as an intimate correspondent of it in its existence at the moment of the interlocution.

In elucidating this structural characterization of Western and Apache and Navajo considerations, we make no statements concerning the rightness or wrongness of either perspective. We merely sketch the differences in approach and thus hope to illuminate some of the fundamental misunderstandings that are apparent in the confrontation of them in metaphysical and in political struggles. Finally, by focusing on these differences we want to dissuade the adherents of the dominant Western perspective from blindly promoting their own view as the only one, or even as the only salutary one (as will become clear in the next chapter).

Notes

1. This chapter is based on a paper written by Claire Farrer and me (Pinxten & Farrer, 1993). Claire Farrer was guest professor at the University of Ghent, Belgium through a grant from the NFWO (Belgian Science Foundation) in the spring of 1990.

2. A good description of the meaning and relevance of difference in the Navajo knowledge system is given in Farella, Chapter 4 (1984) while an analagous one for Apache is in Farrer, Chapter VI (1993).

3. We are unconcerned for the present whether this is an effect or a cause of consistency.

4. This description is inspired by the laboratory studies of authors such as Latour & Woolgar (1979), but it equally matched the prescribed pattern of a learning-in-school situation which may be found in any textbook of pedagogy (see, e.g., Cole & Cole, 1989).

5. See Susan U. Philips (1974) for an excellent discussion of cultural ways of paying attention in Anglo dominated school rooms.

CHAPTER 6

Learning from the Teacher's Point of View. The Case of Geometry Teaching

1. INTRODUCTION

In the previous chapter a sketch was given of the mechanisms and principles of learning in the learner. These mechanisms and principles were shown to differ according to the cultural background of the learner. If this result is valid, then, to paraphrase the words of Shweder (1990), learning is always 'cultural learning'. That is to say, the general and universal human capacity to learn manifests itself in culturally specific ways. A consequence of this finding is that a truly universal theory of learning is simply not in existence. Not only do I meet the majority of critical studies on cognition, intelligence and learning in the current research on these topics in the Western context (the critiques on intelligence studies by Gardner, Sternberg, and others, or the shift from a purely psychological or cognitive approach to socio-cultural perspectives in Cole, and others): except for the reductionist behaviorist school, with its implementation in programmed instruction, no uniform theory of learning is available today. But beyond this point of internal, i.e., Western, lack of knowledge about learning, no foundation can be pointed at so far for a universal theory of learning, that is a theory which would capture the diverse manifestations of the human capacity to gather and transfer knowledge in all cultures. Again, it should be remembered that both the very domain of knowledge needs to be reconceptualized (both for Western notions – see the discussion of work in Chapter 5 – and for non-Western notions), as well as the broad territory of forms, styles or ways of learning. I am very conscious of the fact that I did not offer an alternative theory in the previous chapters, but I claim that I demonstrated the problematic nature of our models and theories so far, especially by indicating their uncritical universalization of decidedly partial and Western insights. If one takes the program of scientific research seriously, even in a minimal way, it is clear that there is a long way to go from this parochial view on a phenomenon (which one tended to 'declare of universal nature' under the guise of 'science') to a genuine universal theory.

A related point concerns the notions of teaching. That is to say, the learner can be helped or trained during the process of learning. The learner can become a pupil and be informed by people who already know, who already developed skills and who are devoted to transfer their knowledge, in a formal or informal way, to the next generation. Subproblems for these teachers can be any amount of things, depending on the demands of the community, the capacities of the pupils or the needs of the environment: the teacher can teach skills, habits or techniques, but also 'facts' and stories, and s/he can teach how to learn ('learning to learn' from the perspective of the learner). The phenomenon of teaching has a whole set of parameters: for example., the technological setting of the teaching (school or other), the social context (classes, gender, etc...), the learning strategies of the pupils and the contents of teaching. In this chapter I will concentrate primarily on the latter two aspects. They provide a link with the analysis in the foregoing chapter on learning.

The question arises here whether and to what extent contents and learning styles (strategies, techniques, habits, etc.) of any particular cultural community should be taken into account when devising a transfer of knowledge by means of teaching. Does it matter what the learner brings into the learning situation, and should one consequently adapt teaching to the characteristics of the learner or not? I answer these questions in the positive. Programmed instruction, based on behaviorist theory of learning, is limited in its capacities. The alternative approach of contextualized learning (in the socio-cultural approach of the Vygotskians and in other perspectives) promises to do the job in a teaching setting where programmed instruction fails. Parallel to the psychologists mentioned I claim that any theory of teaching should be in line with and in fact based on the learning habits and strategies that we find in the learner. In that sense, a theory of teaching should be as 'naturalistic' as possible. Since we have no universal theory of learning, we have to do with more local or partial theories. Moreover, and consequent with my position on learning in the previous chapter, I here defend the standpoint that any teaching program should systematically take into account the cultural specificity of the processes and products of learning. In other words, any teaching program should be adapted in a number of ways to the actual learning contents and styles of the learner in a particular community. Obviously, this can not mean that the learner's knowledge and ability will dictate the teaching program. This would bypass the very notion of learning (where expansion or adaptation of knowledge is a crucial feature). On the other hand, it does mean that my working hypothesis holds the following terms: *due to the lack of a universal learning theory, any teaching theory can only be provisional and circumstantial. Moreover, any teaching program, in contents and types of transfer of these contents, will have to take into account the particular cultural background of the learner.* The validity of the hypothesis can be tested by means of its success or failure in the transfer of knowledge through teaching. The failure of the 'universalized' schoolish form of teaching is being discussed presently both within the West (especially with regard to lower social classes) and in so-called development programs. I will focus on one domain of knowledge transfer within schools only and develop an alternative: the teaching of mathematics. In very general terms, my hypothesis translates in this particular domain of teaching or formal education as follows: *for lack of a general theory of learning, a local theory of teaching is endorsed in each particular cultural setting. Concurrently, the rationalistic 'new math' approach to mathematics education is rejected in favor of a perspective which is imbued by the local or native 'theory of learning' and in line with the intuitionist view on mathematics.* Two points are to be distinguished here: a) a certain view on the nature of mathematics, and b) a certain view on the cultural specific ways of training in mathematics. A forerunner for the Western educational context of mathematics teaching on both points is Freudenthal (1970), some of whose insights were developed to a culturally differentiating approach in Bishop (1988). I will briefly expand on the two points distinguished just now in order to sketch the implications of choices in this matter. The remainder of the chapter will then give a detailed, comparative example of this position, using the insights about learning in this chapter as a foundation for a perspective on mathematics education.

2. MATHEMATICS VERSUS MATHEMATICS

Any choice about a perspective in mathematics education is directly or indirectly linked with a view on the nature of mathematics. In order to teach something, one should know and account for that something. However, since this is not a book about mathematics and since my concern is with elementary rather than high level or creative mathematics in education, I can be brief on the subject. Two important distinctions can show the way to handle the problem focused on here.

In his introductory paper to a volume on *Education, Mathematics and Culture*, Bishop (1988a & 1988b) distinguished between mathematics and Mathematics. The distinction is necessary to avoid a fallacy that is often found in discussions on mathematics teaching and on the nature of mathematics. The fallacy resides in the non-distinction of the 'universality of mathematical truths' on the one hand and the universality of mathematical knowledge in itself on the other hand. That is to say, the 'universality of mathematical truths' states that mathematical theorems, proofs and the like are true in all places and all times. There is no denying this. However, this is very different from the statement that the mathematical knowledge or procedures, rules, ways of reasoning used in or typical for mathematics, are universal. The latter statement is wrong. It denies the cultural basis on which all reasoning, including the mathematical one, rests and hence 'universalizes' a particular format to confound it with the whole domain. Bishop then goes on to point out which types and forms of reasoning can be found in all cultures, manifesting themselves in ever so many different ways. The particular type of reasoning (with axiomatic features, proofs, etc.) found in the European-based discipline and school system of today is called Mathematics (with capital). It feeds on and derives intuitions from the commonsensical practices in this culture, for which culture-specific correlates in all other traditions can be found, which is identified as mathematics. The choice for an educational program can or cannot take into account the latter, and can or cannot focus heavily or exclusively on the former.

What Bishop calls 'mathematics' is the product of six activities, found in all cultures:

1) counting : up to 500 different counting systems are found so far, varying in tools, units or procedures. A basic step forward in this field was achieved through the work of Zaslavsky on African systems of counting (1973).
2) locating: all cultures in the world have ways to orient themselves.
3) measuring: no culture is known not to have a measuring system, be it approximate or precise.
4) designing: 'shape, size, scale, ratio, proportions and many other geometric concepts' (1988b: 149) are found in a variety of ways in the world.
5) playing as a way to explore both spatial and numerical aspects of the world is universally found.
6) explaining refers to the activity of identifying underlying rules, structures and the like. It is the activity which gives mathematical knowledge its meta-level character.

For each of these activities a growing literature of empirical findings is available. Bishop concludes: "*The symbolizations which have evolved through these activities, and reflections on them, are what we call mathematics.*"(1988b, 151). Western Mathematics (the discipline and its results) is then one form of mathematics which was developed in a particular place in the world, with its own history and its specific world view and values. I will use the distinction between M and m; for educational purposes I claim that M can best be reached through the use of m.

In the discussion on the nature of mathematics, Wittgenstein (1956) is often referred to as a primary source. In his now famous *Remarks on the Foundations of Mathematics* he introduces a series of distinctions which undermine the aprioristic view as it was and is popular in the formalist school (with proponents like Carnap, Tarski, and others). He captures a fundamental critique by speaking of: "*The disastrous 'invasion'*" *of mathematics by logic"* (1956, 281). He clarifies the meaning and impact of that characterization by means of an analogy: *"It is almost as if one tried to say that cabinet-making consisted in glueing."* (idem, 282)

In other words, the formalists or logicists unwarrantedly reduced mathematics to a particular aspect of it, which is dealt with directly in symbolic logic. The other aspects, like intuition, elegance, heuristics, and so on, are underestimated or even totally neglected by the logicians, according to Wittgenstein. In the wake of this critique a small but powerful school of thought on the nature of mathematics is growing. I will only mention a few of its adherents in the following discussion. Kitcher (1984) is certainly one of the major representatives here.

Kitcher (1984) divides the arena of discussion on the nature of mathematics in two opposing camps: the apriorists (Carnap, Tarski, Russell, etc.) and the anti-apriorists (initiated by Brouwer and Wittgenstein, but later Wilder, Kitcher, Bishop, Davies and Hersch, and so on). I will present the argumentation of Kitcher at some length, because his book worked as a catalyst in the growing discussion among mathematics teachers. In the first place Kitcher emphasizes the historical and the empirical nature of mathematical knowledge: at the bottom of our knowledge and at the beginning of M, there was practical knowledge:

"... a very limited amount of our mathematical knowledge can be obtained by observations and manipulations of ordinary things. Upon this small basis we erect the powerful general theories of modern mathematics." (1984, 92).

So, on a basis of m we erect M. Historically, the practical m knowledge of Egyptians and Babylonians was systematized in the M theories of the Ancient Greeks. There is no need to project the unexplainable workings of the so-called 'Greek genius' here: rather, the combination of a variety of other influences (Jewish, Phenician, Chinese and Indian among them) in Greece suffices to explain the shift toward a theoretical systemacy which later characterized M (Joseph, 1989).

What then is the nature of M knowledge today? Kitcher returns to his starting point and argues that observation and manipulation is not only the genetic and historical basis of mathematical thought. He stresses the continuity between perception (as a mechanism in empirical knowledge gathering) and mathematical reasoning (which, on the face of it, looks totally estranged from perception). Through perception we in fact enter into a 'causal interaction' with ordinary objects which leads us to discern their structure. In mathematical thought, according to Kitcher, we do something similar albeit in a distancing way. Mathematical knowledge is 'about' structure in the real world; and mathematical structures are *"reflected in the properties of ordinary objects..."* (1984, 107). However, in contradistinction to perception mathematics does not deal with the empirical world in a direct way, but it is rather an 'idealizing theory'. That is to say, it describes and manipulates the ideal forms of things, and not the empirically existing ones. That M and m concern structure of things (be it in an idealized form) is shown most obviously by the stepping stone theory between perception and M: geometry. Kitcher states:

> "Many of the statements of elementary geometry can easily be interpreted by taking them to be part of an idealization which systematizes facts about ordinary physical objects which are accessible to perception." (1984, 124).

A very similar approach to geometry had been worked out already in the forerunner of the Erlangen program, Dingler. In his marvelous little treatise on Euclidean geometry he reasons along similar lines, adding a description of the concrete actions the geometer performs, physically and/or mentally (or 'idealized') when developing and using geometry (Dingler, 1933). Finally, the excellent works by Davis and Hersch (1981 & 1986) offers a wealth of arguments to illustrate the link between M and m through 'experience'. It is on the basis of such insights that Davis can make the step to mathematics education: he proposes that applied mathematics (rather than pure M), i.e. the mathematics closest to experience and empirical reality, would be used as a basis for education and invites educators to make the following principles the foundation of their curriculum:

> "Where and how is mathematics employed in real life? Describe the mathematical beliefs, constructs, and practices that have been justified by the community [...] Describe the social dimensions of mathematical practice." (Davis 1989, 27).

These practical rules for education, professed by an excellent mathematician who believes in the experience basis of M knowledge, offer me the ideal opportunity to leave the discussion on the nature of mathematics and turn towards that of education. It is clear that the anti-apriorists are gradually building an alternative theory of the nature of M, pointing to the role and impact of culturally and socially evolving forms of m in any society. I have a lot of sympathy for this approach and hope to see it flourish in the future. It was mentioned here simply to point to a solid foundation study which can be used to serve as a starting point for an alternative approach to M teaching. The present-day deep crisis in M education urges us to look for such alternatives. The anti-apriorists may be offering a valuable way out.

3. THE DISCUSSION IN MATHEMATICS EDUCATION

In the high-tech society of the future the competence in mathematical skills may become more and more an element for social and economical discrimination between individuals and between groups. Mathematics educators have been rethinking the traditional curricula over the past decade and have come up with solutions that take into account the social and political implications of elitist teaching of these skills. A variety of more or less radical (Frankenstein, 1989) or liberal (e.g. Davis, 1989; Schultz, 1989 or Bishop, 1988c) alternatives to M teaching have developed. It now seems to be a fairly broadly accepted point that the social class of the student does matter for the aspiration level and hence for the success rates of pupils. Liberal and radical pedagogues take the view that M should be taught with the student's background knowledge about the world as a sort of frame of reference for the teacher (see especially in Keitel et al., 1989).

Within this move towards a program of teaching M *to* a subject, rather than teaching *on (or from within)* M, a few researchers have dared to digress from the mainstream and attend the problem of different cultural backgrounds as well. That is, the attention as shifted in some from a view on teaching a curriculum which is or is not socially adapted, to that of rethinking both the curriculum and the teaching strategies in terms of the (different) culture of the students. Zaslavsky's important book on African m (1973) has opened the way to this line of thinking. In recent work she follows this up by suggestive educational programs in M teaching which 'multi-culturalise' curricula (Zaslavsky, 1989). The group of researchers in Bishop's center have taken pioneering steps on this line. I will mention some of this work before I turn to the particular subject of Navajo geometry teaching.

In Europe and North-America a model of M education has taken hold over the last century or so, which *"identified logic as the important criterion in the Mathematico-Technological culture rather than tradition, experience, or personal status."* (Jurdak, 1989, 12). Jurdak thus joins Kitcher in his critique on the apriorist view on M, and its correlated educational system. Only, as a member of the group of Bishop, Jurdak investigates how and why the Islamic cultural groups perform poorly in M. His main conclusion is that they do because of cultural differences: the last criterion for an Islamic pupil and teacher is not logic but the authority of the Koran, and the way to learn something is more often initiation than western-style discovery. This different type of cultural learning forms a barrier to mathematical skills for the Islamic student, according to Jurdak. That is to say, not so much the curriculum in itself (with its implicit definition of M knowledge), but the means of transfer of knowledge are a barrier. The very strategies and ways of learning and teaching differ between Islamic and European traditions and it is these differences of the process rather than the content that explain failure. Dawe (1989) follows up on another insight of Bishop: the latter claims that every culture has a certain strong point in terms of m learning. Curricula for M teaching may be expected to be more successful, the more they take into account and appeal to these strong points. Dawe thus looks for strong points in different cultures of the South Pacific and tries to work them into teaching strategies adapted to each cultural group. E.g., the manifestly great capacity for rote learning in the Australian Aborigines together with their strong visual memory and their dislike of competition, urges Dawe to conceive of a program that takes these fully into account at the expense of other styles (like competitive group work or decontextualized problem solving) that seem to be so dear to the European schooling system. The list of studies could be enlarged, but I think these few examples may suffice to render the gist of the matter. In general then, along with these and other authors I advocate that both learning styles and strategies and the particular use of cognitive operators involved in present-day M teaching are very much particular to Western culture. Other cultures have other ways, strategies and usages, and successful sophistication of the cultural m knowledge to become M knowledge will have to take these into account. A first step to reach this goal is to look for 'strong points' in each and every culture. That is to say, to search for the ways and strategies of learning which are favored in that culture. The Navajo curriculum for geometry teaching aimed at precisely that.

For the sake of clarity, a few last minute warnings must be issued here. I am not going into the question whether geometry or Mathematics is a 'western type of thinking', but I only focus on their *use as prominent ways of reasoning or instruments in reasoning* to secure a place for oneself in the dominant American society. The little information I offered on the nature of m and M can be used in the devising of a curriculum and a teaching style, but the philosophical question about the worth, truth, etc. of neither m nor M will be gone into any further. As far as the problem of the political importance of M teaching is concerned, other researchers, notably those working in less developed countries have discussed the potential discriminating use of mathematical skills to considerable length (e.g. D'Ambrosio, 1987). I want to offer my bit of evidence here and to develop some ideas about the way in which the predicament of 'underdevelopment by means of education' (which might well describe what is happening in many cases) can be altered in the particular case of the Navajo. In that sense, I side with those I called the 'liberal' M educators and will look at the ways and conditions of making M into a powerful tool for the Navajo, along their lines of preference and relevance.

My general intuition about the development of an emancipatory program of Mathematics teaching can be summed up in one general rule of fist: M knowledge develops against the background of a form of cultural learning and feeds on the m knowledge in the culture of the student. Hence, both the particular form of learning and m knowledge should be fully accounted for in the development of a M teaching program in order to optimize results. As has become clear in the former chapter a whole lot of dimensions are involved here. For example, the school system and the definition, use and transfer of knowledge as they are institutionalized in the Western school are foreign to the Navajo children. Hence, a certain amount of resistance exists in them to comply with this profoundly Western setup. (A rather similar experience of alienation by the school context and its way of handling knowledge was witnessed by my collaborators and myself in children of Turkish immigrants in Ghent, Belgium.) The affective, valuational and ideological meanings attached to this institution should be taken into account by anyone who wants to propose educational measures or pedagogical principles for children of another cultural background, I think (see e.g. Schuyten & Vossen, 1986). I realize that such statements may sound revolutionary. On the other hand, they tend to remind us of the socio-cultural and historical specific background of our own institutions and may refrain us from 'declaring them of universal value'.

4. NAVAJO CULTURE AND THOUGHT

a) Navajo thought and Navajo learning

During our fieldwork we came to understand that thinking (and speaking) is never gratuitous for the Navajo: when you think about something you are actually manipulating reality. Thinking has direct impact on reality. Thus, Navajos will say that to think of something with care and affection will help that something bloom and prosper, and to think of it in a wronging (or 'enemy') way is to cause misery or harm to come over it. Knowledge is not parted with easily: the one who transfers or gives away knowledge is weakening himself or is giving away power in the noblest sense of the word; the one who receives it can use the knowledge to trigger certain effects in the phenomena the knowledge is about. Hence, the receiver can abuse or use against anything or anybody else the knowledge gathered (and is then called a witch) or (s)he can use it to the benefit of all and nature in general.

Within these general views on the status of knowledge it is important to focus briefly on certain aspects of this native theory of knowledge:

– knowledge is a highly valued private property, giving power to the beholder (Haile, 1948). Hence, the transfer of knowledge is a danger-laden enterprise. In the context of our present concern, transfer in an educational setting is far from 'obvious' in the Navajo mind.

– giving away knowledge to someone who is not already knowledgeable to a certain extent, or who is not 'ripe' to receive it will entail its abuse by the receiver (knowingly or, as is often emphasized by Navajos, out of stupidity: Pinxten, 1979), and may hence harm the people as a whole. Again, in the educational context, this implies that people will or will not be given knowledge, depending on their individual ripeness (and age): in a general way, nontrivial knowledge is not given to people before old age (say 60 or 65 years of age: Pinxten et al., 1983). It is clear that knowledge is not *mere* information, and that it is *not public property* for the Navajo. However, the latter two aspects are, in my view, implied in the western outlook as it is implemented in the schooling system.

– finally, the basic distinctions between thinking, speaking and acting on the one hand and between these and 'external ' reality are not shared in the Navajo view. Because of characteristics of holism and interconnectedness in the Navajo knowledge system, *thinking is having impact on reality*. Hence, the detached, neutral or 'objective' status of knowledge in the western tradition and its correlate in the western treatment of knowledge as information in the schooling system, is utterly foreign and even wrongheaded for the Navajo (Witherspoon, 1977).

It will be clear that such aspects of the knowledge complex should be taken into account in the educational setup. A second series of aspects are as important: the features of the Navajo way of learning. I summarize what has been said in this chapter:

– Navajo learning is about contextual and changing aspects of the world. Western learning aims at absolute and decontextualized knowledge.

– Navajo learning is direct, and not discursive (as in the West).

– Navajo learning is primarily through perception, hardly ever through questioning. Questioning is essential in Western learning.

– Navajo learning seeks for qualitative order and esthetic features, whereas Western learning stresses quantification and consistency.

– Navajo learning is person- and context-bound, against the depersonalized universalism of Western learning.

– Navajo learning stresses orthopraxy and detail and not orthodoxy.

– A primary basis of transfer in Navajo learning is the experiential material that is transmitted in a negotiation between teacher and apprentice. The text most often induces what is transferred in the West; negotiations take place in the preparation of the text, not between teacher and student.

– In a general way, learning is more IN reality for the Navajo and more ABOUT reality for the Western learner.

With these features in mind, I will now look at the contents of what is to be transferred in the particular case of geometry teaching. Indeed, any M curriculum does not only teach skills but most certainly works with an implicit world view as well. This became very clear in the field work we did on space and geometrical notions. The implementation of a preprogrammed curriculum of 'New Math', which was the standard procedure at the schools we visited, was difficult or even disastrous precisely because the implicit world view in the curriculum did not match with the Navajo concepts. E.g., the strong emphasis on part-whole relationships in M (with sets and elements, divisions, partitions, etc.) is totally foreign to the processual world of the Navajo. In view of the development of a geometry curriculum, I will concentrate on spatial notions first and foremost.

b) Navajo space

Spatial knowledge can be studied in the language and in nonverbal aspects of culture (such as architectural products, objects of art, behavior in space, and so forth). The model of Navajo space constructed on the basis of this research (Pinxten et al., 1983) has the following particularities:

– space is an all-pervasive 'category', but can never be fully separated from the temporal perspective (see also Chapter 5). As mentioned before, the universe is profoundly dynamic and the 'category' of space-time renders a more appropriate view on Navajo cosmic theory than the separation of the four dimensions. In the model of Navajo space we presented this fact is highlighted most of all by the recognition of the primacy of 'movement' in Navajo spatial thought. With Witherspoon one can say that the group of verb stems for 'to go' or 'to move about' holds the status in Navajo language that is reserved to the verb 'to be' in English (Witherspoon, 1977). However, movement is not the only cognitive notion with a primary status in Navajo.

– the Navajo correlates of the notions of 'dimension' and of 'volumeness/planeness' (i.e., having extension along two or three dimensions at once) are equally basic as the notion of 'movement'. That is to say, in the Navajo spatial knowledge system all other spatial differentiations (such as center, in/out, left/right, angle, geometric notions, etc.) are built up by means of at least two of these three basic notions together with other, often non-spatial aspects of meaning (e.g. particular actions, wind or any other semantic constituent which is relevant for the Navajo thinker: see Pinxten et al., 1983 for further details). The overview of Navajo space we thus reached shows a complex structure of cognitive or semantic relationships between Navajo correlates of spatial notions, with the concepts of Navajo 'movement', 'dimension' and 'volumeness/planeness' as logical primitives and the culture-specific characterization of tens of other spatial notions as derived cognitive or semantic constructs. Local circularity occurs (e.g., the notions of boundary being defined by the notion of 'volumeness/planeness' among other ones, and at the same time co-defining the latter). Without going into more detail here this characteristic should be mentioned to contrast the Navajo view on space with the Western one (at least as it is presented in the studies of Piaget & Inhelder, 1947: the spatial knowledge system is built up on the basis of one single 'primitive' notion– nearness – out of which all other spatial notions are gradually derived in a pretty linear order). Again, this contrast is relevant for educational programs, I think, first and foremost those centered on mathematics and geometry teaching. All in all, the Navajo model of space we reached is one in which not one but rather three notions seem to hold the status of fundamental, irreducible cognitive constituents. Moreover, Navajo spatial notions are clearly distinguished from one another, but this distinction can be based on a variety of criteria and does not necessarily fall into the category of formal logical (or deductive) distinctness as is the case for western spatial modeling according to the Piagetian view. Finally, spatial concepts in the Navajo perspective are not exclusively 'spatial' in any sense: cognitive or semantic aspects from any other realm of Navajo knowledge system can be recognized as constituents of the meaning of a spatial term or concept .

5. GEOMETRY CONTEXTS: EDUCATIONAL PRINCIPLES

How, one might ask, will all these findings and these principles be combined in the form of a curriculum that is both adequate and justified in the eyes of the critical and culturally alert M teacher? It will be clear that one curriculum will be very hard to conceive. A plurality of curricula, both following the criteria outlined in the first sections of this chapter and adapted to the cultural group one is teaching, seems more to the point. Because of the advantages of geometrical notions in terms of visualization training (i.e., the mental manipulation of forms, surfaces, volumes, and the like) and because I hold that geometry can best serve as the stepping stone for the child between preschool knowledge and decontextualized M (I follow both Freudenthal, 1970 and Piaget & Inhelder, 1947 on this point), I chose to concentrate on a curriculum for elementary geometry. Moreover, I will not try to present a curriculum for Europeans (or European-derived culture bearers elsewhere in the world), since that work has been done in an exemplary way by the research group around Hans Freudenthal (e.g., IOWO, 1978) and others.

During a follow-up field research with the Navajo, and on explicit request by them, curriculum material for the teaching of elementary concepts of geometry was developed. It was presented in a few articles and a booklet holding a discussion of the technical and educational principles involved and a detailed presentation of four 'contexts for learning' (see Pinxten, Soberon & Van Dooren, 1985 & Soberon & Pinxten, 1985, Pinxten et al., 1987).

The technical and educational principles in our schooling system correlate with the basic insights of major psychological theories. Thus, the thoroughly rationalistic tendency in so-called modern mathematics and in most programmed instruction in European education corresponds with and finds its legitimation in the rationalistic view on psychogenetic development of Piaget (on the latter see e.g., Gilliéron, 1987): the individual child unfolds its primarily cognitive capacities in interaction with a context.

The unfolding or development is believed to be a process of maturation and to follow a strict formal pattern, which can be described in terms of a logical succession. The same logical structure (from the most fundamental and hence abstract to the more specific and hence concrete notions) which is found in the genetic development of spatial notions in the child can be detected in the organization of geometric theories: the most general and abstract concepts of topology precede the more specific ones of projective geometry, which in turn come before those of euclidean geometry (Piaget & Inhelder, 1947). It is only one step for the educational psychologist to suggest that hence topology should be taught first (since it is logically and genetically primary), and euclidean geometry last. I have no examples of this educational strategy for geometry, but the rather general acceptance of 'new mathematics' (or set theory-based M courses) follows the same line of reasoning.

A vigorous opponent of this rationalistic approach is Hans Freudenthal (1973, 1979). His basic claim is that mathematics teaching should be directed at the level of reasoning of the child, regardless what the structure of the field of mathematics looks like. His basic stance is that one should teach children notions of M, not treat them as mathematicians. The researchers in this perspective claim that the child lives and thinks in semantically rich contexts. That is to say, terms in child language may have a variety of meanings and the conceptual or semantic field of terms is fuzzily bounded. The rigor of mathematical terms is characterized by unambiguous and exclusive (or very poor) meaning and the boundaries are as strictly defined as possible: at the limit the mathematician works with pure abstractions, without any reference to a world of experience. In other words, mathematical knowledge is maximally decontextualized. In the view of authors like Freudenthal, Bishop and myself these features make this type of knowledge far removed from or at least different from the kind of knowledge the child is producing and using. The rule of fist of Freudenthal is to start from the child's psychological setup in order to teach it, and not from the characteristics of mathematical knowledge (see his 1970 and especially 1979). In the school setting this implies that the richest possible contexts should be worked with in order to teach, which is the exact opposite of the rationalistic view.

A third approach is the now very popular 'socio-cultural' perspective, which developed out of the works of the Russian school of psychology with such leading thinkers as Vygotsky, Luria and Bakhtin. In a general sense, this group conceives of cognition as social learning. That is to say, learning (or thinking) always occurs in a social or socio-cultural context. Logical operations (such as the Aristotelian reasoning) are both with regard to the premises and to the preference of one operation over the other always set in a socio-cultural context. Thinking and learning are never context-free. I want to suggest to pick up this general view and expand it to cover a cross-cultural situation. This is not done by Vygotsky (who really thought the Others were primitive or living in a historically pre-European period, see Van der Veer & Valsiner, 1991). What is counted as a valid classification or a sensible argument in culture A will not necessarily be recognized as such in culture B. This does not mean B does not have the capacity to think properly, but rather that the categories and the choice of processing operations may be deemed irrelevant (or less relevant) for the particular concepts concerned by culture Cole et al. (1971) have important examples on this distinction in their study on Kpelle classification and mathematical skills. Examples from other parts of the world are offered in the volumes on other mathematical practices, such as Zaslavsky (1973), Bishop (1988b) and Keitel et al. (1989). I take Cole's work to be convincing on this point and want to draw some educational consequences from it. The major consequence is that an educational program will most probably be more efficient if it draws on the native strategies for thinking and learning than when simply implementing the western (or for that matter any other) way. A second consequence is that the particular classifications and notions of a culture will in all probability constitute the best material to work with in an educational setting. My proposal for a Navajo curriculum on geometry is based on both of these consequences.

6. GEOMETRY CONTEXTS: EXAMPLES

In the daily life of a Navajo a multitude of semantically rich or culturally laden contexts can be identified, all of which could be used to become the basis of a first and explorative teaching of intuitive geometric notions (see Pinxten et al., 1987). We worked out in some detail the contexts of the rodeo, the hooghan or traditional house, the school compound, the weaving of rugs and the herding of sheep. Children of the age of seven to twelve all have quite a lot of knowledge and indeed experience with all of these. Let me illustrate one context in order to make clear what is the meaning and intention of my perspective.

The hooghan is the traditional construction which is still used as a home by some and as a ritual building by all Navajos on the reservation. This is more pronouncedly the case in the central and hence more traditional area of the reservation (Rock Point and Rough Rock area near Chinle, Arizona). In a first lesson children and teachers go and visit the hooghan of a relative. During the trip stories are related and the inside and outside features of the building are observed. The Navajo categories and Navajo terms turn up in the stories and explanations: the construction is oriented with reference to the cardinal directions, the smoke hole in the middle of the roof, and so on (see van Dooren, 1989). Back in the classroom teacher and children are rehearsing what they learned: all the Navajo terms are listed, the particular details which struck children are recounted, and so on. In the next move children are now going to make a small scale model of the hooghan. In practice (during 1982-1983) the hooghan was rebuilt several times in the classrooms, at different scales and with different sorts of material.

The hooghan is normally a hexagonal, an octagonal or a circular form. The words or descriptions of these forms are given and rehearsed in Navajo. In practice, it turned out that operations rather than forms were described by the Navajo: the ground plan proved to be made by drawing a rough circle (either by means of a pole and a rope attached to it, or just with a free hand) and by positioning poles in the four directions on the circle. On the basis of this distinction the poles in between can be located and erected. The door is identified in the place of the eastern pole, the walls are erected by means of horizontal beams between the erected poles and the roof is woven on top of the whole construction. The important thing is that children have to discuss and try out how to build the whole construction. In the process they come across problems of proportion, height, width, direction, and so on. By trial and error but most of all by careful a priori observation they manage to construct a first and then a second hooghan. The guiding principle for the Navajo and for the white teacher is: not to interfere. After the phase of construction (and, importantly for the Navajo, after finishing the task in a satisfactorily beautiful way) the teachers pick up cognitive material which has come out during the process, write the Navajo terms used on the blackboard and rehearse them in other examples.

Let me go into this example in more detail still, to make clear how one works with intuitive geometry concepts in the Navajo case. What we did in the classroom could be called "playing hooghan". After visiting the hooghan of a relative and observing what happens where and when in the hooghan (when is eating time and where is it cooked? where do people sleep? where is the fire-place?), the children try to construct a hooghan in the classroom. The observations to start from are rehearsed: people sleep in a circle around the center, they walk around it in a clockwise direction; the fire is in the center; around the center one can detect walls in all directions, except in the east (door). The children construct a (small) hooghan in the classroom by means of cardboard and sticks. The hooghan has to be big enough to hold a small group of children and it has to have the characteristics of the hooghans that were visited. When sitting in it, children will try to determine the center. Their own 'reinvention' of the notion of center is important here: the teacher does not show how to determine the center in the try outs of this curriculum, but rather children gradually conceive of a center on the basis of their actions: by stepping an equal amount of steps in all directions first, by applying a stick or a piece of rope in all directions next, and so on. When in a later phase a smaller replica of the hooghan is built (constructed on a table in the classroom) the action-notion of length (i.c. a rope of a certain length or a stick, applied in all direction) is spontaneously reused by the children. Meanwhile, one or more terms are introduced or sometimes made up in Navajo for the concepts used: long, center, equal length. These terms are put on the blackboard (they are not given here, because the Navajo teachers opposed to their publication). Throughout the teacher and the researcher interfere as little as possible with the children. Their role is confined to that of the supplier of material rather than that of the active teacher or guide. In a final phase the hooghan is drawn rather than constructed in concrete materials. At this level the visualization processes are introduced.

In a similar sense the context of rodeo (very much the favourite one for the boys) is explored, ending in several attempts to rebuild a rodeo ground in the school. In a last stage some of the concepts or terms which occur in both the contexts are recognized as more general or abstract terms and then applied in still other contexts. The latter phase is moving towards a cross-contextual use of categories, remaining within the Navajo cultural scope all the time.

7. WHAT DID WE LEARN FROM THIS?

In my view a few remarkable givens should be mentioned here. First of all the teachers gave us a list of terms which came out of this exploratory way of learning. They gave it only with a lot of reluctance. The list apparently is a set of terms for the Navajo categories of intuitive geometry (such as length, width, circle, etc..) as they came forth of this process of teaching and exploration. The reluctance can only be understood in terms of what was said before on the impact of speech and thought on the world for the Navajo. They were not ashamed or in any other way uneasy about their correlates to intuitive geometrical concepts and terms (which is in fact what it stands for) but, as they told us explicitly, they were afraid we might abuse it, i.e., use it lightly, irresponsibly or out of the proper context. We had to promise indeed not to use the list in publications for non-Navajo. The knowledge which was reached should not be used against the context which generated it. This is most certainly a particularity of the Navajo tradition. Other traditions will have other specifics, we gather. We should respect them and, as is shown to be possible in this case study, build them into our educational program.

In the second place, on the cognitive level, we witnessed that cognition and learning are very much socio-culturally specific phenomena. The school setting and the classroom situation are clearly western import. It remains to be seen what their impact on the learning process is, but unfortunately they could not be altered. What could be organized in terms of the Navajo culture so far (i.e. the material, the conceptual frame and the learning strategies) has been adapted accordingly. The importance of this orientation on the native perspective to as large an extent as possible can only be stated in a very provisional way. We have no follow-up study and we have no really comparative data available. However, taking into account the tremendous difficulties of Navajo children with M (certainly in the pre-progammed format of the usual American curricula) and looking at the enthusiasm and the creative results (the list of terms and the scale models and drawings) I claim that in all likelihood the following major benefit is gained by such a program: children develop concepts for use in a cross-contextual way by sticking with and becoming gradually more conscious of the native categories and terms. The procedure results in the production of further concepts and terms within their own socio-cultural tradition. In my opinion this should enlarge the ground for insightful learning considerably: by developing concepts and terms within their own language and categorization system subjects at the least avoid the alienation of stumble blocks that appear through lack of understanding and untranslatability in the implementation of a foreign curriculum. In other words, I am convinced that it is worthwhile to develop the seemingly exotic (or, from the perspective of the Mathematician, wrong or at least unorthodox) concepts and conventions which emerge out of the native intuitions, because the colossal benefit is that children from that culture can then go from concept to concept or from term to term by means of insight or understanding, and should not draw insecurely on rote learning of cognitive material that appears as alien or nonsensical to them. In still other words, education which draws on vernacular categories and learning strategies is not alienating and hence may be emancipatory. It is clear that at some point in time the adoption of other (primarily western concepts and cognitive strategies) can be opted for. My conjecture is that the strategy defended here is still beneficial, because it is less alienating and allows for insightful learning for the child.

A final point concerns the use of Navajo learning procedures and principles in the school context. Since the school setting could not be completely altered, a compromise is aimed for. First of all, it is clear that contextuality is a basic principle in the choice and in the practical elaboration of a curriculum: all the material worked with is found in the world of experience of the child and is treated as a cultural reality, not as an abstraction. The emphasis is on orthopraxy and not orthodoxy: through trial and error children come to find and understand the abstractions they need to fulfill a practical task. The emphasis on perception and on detail in the Navajo way of learning is fully respected and is used as a vehicle for learning rather than as primitive or avoidable habit. The teacher can, through a minimally directive attitude, allow for adequate speed of learning for each child and for personalized knowledge transfer. Indeed, children learn on their own and from each other, and they can turn for help (in terms of material or information) to the teacher at their own speed. On the negative side, I think that the school context and the institutional authority of the teacher can not be diminished enough to allow for a full use of the Navajo aspects of learning such as negotiation, person-boundness and reality-directedness of learning. Giving up the school setting completely (as is suggested more and more in the Western educational context, see Illich, 1970) seems to be a prerequisite for a fully respectful organization of knowledge transfer in different cultures. It is then that the Western biasedness of the system of knowledge transfer in a school setting will become fully clear and that its possible benefits for some and manifest handicaps for other types of knowledge transmission will be testable through comparative evaluation.

PART III

COMPARISON AND NORMS

CHAPTER 7
Ethnocentrism: Ours and Theirs

1. ETHNOCENTRISM AND THE FUTURE OF THIS WORLD

In a world where Latvians, Estonians and Lithuanians, Uzbekis and Armenians, Hungarians in Rumania, and Turks in Bulgaria, Blacks in South Africa, Indians in the United States and Canada, Sikhs and Muslims in South East Asia and all immigrants and refugees in all host-countries of the world are claiming, among still many other, their right to live their religion and culture against the oppression by the dominant culture felt by them, it seems not altogether without ground to take the questions of ethnicity, ethnocentrism/racism and nationalism seriously. Both the marxist and the liberal hope that these questions would belong to the past and would long be overruled by economic demands and state politics seem to have missed the point: they both underestimated the strength and the meaning of the cultural factor. As an anthropologist I want to add that the small cultures do not appear to be dead - witness the renewals of struggle and of traditional culture (with new technology) in American Indians, in Amazonian Indians and in Australian Aboriginals. My prognosis is that they will not readily disappear from the face of the earth.

This rather long introduction has but one purpose: I want to indicate that the sociopolitical reality of ethnic identity, ethnic and cultural prerogatives, ethnocentric and nationalist drives and eventually racist fights will be with us in the world of the near future rather more than some had hoped and much more than most of us have anticipated. From the point of view of most anthropologists it is ludicrous or simpleminded to think that ethnocentrism will be conquered by the combined means of economic and political impact of western dominance. The rather popular though outdated attitude of negating the other's cultural tradition still underscores the blindness of many intellectuals in the dominant countries (both western countries and Japan, I gather). Why do I call this blindness? What are my arguments? Let us look at two typical instances, both of them 'put over on me' by friends.

When I started out with my field work on spatial notions in Navajo language and culture, friend A once told me that he (as a philosopher) was convinced I would find nothing but trivialities concerning knowledge or thinking in 'these oral cultures'. The attitude behind such a statement is typical of lots of intellectual friends and colleagues. It reads: orality equals low intellectual activity and hence cannot be taken seriously in the struggle for survival in the 'modern world'. The intellectual (philosophical, scientific and hence evolutionary) superiority of literacy is so much taken for granted that it easily leads to blindness with respect to what is really going on in intellectual processes. It may suffice to mention the important book by Scribner & Cole (1981) here: in their *The Psychology of Literacy* they demonstrated convincingly that literacy does not enhance the cognitive capabilities of the subject but rather implements the authoritative attitudes of the schooling systems by means of which it is introduced in oral societies. This devastating conclusion seems to indicate that we should at least differentiate between literacy, schooling and intellectual processes. What is it exactly that we mean when we say oral cultures are stuck at a certain level of 'triviality'? Do we not substitute intellect for the particular authoritarian and written type of culture we are reared in? In other words, can we sensibly mean to talk about the wisdom/stupidity of oral cultures when we have no other categories to understand them than those we draw from a particular literate schooling tradition? How will we not be blind for the learning processes and even the linguistic intricacies of the story telling situation when we have only the school paradigm to think with? (On the problem of the difficulties in describing and categorizing stories in present-day linguistics, see e.g., Hymes, 1981).

My friend B has another angle to the question. His American background may have given him a rather more materialistic view on things. His remark, which is again typical for a good part of the intellectual elite I fear, turns around wealth: he claims that given the proper high level of material wealth any person or group will act in the same individualistic and rather detached way that present-day Americans (and Europeans) do. In other words, intellectual traditions are typical for middle class persons within wealthy cultures. The wealthy persons in that society do not bother with intellectual attitudes anymore, and the poorer cultures (which are all below and 'before' the standard of Europe and the USA after the Second World War) do not really have time and energy for it either. This view reduces cognitive and intellectual performances of high standard to a particular psychological setup which is typical of a particular level of economic wealth. A curious thing with this type of perspective is that it cannot explain the origin of the intellectual tradition in the same terms: would one imply that human beings only started to have 'deep thoughts' from the moment they became (a little bit) prosperous? Surely, there is a historical relationship between a certain level of prosperity and the boom of intellectual institutes and careers, but is this to be equated with thinking or having intellectual activities? The connection seems random and the equation is at the least dubious.

I will not go any further into these examples. My point is that the two popular views on the 'intellectual life of the others' I find among my colleagues are not well founded. The only reasonable and tenable point I can see in them is that they speak about the non-recognition in other traditions of the culturally and historically particular type of knowledge production and 'intellectual life' we know in some western circles for two or three centuries now. This point, however, is a truism. How could it be the same? But more importantly: why would this particular type be more than just one type in one historical and cultural context?

I am reaching the finale of this introduction: if it is true (as I claim) that other traditions will not simply go away with time and so-called development and if it turns out (as I can demonstrate in some cases now and expect on a worldwide scale in the near future) that these traditions play a role in the cultural and the political life of the world to be, then it would certainly pay to investigate them thoroughly, rather than being blind to them. The conceptual cluster under study here -which I term 'ethnocentrism' for the sake of brevity-, should be studied seriously in such a world, lest one opts (implicitly as some of the intellectuals mentioned do or explicitly as the politicians of UNCSTD and other development programs do) for a solution of subordination of the weaker ones by the stronger one. The latter could be an economic and/or a political struggle, giving victory to those who are most powerful now instead of to those who are more sensible.

Ethnocentrism is a deluding concept, since it is both something to be studied in this research program and an attitude of the researchers themselves, I claim. It is to these two aspects that I turn now. They will be worked out in more detail in the rest of this chapter.

Ethnocentrism is a set of attitudes and outlooks in a group vis-à-vis some other group (see LeVine and Campbell below). In my view and again from the perspective of the anthropologist, these attitudes and outlooks will be found in some form or other in all cultures or peoples, but the particular values on these dimensions will differ from culture to culture. In other words, what I call ethnocentric for the Navajo will be akin to but different from what I will recognize as such in the western tradition, or in the Asian case, and so on. If we grant that the world is becoming smaller (meaning more and more peoples engage in more and more contacts with other peoples in the future world) and if we agree that they enter into interaction and communication with their particular biases, then it is of the utmost importance to study these different types of ethnocentrism and to try and develop a multicultural perspective on it. This is the first aspect. Secondly, and in keeping with the lessons taught by critical and reflexive movements in the social sciences (see Chapter 1) as researchers we should be aware that our view on human beings and cultures has been narrow and indeed ethnocentric in itself. In a nutshell and all too shortly put, we can say that we mapped human beings in terms of the social sciences which were feeding heavily on European conceptions of knowledge, culture, society, self, and so on and then projected our models on all other cultures in the world. The uneasiness and the theoretical bewilderment one finds so often in anthropology (as the official knowledge bearers about the 'others' , see Fabian, 1984; Pinxten, 1990) testify to the struggle with this critique. But struggling with something is not the same as finding an agreeable answer. In my opinion, the suggestions for an overarching theory we find in the literature are wrongheaded in that they start from the sole bias of the western view on human beings, thus short-circuiting the image of 'the other' to the benefit of our own ethnocentric model about ethnocentrism. This is a problem of cultural knowledge, though not only that. It is a problem of knowledge in that social behavior towards others also works with images ('knowledge') about the others as well as strategies to reduce dissonance or rationalize an attitude (e.g. Festinger, 1957).

The only way out I can see is to follow the same lines of approach I advocated above for comparative study: a decent perspective will have to be comparative in that sense, or it will fall prey to western ethnocentrism. In other words, I claim we do not have a well-founded and universal model about ethnocentrism so far and hence deal with ethnocentrism in a parochial, that is in a western ethnocentric, way. In order to escape this pitfall I will have to take the long road: investigate what ethnocentric attitudes and outlooks we find in particular cultures (we have some information on our own and on some other cultures as yet) and develop a comparative strategy (as pointed out above) from there. Finally, I will 'operationalize' these findings and implement them in the negotiating process (Chapter 11) and seek to promote egalitarianism rather than subordination through interaction and communication.

2. WHAT IS ETHNOCENTRISM (ACCORDING TO THE LITERATURE)?

Ever since Sumner's book at the dawn of this century a host of studies have been published on the nature and range of ethnocentrism, racism, the ethnic identity complex, and so on. The still useful handbook by LeVine and Campbell (1972) gave a first authoritative synthesis of the field of study. Their general definition of ethnocentrism is not really challenged until now: ethnocentrism is:

> "an attitude or outlook in which values derived from one's own cultural background are applied to other cultural contexts where different values are operative" (LeVine & Campbell, 1972, 1).

The extreme form of ethnocentrism, where the person takes his own values to be reality (and those of others to be illusions) is called 'phenomenal absolutism'.

This definition was, of course, meant to be neutral or technical. That is to say, the authors try to understand how different theories in different disciplines measure and describe 'ethnocentrism' in the meaning designated above. In order to reach their goal the authors distinguish between three aspects: a) a set of different attributes of social life combine to form the syndrome of ethnocentrism, b) this syndrome is functionally related to group formation and intergroup competition and c) all groups show the syndrome. Aspect b) states that the syndrome is not (only) a psychological phenomenon but has a clear social dimension. Hence, studies in social psychology and sociology are listed next to psychological analyses. Aspect c) reminds us of the fact the syndrome cannot be restricted to one group or cultural community. This point is very valuable, I think, but it forms the weak spot of the proposal as well: it has to draw on a representative and universally valid definition of 'ethnocentrism' (which had to result from a)) and it is there that LeVine and Campbell get stuck, in my opinion. What are the attributes of the syndrome of 'ethnocentrism'? LeVine and Campbell give a list of 23 facets, based to some extent on the initial work of Sumner. They subdivide into 'attitudes and behaviors toward ingroup' (dubbed A by me) and 'attitudes and behavior toward outgroup' (dubbed B by me). I give a selection of the list:

– sub A:

1. see self as virtuous and superior
4. see selves as strong
14. obedience to ingroup authorities
16. willingness to remain an ingroup member
18. willingness to fight and die for the ingroup.

– sub B:

2. see outgroup as contemptible, immoral, and inferior
5. see outgroup as weak
7. outgroup hate
20. virtue of killing outgroup members in warfare
21. use of outgroups as bad examples in the training of children
23. distrust and fear of the outgroup.

In an attempt to underscore the usefulness of these criteria or parameters LeVine and Campbell point to the studies of some anthropologists (like Murdock and Whiting) who computed some correlations between sets of these facets over a varied collection of cultures: they got cross-cultural correlations of 4 and 5, and so on. After their discussion of the sociopsychological and sociological contributions to the field the authors return to the problem of cross-cultural research again. They rightly point to the methodological difficulties involved with the delineation of ethnic boundaries: when do we cross the line between one group and the next one? The question is, of course, of utmost importance for a theory of ethnocentrism which is based on a preconceived distinction between ingroup and outgroup: who is 'us' and who is 'them'? The solution offered by the authors is to expand Campbell's theory of entitativity and to define the *"grounds for use in diagnosing the entitativity of aggregates of persons"* (p.105): the four Gestalt principles of (1) proximity, (2) similarity, (3) common fate, and pregnancy, (4) good continuation or good figure. Added to these are a notion of solidness (boundary impermeability, resistance to intrusion) and 'internal diffusion, transfer, and communication'. (idem).

In my opinion this approach to the problem is interesting, but it misses the point. Why is that so?

The attempt to move from a (socio)psychological level (ethnocentrism in one group) to a cross-cultural focus presents a first difficulty; the phrasing of the problem of ethnic boundaries as a methodological question (and hence the solution by means of entitativity criteria) is a second stumbling stone, I think. It is characteristic of a lot of cross-cultural psychology studies to generalize or universalize characteristics which are found in one group (or culture) to other cultures in order to reach a theory which would speak of behavior, attitudes or beliefs of all human groups. This move is by necessity a form of comparative research, I claim. The use of a formal technique (statistical comparison) to reach correlations does not alter its nature. The cross-cultural scholar can only take the data and terms of the one-culture researcher as a starting point and use them (implicitly or explicitly) as a frame of reference for his description and computing of what is recognized as the same data and terms in all those cultures he wants to include in the comparative move. In other words, the initial terms are implicitly granted a universal validity or relevance by most cross-cultural psychologists. However, as is clearly demonstrated in LeVine and Campbell's book, these initial terms are the ones which were construed by the psychologist or sociologist-member of a western culture. Hence, they reflect the presuppositions, attitudes and outlooks of his/her culture. There is no doubt in my mind that the western scholar can do his empirical work in a professional and high standard way, but there is no way s/he can 'step out' of his/her cultural background while doing it. Therefore, the description of ethnocentrism will be limited in its adequacy to the boundaries of that cultural background. When the researcher applies it (as the basis for statistical comparison or in any other way) to supposedly similar phenomena in other cultures, s/he falls prey to the ethnocentric fallacy. That is to say, the researcher describes attitudes and outlooks of the other in terms which are the expression of distinctions and identifications in the researcher's own culture. The latter are given in the list of 23 entries by LeVine and Campbell (1972). The very terms used should have warned scholars to be careful about the cross-cultural universalization of the entries: is 'hate', 'willingness' and so on to be expected to have a universal meaning in any likelihood? Can we claim to have an objective theory of these concepts which would readily and automatically apply to similar ones in other cultures? Then how are we to measure the similarity or sameness of 'hate' or 'willingness' (to stick with these two terms) in American whites, Canadian Chinese, let alone Indians or Africans? And, secondly and most importantly, can we claim or even expect ethnocentric attitudes and outlooks in different cultural groups to be based on these behavioral characteristics in the same way? I will turn to this point in the examples below.

The second stumbling stone is the identification of ethnic boundary description as a methodological difficulty (and the solution of that difficulty by Campbell's entitativity criteria). Again, I applaud the ingenuity of the solution to create some order in the field within the boundaries of say the European group as an entity. But again, the problem lies deeper than mere methodology can reach, I think. Two mutually opposing approaches seem to point in that direction. Anderson's *Imagined communities* (1983) is an attempt to deal with nationalism as a cultural system (like religion, see Chapter 2) and hence as a result of trans-generational imagination of a group. He analyzes the growth of nationalism as an historical outcome of the decline of the religiously founded and dynastic society. In his view nationalism appears only when (and because) the religious reference fades and the dynastic atmosphere (as a carrier of political organization) is becoming more vague in the history of the West. Finally, the link between cosmology and history (dominant in the theocratic political system) loosens and leaves room for an autonomous identification of history and politics. All this happened in Europe and the New World in modern times (17th and 18th century mainly), giving way to the growth of an alternative in the form of nationalism in the New World. This new cultural dimension was then reimported into Europe, according to Anderson. It is not so important here whether Anderson's views are historically correct or not. But his main point seems to be worth investigating: what we call nationalism today is a construal which is recent and which only developed after the theocratic (or religion-based) political views and their social vehicle (the dynasties) faded. Hence, when we use that term, we should be conscious of its highly culture-specific meaning. When I start from there I should ask myself whether I can find similar prerequisites of content in other cultures: religion (i.e., church and beliefs), dynasties, history without cosmology. Moreover, I must be aware that any of these prerequisites is filled in in a particular way since they draw on western traditions and western forms. E.g. with reference to nationalism Anderson states: *"nations inspire love, and often profoundly self-sacrificing love"* (1983, 129). These categories sound very much like LeVine & Campbell's criteria 18 and 20. In other words, we can project that the latter (18 and 20) will be found in 'the guise' of nationalism in a western culture, but can we presuppose that they are present in another guise or with different contents or not at all comparably in other cultures?

Moreover, since nationalism is at least a reality in the western world, can we not expect that our notion of 'ethnic boundary' is a by-product and hence an artefact of our recent history of nationalism rather than a universal trait of humanity? The history of the form of "ethnic nationalism" developed in Rumania for less than a century now seems offer interesting material here: the notion of 'Rumanity', as a nationalistic and as an ethnic category is highly specific for a good part of the population of that part of the world, but can not be universalized in any obvious way. This does not merely mean that nationalism there is Rumanian, but that the particular form it takes distinguishes it markedly from Western European forms, or from African recent nationalisms, or what have you (see Karnoouh, 1989).

Finally, some recent anthropological comments on 'tribal boundaries' seem to point in that direction: tribal units are an artefact of western categorization and not an intrinsic quality of the cultures under investigation (Fabian, 1979 & 1983). The only way out of this morass of conceptual ambiguity is to investigate the concepts on self and other in each culture before going into large scale comparisons.

The other type of approach that seems to be relevant here is that of evolutionary views on society and of sociobiology. In this respect something should be said about two partially opposing contributions: the radical sociobiology of Van den Berghe and the evolutionary epistemology of Shaner.

Van den Berghe (1977) is explicitly devoted to a sociobiological perspective on ethnocentrism. To my knowledge it is unique in this respect. In his view, biological factors are responsible for the self protecting attitudes of ethnocentrism. He claims that kin selection on the basis of 'blood ties' are responsible for the identification of boundaries and the exclusion of those who are not related by kinship. He calls this mechanism the 'biology of nepotism': a group of people organizes itself preferentially in terms of its own offspring. According to Van den Berghe this type of political organization is the first one (in time), to be found in small communities. When this form weakens (because the group grows, for example), one will witness the development of rather similar criteria of inclusion and exclusion for the new group in terms of cultural features: this one is a typical X and that one is an Y. The ensuing patterns of ethnocentrism are not biological in nature, but cultural artefacts; nevertheless, they are the cultural substitutes for a clearly biological mould, according to the author. Van den Berghe thus links the historically grown forms of ethnocentrism with the biological and hence universal predecessor. If we would take his point of view to be valid, we have at least two different interpretations in this one theory for Campbell's entitativity: a biological and hence universal format, and a historical and hence diversified format. The main critique I can think of is that against the blind determinism in such a sociobiological approach. But then, Campbell's entitativity might well be attacked along the same lines in favor of a truly historical or cultural theory (cf. Anderson, 1983).

A similar reasoning obtains when we confront the Campbell solution with another biology-inspired line of research, this time in comparative philosophy. Shaner (Shaner et al., 1989) presents the theory of knowledge of the Japanese philosopher Yuasa. The latter reexamines some basic tenets of western philosophy (e.g., mind-body) from a Japanese perspective. Shaner interprets these proposals in the light of a genuine comparative philosophy. Confronted with contemporary neurology he claims that it now becomes clear that universalism and cultural relativism are no longer exclusive positions (and this is one of Yuasa's positions as well): contemporary neurology seems to isolate more and more the universal features of the human brain and hence to point to the foundations of the mind. Combined with evolutionary theory this offers us a solid base of universal characteristics of the human agent, the knower, and the social being. However, at the same time neurology shows us that from the first days on neuronal connections do or do not develop (i.e., come into being or disappear) depending on the cultural context of needs, demands, inspiration or lack of impulses the organism is placed in. Thus, the universal basis is one aspect, but the cultural guidance and imprinting is seen to be active as well from the very first moments of existence. This very fact is the reason for Shaner to defend the necessity of a thorough comparative study together with (and not in opposition to) a biology-based universalist approach. When I confront this theory with both Van den Berghe's and Campbell's proposals I draw the following provisional conclusions on the matter of ethnocentrism: ethnocentrism is a cultural phenomenon, which may or may not have a universal basis in some initial and highly restricted set of biological features. So far, the controllable and empirically sustained neurological minimal basis indicated by Shaner seems to be scientifically more defensible than the vague and broad sociobiological foundation Van den Berghe is pointing at. However, in both (biologically based) theories the formation of particular concepts, attitudes and outlooks in human beings and in groups is largely attributed to the domain of cultural or social-historical factors, rather than biological ones. Hence, even in the explicitly universalist theories (such as Shaner's and Van den Berghe's) there is no strict determination of the form or outlook of a social phenomenon (like ethnocentrism) by any a priori and hence universal features. This state of affairs leads me to make a strong point for the type of comparative study I advocate in this book: one should study the culture specific features of ethnocentrism in any particular group in depth first, then compare the results with similar studies on other groups and lastly decide on whether and what could be called universal with regard to the subject (i.e., ethnocentrism). By means of the examples listed below I will try to make clear the range of such an approach.

3. EXAMPLES

Although the studies mentioned so far have their merits as analyses of attitudes and outlooks of an ethnocentric nature in the western society, they are clearly too limited in scope to qualify as proposals for comparative research, let alone as universal models or theories. The problem seems to be that they all conceptualize ethnocentrism from one perspective only (in casu the western one) and then proceed to use that perspective as a universal frame for comparison. Some examples will help to show what I mean.

(a) One of the striking things for the western observer in India is that people differ from each other in color, outfit and language. Looking closer it appears that they belong to different castes (whatever that may be) and to different religious groups. The Sikhs stand out among all others in their singular way of dressing (long coats of one color and the headband) and in their quite separate religion. The Hindi will be found in every possible job, from the lowest to the highest social status position. They will be seen bathing in the river Ganges, making offerings in one of the many temples, taking part in processions or contemplating the sun in complete isolation. When the noise of the day dies down and everybody goes home, the most amazing phenomenon hits the western observer: members of all castes, Sikhs, Muslims, Hindi and foreigners live in the same street, mixed among each other. I mean to say that, although the society appears to be stratified (in castes) and segmented (in religious groups), certainly the residence rules do not show ethnocentrism (personal communication: Balu). At the same time, at the level of India as a whole, the Sikh community fights for its independence and claims to be segregated or discriminated by the Hindi majority. Also the Muslim minority has specific revendications against the Hindi. Violent clashes between different groups occur more and more often in different parts of the country.

In Europe and the United States of America every city has its neighborhoods: the Jewish ghettoes throughout Europe's history have had their place and their connotations, but the same can be said about any settlement of a foreign community in a city. One can often find a Spanish, an Italian, a German, a Russian, an Arab, a Turkish or a Black neighborhood or quarter in the European cities (even medium-sized cities like Antwerp, Brussels or Amsterdam show this pattern, while Paris or London are structured according to ethnic zones). The growth of ghettoes is a consistent phenomenon: with the arrival of new groups in the 70's (Moroccan and Turkish immigrants) new ghettoes appeared. American cities have their quarters or suburbs of uniformly Black, Jewish, Polish and so on population. New York's West Side, Chinatown in different cities, the Chicano neighborhoods in the South and the Southwest, Black suburbs in all major cities and in the South, Indian reservations primarily in the West and so on, are ever so many examples of ghetto formation in the USA. Moreover, in Europe and in the USA rich people live in nice, lush suburbs outside of the center of towns or in the newly rehabilitated luxurious condominiums in old parts of the city (as has become fashionable over the last years, for example, with the London Docksides). The poor do not mingle with them in these neighborhoods: they live in shabby, uncomfortable and cheap quarters, mostly in older parts of big towns, near harbors or factories. The builders of the nineteenth century designed it that way, but they were only continuing a long tradition of ghetto formation in the West. A peculiar sign of the obviousness or 'naturalness' of segregation is apparent in the psychological studies of geographers: the studies by so-called 'new geographers' analyzed the way people structure cities in their mind. It appeared that roads are seen as markers to indicate the boundary of quarters (between 'us' and 'them') and that what is known to the subject is mostly only one's own neighborhood and not 'their' territory (Lynch, 1960; Gould & White, 1974). Neighborhoods or ghettoes in Europe and the USA grow on the basis of the social and economic status of the population (see also the new better quarters for the party members in the eastern European countries), and/or along the lines of different religious backgrounds (Jewish quarters, Catholic towns versus Protestant ones in Holland, etc.), and/or racial or cultural differences (Polish quarters, Asian townships, Turkish neighborhoods, Indian reservations, etc.).

When I try to compare the residence types in India and the West, I can conclude that ethnocentrism is clearly apparent in the rules of conduct and the attitudes vis-à-vis settlement in the West. This seems not to be the case in India. However, the violence between different 'religious' groups there might be interpreted as a sign of ethnocentric attitudes in the case of India. What would ethnocentrism be in each of these societies and why does it appear differently or in different realms of social life? What are the 'sensitive' points for one culture and for the next, or why do Europeans especially mind living in physical contact the 'other', whereas they promote mental or spiritual uniformity? How else can we explain the eagerness of the White man to convert humanity to his way of thinking and believing, even to a point of sending special missions to spread the word and 'civilize' the innocent savages? Surely, the economic impulse is not enough to explain the worldwide expansion of the foregoing centuries. How then should we understand the lack of zeal to convert others in the case of Hindi, but also the apparent incompatibility between their social behavior in terms of settlement and that in terms of equal opportunities for power? What is the relationship between power and ethnocentrism there? This is the type of question we should address,

I think, if we want to understand ethnocentrism in different cultural settings.

(b) When we (i.e., my wife and I) were asking about our *ana'i*-status, we were reassured that we would remain enemies to them, but at the same time that we were really very dear to them (Pinxten et al., 1983). How can this paradox be understood?

The situation is only paradoxical when we stick to our own attitudes and outlooks on enemyhood and friendship, or, maybe, when we are unconscious of the 'root principle' that is implied. Just as with our Western notion of ethnocentrism we may conceive of Navajo enemyhood in this example primarily as of a personal or social psychological phenomenon: in our mind, it then concerns the person-to-person relationship between the interpreter-human being and the ethnographer-human being. Within that conceptualization the paradox arises: how can one be an enemy and a friend at the same time? The paradox does not exist in the mind of the Navajo, though: according to Navajo lore you are born a Navajo or an *ana'i*, that is a non-Navajo and hence an enemy to the Navajo people or to Navajohood. In still other words, each and every non-Navajo is a potential threat to the Navajo since the former does not know the way of the people as the latter do and hence 'contaminates' the latter in contact. Navajos know a whole series of healing ceremonies which are explicitly meant for the curing of those Navajos who have been in contact with others. For each other 'tribe' they have a separate ceremony, in which elements of that 'tribe' are used to counteract the harming influences. Thus, Whites, Pueblos, Apaches, Utes and so on all figure in the appropriate 'enemyway' ceremony which is sung over the Navajo who is touched with the enemy's deficient traits (see Wyman, 1983, information from F.H.).

The traditional ideas about Navajo witchcraft corroborate this native model of ethnic identity. When a Navajo abuses knowledge about the tradition s/he is accused of being a witch. That is to say, s/he has grown into such a mental setup that the knowledge gathered can only be used in the way of an enemy: s/he has become a non-Navajo. When the accused person recognizes this status of witchcraft, suicide follows. Indeed, being a non-Navajo is being a nobody, or is falling from Navajohood, hence the self-annihilation. Hence, a Navajo can become an enemy for his own folk, but this entails suicide since s/he cannot become anymore what s/he has been before (Kluckhohn, 1944). The lore about enemyhood is consistent: somebody who was born a non-Navajo and hence is an enemy (*anà'i*) with the potentiality of harming the Navajo, can never become a witch. Indeed the enemy (by birth, so to speak) will never be acquainted enough with Navajohood or Navajo knowledge and tradition to the extent that s/he can be as systematically harmful to the people as a Navajo who turned witch. For the former a cure (an enemyway ceremony) is available, by the latter (who knows both sides) the power of the ceremony is endangered. Also, non-Navajos can marry Navajos and can even become medicine men within the Navajo community: these statuses imply the transfer of technical and restricted bits of knowledge, not the sharing of Navajohood. Evidently, the foreigner who marries a Navajo or becomes a medicine man remains a foreigner, however friendly and warmly s/he is treated by the people.

In the present-day situation a few interesting changes can be mentioned. In recent field work I investigated the concepts of ethnocentrism (and in particular that of *anà'i*) with several Navajos. A Peyotist told me that the real enemy nowadays, that is 'those who are dangerous' are the schooled Navajos (informant G.M.). My consultant explained this in the following way: the Anglo's (white people) have an education that teaches them about the Anglo way, the traditional Navajos had an education in and about the Navajo way, but the schooled Navajo belong through their education neither here nor there. They are without a genuine cultural root, homeless. Graphically, they occupy a middle-ground taking a few elements from the old Navajo tradition and a few from the foreign Western world view and producing a strange mixture that is part of neither of the foregoing ones. This makes them hybrid or 'nothing really'. Therefore, they do not understand and reject (Navajo) tradition and thus constitute a danger for the people.

A second shift can be seen with very educated Navajos. Some of them are westernized to such an extent that they will not bother anymore with tradition or with the difference between Navajo and Anglo. Others, however, seem to have been very disappointed over the last decades (i.e., with the failure of promises by the White governments, mainly under Republican Presidents) and to have lost faith in equal chances in the dominant culture. They are the ones who 'turn traditional' again and promote programs in Navajo language and culture, defend self determinacy of the Indian, and so on. They can be (and mostly seem to be) part of the Native American Church, which is by now an indistinguishable mixture of traditional and peyote elements and forms a forceful alternative for the merely 'westernized' Indian. Consultants from this section of the Navajo people told me that the old view on *anà'i* did not hold vis-à-vis white people only: certainly since the contact with the Anglo's there has been fighting, betrayal, inimical acts between Navajos (using the same term *anà'i* in some cases; F.M., D.BG., M.M., D.B.). Even further, some consultants claimed that Navajos who aimed to be on their own without any compromising intercultural interaction with other Indian groups or with the surrounding Anglo culture, are guilty of 'Navajo racism' (G.M., F.M.).

This way of conceptualizing the 'enemy' is different from, yet somehow consistent with the traditional notion outlined above. Indeed, in the view about alienating through education part of the own population is now identified as dangerous (the schooled youth, or the isolationists respectively). The criterion to evaluate them as a danger for the tradition has shifted from the traditional Navajo one, but remains nevertheless very similar to it: the schooled youth is born Navajo, but they are loosing their roots through education. More than that even: they loose ALL roots through the mixture they produce on the basis of formal education. What is different from the traditional view is that the determinism which was founded in birth according to tradition, is now explained by the role of formal education. The view about Navajo ethnocentrism condemns the nativism implied in the old conception of Navajohood and redefines racism and ethnocentrism in Western terms, i.e., as an interpersonal or relational phenomenon. The proponents of this view seem to move away in a radical sense from the traditional notions of self identity and foreignness. However, I want to stress one point of 'Navajohood' here that allows for and even promotes this kind of attitude: throughout the history of the Navajos they have been known to successively integrate objects, ideas, religious practices and the like from a number of other peoples. This cultural osmosis is so typical that the very notion of 'Navajo tradition' can be understood to mean 'change' (and certainly not static continuation, see Farella, 1984). Looked at from this angle, the reaction of the consultants cited above is consistent with tradition: the closure of the Navajo culture against other influences has always been condemned and avoided by Navajos, so the 'real Navajo way' would be to allow for intercultural contact and the aberration would be to turn to the past forms in order to avoid new contacts. Again, in this sense, those who call the isolationists 'racists' have a point which is founded in tradition and do not, on second thoughts, run counter to it.

4. HYPOTHESES FOR THE COMPARATIVE RESEARCH OF ETHNOCENTRISM

The above examples at least illustrate that the recognition or measurement of individual or group feelings (in attitudes) and convictions (in outlooks) will not necessarily yield the information one is trying to retrieve. The fact that an individual Navajo feels hatred for a Ute or a White man does not determine the enemy status of both latter persons, and even less adds to his membership of a clearly identifiable tradition. The supplementary fact that Navajos have been noted to have integrated rapidly and smoothly any amount of 'foreign' habits, beliefs and religious practices (from Pueblos, Mexicans, Whites, and so on) complicates the situation even more. Tradition for the Navajo is a highly dynamic and supple system of give and take relationships with others. The others remain 'enemies' in this network, but their valued habits and practices, if not the values themselves, are incorporated by the Navajos. An example of the latter is the fact that horses and sheep, introduced during the 16th century by Spaniards, are cherished as very valuable now: it is a high value of any Navajo to ride a horse and walk the sheep. Thus, sheep are addressed as *shimà* (my mother) and ranked among the most valued beings in the world, from whom human beings can learn a lot (F.M.). Horses, on the other hand, are the dream objects of boys, whose umbilical cords are often buried in a horse coral in order to make the boys into good 'cowboys' (Chisholm, 1980).

My suggestion is that we cannot simply apply the set of 23 characteristics defined by LeVine and Campbell and 'measure' or even 'describe' Navajo ethnocentrism by means of it. Our procedure should be different in order to reach a justifiable analysis. I propose to follow four steps; I will illustrate them to some extent by means of the Navajo example to make clear what differences in approach result.

the four steps:

a-b) first ethnography and preliminary identification of the cultural intuition: the very notions of ethnic identity, enemy, and so on differ from one people to another.

The boundaries between peoples may remain fuzzy, but that is not altogether problematic, provided any local group can identify with the picture of self and others that is reached. It is clear from the examples that Hindi, Sikhs and Indian Muslims seem to have strict conceptual demarcations which are explicitly formatted in religious exclusivity for some (e.g. Muslims, probably Sikhs) but not for others (Hindi), and which are expressed in power facilities (possibly for all concerned) but not in residential segregation. On the other hand, ethnocentrism clearly expresses itself in a combination of religious and residential exclusivity (ghettoes) together with intolerance at a more behavioral level (i.e., with regard to clothing, food habits, etc.) in the West. In the former something like 'tradition' (meaning at the least belonging to a certain descent line which shares a history of habits and attitudes) of the group seems to serve as a bedding in which ethnic identity and ethnocentrism versus others are built. In the case of the West (at least over the last two centuries) both identity and ethnocentric refusal of others seems to be conceived as an aspect of the individual (or the small group): one has certain feelings, attitudes, concepts, etc. in a person-to-person relationship. The way the 'problem' of immigrants is handled in political and media circles expresses this very well: it reads as if 'the immigrant' has the (private) choice to adapt himself as a member to the rules of the host community, just as the host claims to adapt to the foreign culture when going abroad. Often the notion of citizen or free choosing individual is brought in to define the arena of discourse: each individual acts and reacts, believes (in a particular view on religion as a system of beliefs), sins, has a sense of dignity, and so on. This definition of ethnocentrism does not necessarily apply in the case of the second party, in casu the immigrant. As was shown above with Hindi and Navajos, personal attitudes and outlooks may be next to irrelevant. Summing up one could say that the cases of the West and India differ widely in the definition of ethnocentrism. The category is each time conceived of in a totally different world of experience and behavior: the locus of ethnocentrism and identity is either a tradition or a (presupposedly) free willing individual.

In the Navajo case it seems (at first glance) as if the people as a whole form the locus of operation and within the people what is recognized at any moment as the tradition. Individual or group preferences, attitudes and beliefs matter very little. The very fact that beliefs are not the essential binding matter of Navajo ethnocentrism is illustrated by their tremendous capacity to change habits, adopt foreign uses and so on and 'make them their own'. The latter is a second major distinction between Navajo and western ethnocentrism: anything foreign will be adopted provided it proves beneficent and is introduced by a member; there are no fixed beliefs on which to base a judgment for or against something. This does not mean that 'anything goes', but rather that negotiations, deliberations and judgments about identity or foreignness are made in different registers than in the West (in casu, nature will show whether something is beneficent or not, according to Navajo lore; one cannot decide in advance). Finally, to finish this very preliminary sketch, a double system seems to operate within this Navajo way: others are potentially dangerous or contaminating (see the 'enemyway' ceremonies), but 'tradition' can change all the time and is structured to allow for adaptation. This system should be taken into account as well in the description of Navajo ethnocentrism.

I hope these remarks make clear what is at stake: before we start describing or measuring something at the object level (what attitudes, feelings, beliefs, etc.) we should have an insight into the presuppositions, the 'root principle' behind behavior, habits and explicit lore in that community. This 'root principle' will then guide the researcher in the procedures for step b, after which we will be able to characterize the principle more adequately.

c) the second ethnographic description

At this level the researcher will elicit and describe in depth the problem area. Hostile reactions, indifference, support in behavior and in language will be recorded, questioned and discussed with the consultants. Any type of auxiliary technique for this study can be used (e.g. questionnaires or experiments), but the researcher should be fully aware of the translation gap and of the possibility of more or less great differences in attitude and outlook between his and their culture. The best way to reach dependable results, I think, is to have one's own interpretations and conclusions constantly controlled by consultants and to check any answer by individual consultants as well (see Pinxten, 1981 for more detail).

The 'root principle' which was arrived at in the first step will be used as a rule of guidance for this ethnographic research. Of course, results from the field work may induce changes in the insights on a particular root principle. In this sense ethnocentrism with the Navajo will be analyzed much less in terms of the person-linked criteria advanced by LeVine & Campbell. Instead, the main focus will be on the operations of tradition and on the explicit and implicit image of self and 'enemy' in Navajo oral culture. This analysis will be supplemented by observations of behavior vis-à-vis foreigners. However, if I am right in my intuition about the Navajo notion of 'enemy', again particular behavioral attitudes about individual 'enemies' matter less than the basic and transpersonal view on Navajohood and enemyhood, combined with the particular understanding of tradition. Hence, the analysis of feelings and beliefs about the 'other' yields information about a *cultural* syndrome, rather than a psychological or social psychological one. When I interpret my empirical research along these lines, I can project that the structure of 'Navajo ethnocentrism' differs from that of White ethnocentrism in some remarkable ways:

–the fact of being an 'enemy' is a cultural given, determined by birth or by education (according to the traditionalist or the modern version). Feelings of hatred or esteem are not necessarily implied, but 'contamination' by a member of any other culture may be more relevant as a by-product.

–the fundamental harmfulness of enemies correlates with their stupidity and invites protection of the Navajos by a specialist-healer; this protection can eventually be provided by a foreigner (as medicine man).

–enemies should not necessarily be killed: they only imply more risks on the side of the Navajo. Navajos enter a dangerous and, according to their standards, sometimes 'stupid' path when intending to kill enemies. It really depends on the circumstances whether killing is wise or stupid; it is never brave in itself. In other words, the virtue is not in the killing of the enemy, but in the correct judgment of the opportunity, the risks involved and so on.

My point is that the identification of Navajo ethnocentrism (to stick to this example once more) will yield a list of criteria which will supplant the 23 items list of LeVine & Campbell. This list will have other entries than the ones recognized as universal features by the latter. Finally, the basis of analysis will be different: I start to describe and analyse Navajo ethnocentrism in terms of the Navajo 'root principle' in this conceptual and behavioral complex. Hence, the Navajo intuitive understanding of people and tradition, instead of their attitudes and outlooks with reference to the individual or the small group (which is the Western focus) is the fundamentally relevant issue. Ethnocentrism in thought and behavior is a consequence of a 'given' cultural condition, irrespective of interpersonal or individual feelings or attitudes. In a nutshell: habits, attitudes, thoughts, and values either belong in the tradition or with 'the people' or not. When they do, they are identified as 'Navajo' and hence beneficial, harmonious or otherwise 'according to the orderly way'. If they do not, they are considered non-Navajo and hence dangerous, disharmonious or inimical. The fact they appear to change position over time is not relevant. Every generation has to redefine its place in the universe and (tacitly or explicitly on seers' or speakers' advice, see Pinxten, 1979) hence the content and extent of Navajohood and 'enemyhood'. Navajo ethnocentrism is thus framed in terms of the 'root principle' which is the final reference in these matters: Navajohood (defined in terms of birth or tradition). Psychological or social psychological features are irrelevant in this respect.

A still different identification is to be expected in the case of Hindu ethnocentrism. I speculate (since empirical data are not known to me so far) that a social and historical belonging, a membership of the same or different traditions defined in such terms, is the 'root principle' here. Individuals, groups or peoples who do not belong in the tradition of the Hindu will be foreign, again irrespective of the psychological or social psychological aspects. In contrast, the sharing of the same religion, the same language and the same territory in the West form the 'root principle' for the identification of Western ethnocentrism. Given the terms of this principle, ethnocentrism has a more prominent psychological and social psychological aspect there: beliefs, communication strategies and linguistic content, and territorial property are more directly tied to individuals and small groups in the West than elsewhere and hence can be felt first and foremost as personal and interpersonal matters. Again, in my view, this is a cultural feature of the West, but it could explain the narrow focus on psychological and social psychological features of authors such as LeVine and Campbell. (A further example of the value of such a 'cultural' approach is given in the study of European-immigrant forms of ethnocentrism by Erkens & Balagangadhara, 1990).

d) the comparison of different cases.

On the basis of the foregoing steps a picture will result about ethnocentrism in culture X, and in culture Y and in community Z. Of course, X, Y and Z can stand for dominant groups and subordinate groups, for immigrants, for different cultures, and so on. The important point is that a genuine picture can only be reached in the painstaking way outlined so far. Comparison then becomes possible, although it will not be as simple or straightforward as it appeared (rather too hastily and onesidedly, as I have been trying to show) in the views of LeVine & Campbell or of Van den Berghe for that matter. Let me draw a few lines, again mostly of a speculative nature.

The (social) psychological characterization of ethnocentrism entails the existence of difficulties in settlement, joint schooling, and so on which are not found in Navajo ethnocentrism. The latter yields a principal (innate) disrespect for others which does allow at the same time for practical collaboration on several domains (living, working, schooling, marrying, etc.), and total exclusivity on other points (knowledgeability, nationality, etc.). In actual policies these differences should be taken into consideration: e.g., my prediction is that it will be impossible to have a joint Navajo-Hopi nation, but it will perfectly possible to have a joint Flemish-Walloon state in Belgium. On the other hand it will be highly improbable to have a peaceful community of Catholics, Protestants, Muslims and atheists in one neighborhood in Belgium or Holland, but it will be no problem at all to have this variety living in one place in a Navajo tradition.

From these studies a sharper and better documented view on the different cultural forms of ethnocentrism should result. The views or models, and the correlations of features within these views, may be subject to comparison rather than individual characteristics in different communities.

e) the IMF, differences and overlaps, and looking for universals a posteriori.

The results of description and analysis in the former steps are mapped onto what I call the IMF (or Intercultural Meta Frame). The IMF contains all relevant information of all the groups involved, checked and controlled throughout the research process by these groups. Putting all this information on one common date base it will be possible for all involved (and for the researcher or policy planner) to look for overlaps, separations and oppositions between the cultural frames of 'we' and 'they' for all parties.

Finally, and as a result of the foregoing steps, universal features (if any) will be yielded by this type of research. The universal characteristics will be based on and produced by empirical research, though, based on the identification of 'root principles' in each and every community under comparison. I can refer the reader to the beautiful chapter on *Local Knowledge* by C. Geertz in his book with the same title (1983) where he develops a rather similar suggestion with regard to law and juridical 'sensibility' in three different cultures. In the end there is no clear-cut positivistic definition of law or rights, bur rather a better understanding of the hidden unity in the fascinating diversity he has been discussing.

f) intercultural negotiation.

Eventually, both the researcher and the parties involved can determine on the basis of this type of research if and where space for intercultural negotiation, conflict and/or conflict management or resolution can be found. This point will be elaborated upon in the last chapter of this book (see also Rubinstein, 1993 and Pinxten, 1994).

4. CONCLUSION

My aim in this chapter was to show that comparative research on ethnocentrism has been done in several ways in the past, but that it is up for a serious reconsideration now. The basic novelty (although it is as old as the term itself suggests) is to focus on the importance of the implicit knowledge, in behavioral attitudes and in speech acts, which is termed here 'root principle'. This emphasis stresses a provisional deeper understanding of the cultural phenomena first (to reach the 'postulate' level) and to use the intuition as a guiding principle in the actual empirical research. This approach will permit the identification of cultural phenomena in the terms of the culture (instead of in those of the researcher) and will guarantee closer control on the results of analysis (since the representativity of the 'root principle' will show in any object level description and hence in model and theory formation). This approach is then elaborated on to some extent with regard to ethnocentrism studies.

Finally, the relevance of a focus on cultural knowledge (in casu, through the identification of a root principle) for the study of cultural phenomena (be they primarily 'religious' as in the cosmology research or political as in the case of ethnocentrism) remains a major feature of my position.

PART IV

PHILOSOPHICAL ISSUES AND ANTHROPOLOGY

CHAPTER 8

Objectivism versus Relativism:
What Are We Arguing About?

If we stand a chance at all of saying something sensible about cognitive relativism, it will largely be because of the qualities of my audience and the charm I may add in my attempt to seduce it. If this chapter suffers the fate of so many others and goes unnoticed, it will largely be due to my misunderstanding of the parties in the debate. I see myself taking an odd stand in the debate referred to in the title: I am a universalist (or objectivist), who professes the heuristic importance of at least one kind of relativism. This is the essence of my message.

1. ON WHAT THEY SAY

I distinguish between objectivists (instead of absolutists, etc.) and relativists. Within both categories one finds a wide variety of forms. For example, relativism can be global or local (Weinert); epistemological or propositional (Knorr-Cetina); cognitive or cultural; moral or reason-bound (Lukes); and so on. Instead of summing up the vast range of possible variations, I will focus on the particular positions of some authors while neglecting others. However, I want to emphasize that a comprehensive overview and appraisal of the field would help us a lot in sorting out just exactly what it is that is being talked about in the heated debate between the objectivists and the relativists.

Objectivists traditionally seek universals, that is statements about the world that are true irrespective of the psychological, sociohistorical, or cultural context of their producers. Depending upon the nature of the 'rock-bottom' that one identifies, one could discern two main positions within objectivism.

Firstly, there is the more traditional objectivist who wants to determine the truth of a statement by referring to the ontological reality. Secondly, there is the latter day (post-Kantian) objectivist (Weinert, 1984), who is hesitant about an ontologically founded argument and would rather situate universal truths at the level of theories about the world, that is, in the apparent consensus regarding the scientific explanations of phenomena. Popper and the logical positivists are recent examples of the latter version. In a sense, the second form is a weaker version of the first, since no ontological commitments are required. Though in recent debates some further positions have been put forward (Quine, Putnam), I do not think that they go beyond the basic couple presented here in any substantial sense. On the basis of such an ontological/theoretical rock-bottom, one proceeds to test the truth of statements/theories or evaluate the models, be they from one's own culture or from elsewhere. An example that has become famous because it is used extensively in discussions of this sort is the Azande oracle as reported by Evans-Pritchard (see Barnes, 1974, Chapter 2, for an overview). Although the oracle uses systematic, rational, tested, and efficacious knowledge from an (internal) Azande point of view, that knowledge is not accepted by us Westerners as valid, because it is neither simple nor falsifiable and, moreover, incorporates *ad hoc* beliefs of the sort that we traditionally classify as irrational. However, as Barnes (op.cit.) suggests, the sociology of science since Kuhn has shown that several scientific procedures may then not qualify as rational either, and consequently will not yield the type of true statements we believe they did. An extreme example is provided by Campbell (1979), the methodologist of experimental psychology, who likens the scientific experiment to a divinatory oracle, thus suggesting that its product (knowledge) is somewhat similar to oracular knowledge.

This brings us directly into the relativist literature. A lot of relativists have been refuting particular claims of objectivists. I will not follow this line of approach in the present paper. Instead, in order to gain some clarity, I will identify four distinct versions of cognitive relativism and deal with the most interesting of them in some detail. Before doing so, however, I would like to say that 'cognitive relativism' is used as a generic term here, encompassing claims about the relativity of knowledge, perception, conceptualization and the like of which Kuhn's (1970) incommensurability of paradigms is probably the best known version. To understand the epistemological implications of this point of view better, one would do well to look at Hesse's analysis of the foundations of this type of relativism. According to her, theories or paradigms are validated by facts, which, in turn, categorize experiences. Factual statements can only be universal if one has an independent (and thus universal) observation language at one's disposal. This is the old logical positivist prerequisite. Hesse (1970) claims that we do not have such a language, and, consequently, cognitive relativism validly states the theory-ladenness of facts. In my view, this is a clarifying interpretation of the claim of cognitive relativism in Kuhn's theory. Another version of cognitive relativism points to the influence of the *Weltanschauung* of the scientist's community on observation, meaning and the construction of facts in science: "In short, science is done from within a *Weltanschauung* or *Lebenswelt....*" (Suppe, 1977, 126). This form of the hypothesis focuses on the cognitive background, the worldview or common sense of the scientist as a member-of-a-culture. This emphasis complements the former where the main concern was with facts and theories, while remaining within the boundaries of what are considered scientific aspects proper.

A third type of cognitive relativism is linked with the names of Lukes, Hollis, and Horton. Lukes does not deny the relativistic nature of world views, theories or paradigms. However, he sees the observed differences as superficial phenomena. Underlying these differences one obtains an (a prioristic) universal criterion of rationality. This criterion should include rules for truth, in its semantic or correspondence version, and the elementary rules of logic (1973, but also 1982). It is this infrastructural rule system that allows for cross-cultural understanding serving, as it does, as a universal 'bridgehead'. Barnes (1974) offers an interesting critique of this proposal and suggests an adoption of a universal foundation. Neither truth nor rationality can be solid universal bases, but:

> "The manifest variability in institutional natural beliefs is to be made intelligible by being set against an unproblematic baseline of normality..." (1974, 41-42).

What this baseline would consist of is vaguely identified as patterns that are 'culturally given' (ibid). I grant that Barnes spotted the difficulties in Lukes' proposal, but I have difficulties with his alternative: what is 'normal' is either again subject to particular cultural norms, and is thus subordinated to a relativity principle on a meta-level, or it is trivial, in which case it has no relevance for epistemological problems. For example, we all have stereoscopic vision, we are bipeds, but the link between these givens and the level of sophisticated knowledge is at best indirect.

The final, and in my opinion the most interesting type of cognitive relativism is to be found in a small circle of theorists of science, that is people studying other great civilizations. (It is amazing that members of different circles notwithstanding exceptions like Restivo, Bloor, or Elzinga know so little about each other). Scholars in this line of research try to determine whet her and to what extent science may have cultural components (Elzinga & Jamison, 1981). In profane words: Is there a Chinese or an Islamic science, as some have claimed, and, if so, in what sense do they differ from Western science? An outstanding figure in this debate is Needham. In his monumental *Science and Civilization in China* (1961, Vol. 5) he challenges the relativistic distinction between Eastern and Western science. One could say that his basic tenet is that modern science is one and is universal. However, traditional science (i.e. medieval or Chinese or Hindu science) produced dependable knowledge on particular problems within a particular socioeconomic and cultural setting. It did not achieve the level of universality characteristic of modern science, because it remained subordinated to the particular religious world view or natural philosophy it grew in (e.g. Needham, 1969). Some of those who have discussed his work have suggested that the relativism which Needham discerns in traditional science holds for modern science as well (e.g. Restivo & Zenzen, 1978; Sivin, 1984). Elzinga and Jamison pick up this line of thought: any particular scientific tradition develops in a cultural context, which defines *"the basic understanding of the man-nature relationship"* (1981, 21). Thus the dominant harmony and equilibrium model of the dominant Confucian class in China expressed itself in a philosophy of organicism. This in turn led to a use of science and a moderate development of scientific development through innovation in China. In the 13th century, when science was seen as having served its purpose of satisfying the perceived needs, a state of equilibrium was attained. On the other hand, the mercantile ideology of the new dominant class in Europe (in the 16th to 18th centuries) used science more and more as an instrument to develop its own power through the worldwide exploitation of nature. Or, to cite Needham:

> "Interest in Nature was not enough, controlled experimenta-
> tion was not enough, empirical induction was not enough,
> eclipse prediction and calendar calculation were not enough
> –all of these the Chinese had. Apparently a mercantile culture
> alone was able to do what agrarian bureaucratic civilization
> could not– bring to fusion point the formerly separated
> disciplines of mathematics and nature-knowledge." (1972, 44).

Thus particular internal features (e.g., the fusion Needham refers to) are influenced by particular cultural (in this case socioeconomic) factors. The socioculturally induced *values* (e.g., mercantile moral values) have to be taken into account in the discussion of relativism. This reminds us of the features that Merton (1972) refers to as characterizing modern science: values of universalism, communism, disinterest, and organized skepticism.

2. ON THE WAYS TO ARGUE

Unfortunately, philosophy is as much in the grip of the division of labor as any other human activity. This had led to the genuinely deplorable situation where philosophers of science do not know (or, worse, do not care to know) about empirical epistemologists, or about rhetorics (i.e., the theory of argumentation). I believe that the new rhetorics in particular can be useful in our debate. In a nutshell, I claim that objectivists and relativists can benefit from a short excursion into the theory of argumentation in order to gain clarity as to what they are arguing about, or perhaps even to become clear as to whether they are arguing at all.

Perelman and Olbrechts-Tyteca (1958) took up the task of reviving interest in rhetorics in the classical sense of Aristotle's *Topica*. They used modern psychological, sociopsychological, and cultural anthropological data and models to develop a systematic, modern *Treatise on Argumentation* (1958). The two volumes comprise an almost complete classification and typology of all relevant concepts. This new rhetorics has now developed into a flourishing branch of philosophy. However, argumentationalists around the world have created their own circles in close connection with students of law. I was inspired by Geertz's search for parallels between his relativist epistemology and legal theory (especially the last chapter of his 1983) to try to apply the new rhetorics to the problem area of this paper. Perelman and Olbrechts-Tyteca's now classic work starts with the basics: any argument develops between a speaker and an audience. The speaker can only be effective if certain conditions are fulfilled:

– the speaker should have an adequate understanding of the audience (in terms of its composition, prejudices, etc.). The more he can represent the view of the audience, the more successful he will be;
– the speaker should be clear in the use of his terms;
– the speaker should be aware of the type of argument he is presenting: for our purpose, he may aim to *convince* the audience or may aim to *persuade* it of a point of view.

Conviction is predicated of that type of argument which claims to present a rational, universal truth and thus focuses on a universal audience (humankind).
Persuasion is possible with that type of argument which claims to be true for or acceptable to a particular audience.

Perelman and Olbrechts-Tyteca demonstrate that speakers in philosophy (or science) always address a universal audience. That is, they focus on gaining the largest possible adherence to their arguments. Historically, the arguments addressed to a supposedly (in the mind of the speaker) universal audience are of a special brand: they are believed to be true, unavoidable, or as close as possible to objective reality. The use of this sort of argument (here termed 'to convince') implies the (mostly implicit) *exclusion* of those in the audience who do not subscribe to the '*objectivity*' or '*universality*' of the arguments by calling them mad, old-fashioned, queer. Sociologically speaking, an elite audience is declared to embody or stand for the universal audience in this type of argumentation (see especially op. cit., par. 7). Thus, in actual fact, because of the objectivity of the argument, a specific philosophical and scientific audience is identified by the speaker as standing for the universal audience (humankind). The authors point to a case that interests us especially (op. cit., par. 10): the scientific discourse. Here, a priori knowledge (as in logic or mathematics) and hard facts (as in some experimental sciences) are declared true (or highly probable) in themselves, and those addressed are ipso facto a universal audience. Within the framework of argumentation theory, the authors appreciate this as 'a fiction' (op. cit., 60). Indeed, from their point of view, the sociohistorical reality is such that a certain set of speakers and a particular audience (the scientists) declare certain types of arguments to be universal truths. From an argumentationalist point of view, scientific groups thus *act* the way theologians are used to acting. The shock of relativistic statements (notably that of Kuhn's timely point) then comes from the fact that the proclaimed objectivity of knowledge is questioned. With this move, the claims regarding the universality of these arguments and the representativity of the so-called universal audience (of scientists) are called into question.

Now, the fundamental point which the intelligent audience I am addressing has seen coming is that of *values*. According to Perelman and Olbrechts-Tyteca, both the premises and the steps of the argument must solicit the agreement of the audience. To this end, a given audience will subscribe to concrete values: a Western audience may generally agree with such values as loyalty, solidarity, discipline, while Confucians point to a particular set of life values that they acknowledge (op. cit., par. 19). The universal audience will base its adherence on abstract values, such as the perfection of God, or a priori truth. The more the arguments attack the latter values, the more they are seen as 'revolutionary'. I will now apply some of these insights to create order in the chaos of the debate between objectivists and relativists.

3. ARE WE ARGUING?

It will be obvious that objectivists fall nicely into the category of the 'universal audience'. The ontological objectivist declares that reality-in-itself is revealed in a certain way, and thus forces 'anybody in his right mind' to subscribe to a certain point of view. That is to say, the speaker and the audience who identify with this position state that there is perfect correspondence between reality and the message that is brought forward. I think that this correspondence can only be demonstrated in one of two ways: either it is revealed in some way, or it can be shown to be the case by applying a valid search procedure. Since revelation is not accepted any more in the contemporary philosophy of science, which is what concerns us here, the objectivist is led to convince the critic of the well-foundedness of the abstract values he shares. This gives us an interesting variation of objectivism we know about: Bohm's plea for multiple realities (see the excellent presentation in Restivo, 1981). Bohm claims that sciences produce universally true knowledge of that type of reality which can be known at that moment. If my interpretation is right, this introduces a fundamental ontological relativism in order to save the claims to universality that the scientific group has at a given moment. In fact, since this position drops the highly valued and safe assumption about the one and only ontic reality, it threatens to lose most of its adherents to objectivism. (This may be the reason why Campbell, 1977, speaks of ontological *nihilism* instead of ontological relativism). Bohm and Restivo have a logically tenable position, to be sure, but its values are hard to share.

The epistemological objectivist, of the second type that I distinguished, retreats one step in his commitment: adherence to the message does not depend on an ontological commitment, but on subscribing to a set of statements (a theory, a paradigm) that are necessarily true. Within present-day epistemology, I think that this position requires a sharing of truths, which are seen as universal either because they are true a priori, and thus without reference to empirical testing of any sort, or because they are *"the fully accepted beliefs of our current science"*, as Barnes would put it (1974, 6).

None of the relativists actually questions or argues against the ontological objectivist (realist). This, again, is the reason why Campbell (1977) can reasonably claim to be both an ontological realist (an ontological objectivist) and an epistemological relativist: all types of relativism that I have distinguished deal with an epistemological problem. The relativists of type 2 and 3 (*Weltanschauung* and bridgehead types, respectively) discuss not so much ontology as the type of correspondence theory that we should adopt.

Type 1 (incommensurability) seems to discuss internal epistemological values: should we share consistency as a value in order to be a universal audience? Type 4 discusses an overarching set of values: should we value a certain type of usefulness, contextuality or justifiedness defined in terms of other socio-cultural values? In what sense is science itself a cultural phenomenon (local knowledge), and if it is, how can universal truth be conceived?

If this analysis is correct (i.e. if it wins your adherence), it follows that the opposition between ontological objectivism and any type of epistemological relativism that I have so far distinguished is a false problem. Both can coexist and can be combined in a respectable way by the same audience. Note that I am not convincing you or persuading you to adhere to this combination, even though I myself am a realist. I am only arguing on a meta-level: they are not mutually exclusive because they speak of different things. When one claims that ontological objectivism necessarily entails epistemological objectivism, one actually says that some version of correspondence between reality and theory is a conviction that should be shared. The existence of such a correspondence can only be presupposed. Hence, it is a value that one is asked to share in order to qualify as a truly universal audience within that context of argumentation.

Do epistemological relativists actually argue against epistemological objectivists? I think that they do. In fact, in this discussion we can discern oppositions between value statements within one and the same level of discourse. However, I think the *gradual* diversifications in belief are more numerous than the opposition. For example, if Lukes, Horton and others of the same persuasion claim to adhere to some notion of bridgehead, they in fact express the high value they attach to the existence of some beliefs, which have a similar status for the universal audience as the a prioris or law like statements have for the objectivists. Lukes claims that some universal criteria of rationality should be accepted, if one is to explain to some degree the prevalence of organization in any society (1973). That is to say, from within the frame of argumentation theory, Lukes claims that a 'real' universal audience 'in fact' shares a certain type of rationality (across cultures) which constitutes the basis of universal truths. Or, humankind is said to factually value some kind of rationality, which is what makes the development of systems of knowledge (in the present case: common sense) possible. I believe that Barnes' normality notion serves the same purpose. Thus, these approaches are not relativistic in a genuine sense, but only challenge a dominant ('scientific') view on epistemological objectivism in order to replace it with a cross-culturally founded one.

A similar argumentative move can also be discerned in the *Weltanschauung* version of relativism. Let me elaborate: the proponents of this version suggest that the content or the premises of different knowledge traditions are different, but that their rationality is the same. This comes down to an 'objectivism' along the lines of Lukes. Alternately, if they claim that both content and rationality criteria differ, they belong to the fourth version (see below).

The incommensurability argument of Kuhn and others is clearly internalist in my view: it questions the value of consistency which was/is shared as an abstract value (in Perelman's terms) by the universal audience of scientists. As such, it is a critique of the long dominant view that consistency should be shared as a value by the universal audience of scientists, but it does not imply a genuine relativistic view. Rather, it makes the point that one of the values formerly held needs to be dropped without, however, giving up the objectivist position.

Finally, we turn to the 'great civilization' version. I suspect that this type of comparative studies, together with the history of science and the sociology of science, is likely to yield the most fruitful insights. At one level, it may provide us with criticisms of the a-temporal, self-declared universality of an audience. While such criticisms are, by themselves, both valuable and healthy, what is more important in this version is that it may deepen our awareness of the values we actually share and (sometimes coercively) thrust upon others in the course of an argument. Needham himself does not join us here: he sees a clear rupture between traditional science (with local knowledge) and modern science (with universal truth), even though his critics have pointed to difficulties with this stand (e.g. Sivin; Restivo; op. cit.). The analysis of a system of knowledge as a particular cultural system with a particular audience sharing a particular set of values has hardly begun. The comparative work can only be carried out after such an analysis. I am personally of the opinion that this type of research may somehow yield a more documented view of the (im)possibility of a genuine relativistic epistemology. However, it will require a lot of empirical (descriptive and comparative) work. We may then eventually be led to accept what I call 'universals a posteriori'. That is, I suspect that we are able to communicate and interact with each other in order to arrive at some common understanding regarding the way we see and think about the world; about the limits of and constraints on well-founded or dependable knowledge; and, perhaps, even about "good" (i.e. commonly cherished) ways to use it. But all of this will only be ours gradually and as a result of a long, more or less open-minded, empirical epistemological analysis, conducted with an awareness of our criteria of adherence and with a willingness to change commitments.

It is thus that by traveling the long and hazardous road of providing an empirical foundation for a possible relativistic epistemology (of the fourth type) that we will have the universals for an objectivist epistemology on an a posteriori basis. Meanwhile, the relativistic attitude can be used as a sensible heuristic in epistemology though such a use is not without its dangers, as witnessed by the postmodernists. I claim that this is its main value, and one which I want to share.

CHAPTER 9

Philosophical-Anthropological Speculations: Intercultural Negotiation

1. THE WORLD OF THE FUTURE

In 1989 practically nobody foresaw the collapse of the Berlin Wall, neither were there realistic prognoses on the disintegration of the Soviet Union, the civil war in Yugoslavia or the many other nationalist movements that have since won the front-pages of our newspapers. A year later the rather sudden outbreak of the Iraq war shook the whole world and certainly forced Jews, Muslims and Christians to face each other as social and political reality. Most probably this war led to feelings of humiliation and hatred (in many Muslim groups), possibly it yielded some hope for a sovereign state (in Palestinians), and certainly it triggered an attempt to impose a 'global culture' idea which would embody 'basic human values' in the eyes of the victorious parties. Without doubt the future will have to tell us what became of the dreams and of the effects of New Order ideology. However, already in 1991 the Soviet empire is actually crumbling, notwithstanding the warnings and the expressions of agreement of the formerly most powerful leaders of the world. At the same time, immigration from Eastern Europe and from African countries to Western Europe is escalating (amounting to over 400.000 refugees in 1990 alone). This dramatic evolution is countered by a smaller and silent movement in Europe: Vietnamese immigrants are organizing their own re-immigration into Vietnam now, since in their opinion the beginnings of the same decentering and disintegrating breakdown are to be spotted in Vietnam and China. If they are right (and I honestly think we cannot say they are not, taking into account our serious misjudgment about Eastern Europe) a good part of the world is in a very serious turmoil and nobody can predict the end of this as yet.

Together with this perception of a growing turmoil it is obvious to anyone who travels in the world of today that products and techniques, sometimes also values of the dominant West are spreading rapidly: soft drinks, television, video games, clothing, and what have you originating in the West are sold and produced the world over. Beyond that, Japanese and South Asian firms produce and sell 'clones' of these products in a vaster amount than any western firm may ever have thought imaginable. The world of finance is becoming more international-intercultural than ever before, and the production of weapons has long stopped to be a western privilege. Fashions and threats (be it with drugs or with epidemics) are perceived more and more to become 'global' rather than western. All this may lead us to forget that globalization or culture borrowing trends have been a marked phenomenon as well. Only the speed of diffusion, and possibly the scale of the spread differed. Indeed, both technologies (see Needham 1965, Vol. 1) and material goods have been imported in Europe from days immemorial (with notable peaks during the Roman empire and after 1400) causing the Westerner to dress in Asian and African material, to eat, drink and smoke Chinese, Indian, American Indian and African goods in different forms and in vast amounts for centuries. The perception of this inward movement seems to have differed from that of the outward movement, though: whereas the former does not lead us to consider ourselves becoming 'Africanized' or 'Indianized', the latter does prompt some of our thinkers to profess that the whole world is gradually 'westernized'. It is, in nobler terms, developing a European-based 'global culture' according to some.

The foregoing paragraphs are not meant as an analysis of the political and ideological situation in the present day world. If Kremlin watchers and other specialists in the field are unable to produce decent and dependable analyses, who would I be to try my hand at it? This short description of 'faits divers' is only meant to highlight what looks like two main options now in the prospective views on the world: one believes in global culture, a unified world, basic human needs and values and such like; the other emphasizes the growing diversity and the utter disintegration of greater units to yield national or even regional independent entities. I think a third way is more likely. Let me expand a little bit on all three alternatives.

a) global culture

One view on the political future of our planet is that, notwithstanding local differences at the present time, the world is gradually developing into a basic monocultural world with a solid foundation in universal values and universal truths. This perspective on humankind is expressed in the political views of today by the President of the United States of America (State of the Union of 1991) where he professes that a New World Order is growing and should be implemented everywhere. The New Order would feed on a cultural foundation which is gradually becoming global, that is shared by all peoples in the world. One thinks of the culture of highways, television, hospitals, telephone and so on. However, this globalization view is not only held by politicians of a powerful nation. It is shared by a group of scientists and philosophers who are engaged in global studies and research into worldwide systems. In the domain of the social sciences and philosophy two better known groups can be mentioned: the traditional positivists and the 'global culture' adherents.

Traditional positivists claimed that the knowledge and technology of the West is spreading all over the world and will soon be determining the tastes, habits and thoughts of all citizens of the world. Their question is not whether one perspective on humankind and culture will reign supreme and supplant all other, so-called primitive or less-developed views on the universe, but rather when this 'glorious' stage will be reached and by what measures it could possibly be enhanced. The latter questions are not arrogant, though they may be one-sided and overzealous. The basic belief is that scientific knowledge -as a decontextualized and universally true type of knowledge- is one pillar on which to found a culture of humankind, a watered down version of Christian values (as expressed in the Universal Declaration of Human Rights) being a second one. Both science and basic human values would be guarantees of the superiority of this view on humankind, and this superiority will hence bring forth the unity of the world in and by itself. The knights of this idealistic view fight the 'backward' and 'misunderstanding' proponents of other perspectives in the name of and by means of these two 'universal' means. In science and philosophy this perspective is known as the 'received view' (Suppe, 1977), and although it had to deal with a series of blows over the last decades it continues to be very popular among the elites of the West. The critiques have been various and (in my view) damaging: postmodernism accuses the defenders of the positivist view of blindness and rashness in their beliefs, indeed of a sort of dogmatism; social studies of science have shown that ANY form of thinking is contextual and historical and hence fallible (e.g., De Mey, 1984; Campbell, 1979); moral philosophers attack the very notion of universal value and question the universality of ideas of progress, human rights and the like (Claes, 1991; Pinxten & Claes, 1989); philosophers question the very notion of knowledge as universal truth in progress (Feyerabend, 1987; Laudan, 1982).

The 'global culture' group is a somewhat related stand. The group around Wallerstein, Featherstone and others (gathered in the journal Theory, Culture and Society) is a powerful representative of this viewpoint. Being social scientists and historians first and foremost, their analysis is more careful and more subtle than that of the positivist philosophers. In the volume edited by Featherstone (1990) a series of positions and arguments of the group are brought together. A particularly interesting chapter, I think, is that by Robertson (1990): he emphasizes the ongoing phases of globalization rather than any static or 'finished' version of global culture. With the growing disintegration of the nation states as indisputable units of social order and ideological meaning in the present era Robertson sees a further phase of globalization setting in. He develops a five phase model of globalization which catches the historical shift from regional political units, over nation states towards a global culture (up to this day):

– phase 1: the germinal phase from around 1400 till around 1750 in Europe with the down playing of the medieval society and the emergence of national communities. On the ideological level we see ' Accentuation of concepts of the individual and of ideas about humanity.' (1990, 26).

– phase 2: the incipient phase between (roughly) 1750 and 1870 with the actual growth of national states. Nationalism-internationalism becomes a major theme.

– phase 3: the take-off phase between 1870 and 1920: inclusion of some non-European states in 'international society'. The rights of individuals in a nation are thought about, and the international order is gradually implemented. Special indicators for the latter are: *"Rise of ecumenical movement. Development of global competitions- e.g. Olympics, Nobel Prizes, Implementation of World Time and near-global adoption of Gregorian calender. First World war. League of Nations."* (1990, 27).

– phase 4: the struggle-for-hegemony phase: till the 1960s. Nationalism at its worst, with many international conflicts. Dominance of a few Superpowers.

– phase 5: the uncertainty phase lasting into the 1990s: the Third World is included in global consciousness, the prospects of nuclear annihilation and ecological disaster are seen as global problems. More and more societies become multicultural and polyethnic.

It is difficult to assess the depth and the long term effects of such trends of globalization. The long term aspects are most readily seen when considering an archeological or evolutionary timespan, rather than a historical one. In one of his most cited papers Lévi-Strauss (1987) remarks that the differences between cultures living today seem to be smaller than between the latter and the ancestral cultures living thousands of years ago, certainly in the minds of contemporaneous people (p.25). Hence, in the minds of the peoples and in the model of the archeologist the gaps seem to be narrowing. Going from there to concluding that a global culture is emerging, is, also for a universalist like Lévi-Strauss, a shift in thinking: within the foreseeable future intercultural differences (and the ethnocentric or racist discourse correlating with them) will be the dominant features of sociocultural life, rather than global culture. Just like in the foregoing centuries the survival or decline of cultures will be dependent upon the power of one or more dominant society; hence, Lévi-Strauss's appeal near the end of his paper to all anthropologists and biologists to join forces in order to safeguard a sociocultural atmosphere of tolerance for 'otherness'. Archeological, let alone evolutionary, comparisons of this sort are highly speculative and often tell us more about the ideology and cultural history of the proponent than about the cultural reality focused on, as Lévi-Strauss argues at great length (idem). Falling back on historical time, which at the face of it looks more manageable, we are confronted with multi-interpretability of facts and trends as pointed out above. In short, the predominantly unilinear development which is implied in the globalization idea can not easily be recognized or measured in a serious way, and may well be an ideological stance in disguise.

The depth factor adds a supplementary difficulty for the researcher. Indeed, how are we going to determine the relevance or importance of a feature or a trend? To what extent are merely ideological factors at work, or to what extent is the futurist in the social scientist playing along in a game of perpetuation of power dominance and hence of blindness for ethnocentrism in his own views? Let me illustrate this point a bit.

Is the material change of a culture –e.g., the fact that all world citizens adopt soft drinks and television– a sign of the decline of little or native cultures, or is this only a superficial effect which is then taken to be fundamental by the exporters of these cultural goods? In still other words, how can we measure or evaluate the impact of cultural changes and the adoption of imported goods and habits on a culture? Citing a striking example, a Japanese who marries in a catholic church (because the ceremony is charming, according to some of my informants), is buried according to a Shinto tradition (because that is the custom, according to the same informants) and practices Zen (because that is efficient in a stressful society), is living up to Nihonjinron (i.e., the typical Japanese tradition) while adhering to all these, apparently different traditions. Whereas such mixture of 'religions' (whatever that term may mean, Balagangadhara, 1993) would be regarded as paradoxical, heretic or otherwise unacceptable in Judaic, Christian or Muslim religious circles, it is said to be typically Nihonjinron by the Japanese. They need not believe in the Christian lore, and feel no urge to subscribe to any Buddhist or Shinto doctrine in order to be 'typical' Japanese in this scheme. What is adopted is a practice, a fashion, or a habit. On the basis of such examples (and they can be multiplied for numbers of cultures outside the European sphere) it is not obvious at all what westernization or globalization of culture will mean, other than superficial borrowing of goods and techniques. Like all superficial phenomena they can disappear as fast as they come, to be superseded by import from elsewhere or by internal innovations.

When this analysis holds water, it follows that both historical and structural assessments of the growth of global culture in the present era are less than convincing. At least, in historical time, e.g;, for the next decades, and at a non-trivial level of culture change such a stand can not decisively be argued for.

b) a scattered world

A second school of thought in these matters holds the opposite view that empires are crumbling and that the revival of nationalism and regionalism is to become the central theme for the decades to come. The breakdown of major units and spheres of influence in the last decade of the twentieth century is interpreted in this way: not only is the Soviet Union disintegrating and giving birth to the 'old' states of Latvia, Ukrania, and many others, but a variety of peoples and proto-nations all over the globe are ready to demand or declare their independence from larger units. A visionary critic like Schlesinger (1991) professes that a similar process of internal split (e.g. through civil war) is to be expected in the USA as well. Whatever the value of such analyses and prophecies may be, it is clear that a different picture of the future world emerges from this perspective: the globe will turn out to be a patchwork of many different little political units. The units may define themselves in terms of languages, religion, ethnic origin or what have you. They may be trading with each other or warring with neighbors. In any respect, the grand scheme of a world culture will be next to nonexistent for decades to come in this prospect.

A few remarks are in order here. First of all, it looks as if the reaction of national and regional identity movements may indeed just be that: a reaction to former dominance by a superpower or great nation, which was never really accepted by a myriad of smaller ethnic or language groups. The Russians dominated the catholic Balts, the Muslim Azeiris and the Asian peoples in the Soviet Union, just like the white protestant kept on ruling over the blacks, Indians and Chicanos of the USA (whatever legal standards have been adopted meanwhile). This position of subordination is overcome by revolting against the dominant culture. However, the force and identity which triggers a revolt may not in itself suffice as a basis for a future political unit. The many cases of the past come to mind here: Belgium grew out of a revolt against foreign dominance, but does not constitute a solid basis for nationhood for the people concerned; the same can be said about many former colonial regions which keep on struggling for internal stability and anxiously seek for a national or religious unity which could withstand or overcome the traditional factionalism in terms of languages, tribes, and so on (by way of example Israel, but also Iraq, Mauritania, but also South Africa, etc. can be mentioned).

Recent overviews of literature on nationalism and culture add a series of important remarks. First of all, Foster observes that both anthropologists and politicians have come to look upon nations as *"cultural products, and of nationalism as a cultural process of collective identity formation."* (1991, 235). Hence, the contemporary and conscious promotion of 'national cultures' in different parts of the world. The apparent success of this political theme seems to testify to the fact that the 'scattering' process referred to above is a reality to stay with us for several decades to come. On the other hand, however, the fragmentation is not the sole trend. The growth of a global culture (at least at the material and economic level) can not be ignored. Hence the suggestion that *"globalization and localization of cultural production (may be) two moments of the same total process..."*(1991, 236). Such a view opens up a new avenue for thinking about the present world situation, since it dissolves the unlikely dichotomy which forces to choose between a global culture and a myriad of local cultures as a viable model.

c) the third alternative

In my view a third perspective should be added. It is as speculative as the other two, and yet it does not hold the exclusive view on the world (implied in the dichotomy of globalization versus localization) which is characteristic of them. In my view, a third movement of cultural integration can be discerned in the world of the near future (some of these speculations are inspired by the dynamic model for political evolutions which was developed by Adams, 1988 & 1991). Together with the movements for local or regional independence one can witness a marked change in moral, cultural and political dominance of cultural areas. Thus, the Gulf War made clear that, although the West (and mainly the USA) may be the greatest military power of the eighties and nineties, the appeal of the Western ideological model is fading both in Islamic countries and in black Africa. Some hold that both in the West and elsewhere in the world the era of ideologies may be over. Not only have both the major nineteenth century ideologies (liberalism and Marxism) lost their appeal, but no new ideology has come to the fore. Not one encompassing ideology or world view seems in order, but expression of stands, preferences, and so on on particular issues and problems. Negotiation then matters rather more than conviction, situational and person-bound values override global ideologies or world views. If this analysis holds water, then all communal or global problems will have to be handled through knowledge of each other and by means of negotiation. It is in this perspective of a post-modern world (politically speaking post-imperialistic and post-communist) that this book is meant to convey a message.

What I see on the international scene is a breaking down of the grand and globalizing ideologies and their temporary replacement by local (and often still older) practices and urges. Thus, whatever Sadam Hussein may have been, and in whatever way he was represented to the Western public, it appears that his reception was very different in Islamic countries and in the poor Black communities of the South. Field workers in these areas invariably point to these differences. In a similar way, Islamic groups and states in the southern part of the Soviet Union seem to be turning away from Moscow and at the same time attack the 'Christian' populations to the north and the west of them (Armenians, Ukranians, and the like). Simultaneously, the formation of a more or less 'Slavic' union to supplant the Soviet Union over he latest decade gives a hint –whether or not it will persist is less important than the fact that it appears as a culturally viable solution for the peoples concerned– of the larger political units that can be expected in that area of the world. In the Turkish immigrant communities of Western Europe these evolutions are the subject of lively debates. The humiliation felt by Muslims during the Iraq war is translated in higher ethnocentric thresholds between European natives and Islamic immigrants in Europe and elsewhere (for example, in the typical tourist destinations of Morocco, Tunisia and Algeria). The substantial braindrain from the Soviet Union and other Eastern European countries enables the new industrial countries (like Thailand, Korea, and so on) to buy highly qualified scientists at a retail price and thus enhance their jump forward on the world market of political power. Meanwhile, the Japanese sphere of influence is growing slower than before, but at the same time a clearly powerful and appealing area of Southeast Asian economic and cultural center is coming to fruition: Korea, the Philippines, Thailand, but also India are growing out of serfdom and defining their own course in culture and politics again. A somewhat similar trend can be pointed at both in Western Europe and in South America. In both cases, growing or manifest economic power is being translated into a cultural revival and slow, but steady political unification or collaboration. Within each and every of the units mentioned a diversity of ethnic, religious and cultural groups at the lower level of extension can be mentioned (be it Sikhs in India, separatists of sorts in Europe, and so on), but at the same time a crystallization of large cultural areas seems to emerge. That at least is my view on the situation.

When one would try to project these trends in the near future, a particular picture is shaping up. The world of the next decades will not be characterized basically by one global culture, even though one may hope and expect that some global programs of research and political decision making may survive the present era of turmoil. Neither is it the case that the world will be hopelessly scattered in 400 or more little states that will wage war on each other. A more likely pattern, it seems to me, is that both these trends will continue to develop at the same time, but at a rather low pitch or with regard to particular problems only. A third, intermediary political structure will emerge, according to my speculation, based on a broader cultural layer of common values and preferences for a group of (former or new) nations. What is new to us, Westerners, in this third trend is that it runs counter to our rather naive or ethnocentric expectation that 'all will become like us' in the end (the globalization belief).

What larger units or blocks do I see? Provided the USA and the EU (possibly expanded with parts of Eastern Europe and Russia) will subsist and continue as they do now (in 1992), I foresee the rapid development of one or two Islamic blocks (maybe a North African one and an Asian one, the latter possibly including parts of the present-day USSR), a South East Asian block (possibly with Japan), India and China, South America (with dominance of Brazil and Argentina), a Pacific block, a black African block (at some point in the distant future). These different large units may have more or less strong relationships, confederacies, defense treaties and so on with particular other ones, and less of that with some others. The net result may be that at one point in time from three to ten blocks may be actually operating on the world scene. The important point, however, is that at least some of them have a particular cultural view on the world and carry a particular set and a particular hierarchy of values, which are not necessarily shared by any other block in exactly the same way. In actual practice, over half of these blocks (and certainly more than half of the world population) are non-western in tradition and lifestyle and have a different perspective on values, politics, religion and the meaning of life. Of course, this is and has always been the case so far. The major difference that will occur, in my speculation, is that over the last four or five centuries the West has been progressively more successful to impose its own political and economic rule upon all other cultures and states and has come to believe that hence European values could safely be used as THE bottom line (to be) shared by all participants in intercultural interaction and communication, on an individual basis and on the scale of the world (through the formation of nation states and of international organizations of states). The continued use of Human rights as a sanctioning universal instrument in international politics and in trade testifies to this effect. This dominance of one superpower is decaying rapidly, without there being an alternative superpower to take the lead

(Huntington, 1995; Kissinger, 1994). The net result is that different cultural-political areas fall back upon themselves and question or turn away from 'westernization' at a fast rate. The best examples are Japan and the Islamic countries, but in my sketch I generalize this trend to cover the whole globe.

Notwithstanding this trend toward medium-large blocks, as I see it, some global problems and worldwide needs will persist, and even grow in urgency. Population growth, hunger, ecological threat, military overspending, and so on, are global problems which demand a treatment in unison of all powers in the world. With the disappearance of the one paradigm or the unique and dominant cultural-political perspective, these global problems will have to be treated in a frame of mind of negotiation between cultural value systems that differ and are often radically opposed. It is here that the sort of comparative study that I advocate in this book becomes essential as a tool to reach negotiation. In order to illuminate this point, I have to turn briefly to a discussion of negotiation first, and try to sketch a view on intercultural negotiation afterwards.

2. ON NEGOTIATION

Negotiation studies that are relevant for the present study can roughly be divided in two categories: formal treatises and qualitative analyses. The formal treatises originated in the mathematical subdiscipline of game theory, but gradually expand to become a discipline on their own. I will mainly draw on Raiffa (1982) here. The qualitative analyses can be found in political theory, business and management research and intercultural studies. The so-called Harvard Negotiation Project may be one of the better known examples in this area (Fisher & Ury, 1981), but contemporary analyses of intercultural negotiation will hold my attention primarily (e.g., Hofstede, 1991; Rubinstein, 1992). I will consider the contributions from both approaches consecutively.

a) what is negotiation?

    In a general way people solve disputes by means of a variety of procedures and techniques. Tradition or habit is one such type: we choose a certain option rather than a second one, because we always used the first one in the past (it is typical for the house, the tribe, the club, etc..). Negotiation is another avenue to settle differences or disputes. I exclusively focus on negotiation, because in my view different traditions will persist and hence render agreement between cultural blocks by means of (one) tradition next to impossible.

    First of all different kinds of disputes can be distinguished from each other. Raiffa (1982, 11-19) sums up a series of twelve formal characteristics for disputes: two or more parties, monolithic parties or not, unique or regular negotiation, one issue or several topics of negotiation, linkage between issues or not, need for an agreement or not, need for ratification or not, the possibility of threats, the presence or time constraints, the binding character of contracts, the private or public nature of negotiations, and the possibility of intervention of an outsider. The different values on these dimensions call for a different approach to each particular process of negotiation. For example, when three parties are involved it is sometimes possible to make coalitions, which is of course excluded in a two party dispute. Each particular negotiation situation is a specific combination of each of the twelve formal features Raiffa lists. Since these features are so obvious, an analysis in detail is unnecessary.

    More important for my purposes is Raiffa's treatment of auxiliary elements in the negotiation situation. This analysis is directly relevant for the rest of my argument, provided I can fill in the categories in a more empirical way. One option Raiffa defends is that the role of external interveners should be considered as much as possible, such that these interveners *"behave in order to help the negotiating parties in some impartial, balanced way."* (1982, 22). The intervener can facilitate the negotiation process (in bringing the disputants together around the table): one distinguishes between types of interveners such as the mediator, the arbitrator and the rules manipulator. The mediator is the more neutral intervener who tries to aid negotiators to find a compromise agreement.

He cannot force or even suggest a solution, but should rather help the parties in finding a common ground to continue talks and plan for an agreement. In the case of a multicultural world mediators would operate as anthropologists-diplomats: they should know about the value system of both (or all) parties and point to possible grounds of communal interest. No global solution (of a scientific or a religious or an ideological nature) can prevail, but parties are made conscious of each other's traditions, backgrounds, interests, and so forth. In a following paragraph I will dwell upon the way such a mediator can work in a negotiation process.

The arbitrator can do the same as the mediator in helping the parties to find a common ground, but *"if these preliminary actions fail, the arbitrator has the authority to impose a solution."* (idem, 23). Such instances as the judge in the Western judicial system come to mind. It is clear that in the multicultural world sketched above, only supranational organisms could have such a role. The present institute of the UNO may be a candidate here, although its authority 'to impose' a solution has always been slight. In that respect, no rapid and drastic change is to be foreseen, nor is an alternative announcing itself.

The manipulator has the authority to alter the rules, and hence to change or constrain the process of negotiation (idem). In cases of deadlock such an authority may manifest itself and unlock the negotiation process by suggesting a change of rules such that all parties can be satisfied in the new game. In the subject under consideration in this chapter one can think of scientists (anthropologists or others) or politicians who are not directly involved in the dispute and can be acceptable at some point for all parties involved as rules manipulator. No general prediction seems possible, however, and each case will have to be looked at separately.

Raiffa stresses that for each and every negotiation situation (and of course for the introduction of any of the agents mentioned) a thorough and rational analysis of the situation is a first requirement:

> "The principle theme of the book is that analysis – mostly simple analysis – can help. It can help a single negotiating party as he thinks reflectively about what he (prescriptively) should do, given the assessment of what others, in some quasi-rational descriptive sense, might do." (idem, 359).

A major contribution from the qualitative approaches is that of Fisher and Ury (1981), the protagonists of the Harvard Negotiation Project. Rather than disregarding the (obvious) formal characteristics of negotiation they add a further level to the research (and the practice). In that sense, their book may be characterized as being concerned with 'meta-negotiation' (Rubinstein n.d.). Fisher and Ury claim that a lot of the bargaining or negotiation that goes on in the world can be identified as 'positional bargaining'. That is to say, the parties take and defend a particular position which is then guarded with such engagement that most energy is often spent in holding onto or defending the position, rather than negotiating for an 'objective' issue. In a sense, the party identifies itself with the position. The position can hardly be left or modified without loss of face, dishonor, and so on, and the negotiation can be seriously blocked or even made impossible when positions are seen to be opposed, exclusive or contradicting. In the end, the real interests of the parties is overshadowed by the positions defended. In the context of the present book, I think this positional negotiation is easily recognized as a trap for parties that have a conscious and explicit ideological or religious character. The fierce and seemingly endless religious wars between different Christian denominations in the 16th and 17th century come to mind, as well as the bloody wars between Christians and Muslims (in the Middle Ages and today). Finally, antisemitism, fascism and Stalinism can be pointed at as ideologies which drove parties to hang on to positions, at the cost of many lives. The list is of course not exhaustive, but the examples are the ones most readily agreed upon by any political group today.

In contrast with this type of negotiation Fisher and Ury develop the method of 'principled negotiation'. They say (1981, 14):

> "in contrast to positional bargaining, the principled negotiation method of focusing on basic interests, mutually satisfying options, and fair standards typically results in a *wise* agreement. The method permits you to reach a gradual consensus with a joint decision *efficiently* without all the transactional costs of digging into positions only to have you dig yourself out of them. And separating the people from the problem allows you to deal directly and empathetically with the other negotiator as a human being, thus making possible an *amicable* agreement."

The four principles of principled negotiation are discussed at length in the book:

a) separate the people from the problem: what one should address is the problem, as an outside given, not to be identified with.

b) focus on interests, not on positions. Some of the interests may be common to parties, and the solution of the problem should be one of them. A position is a solution in the interests of one party only (at least in the perception of that) and not necessarily a solution in the interests of all involved.

c) generate alternatives, look for many possible solutions before embarking on the negotiation talks.

d) have results checked against one or the other objective standard. That is to say, the interests of all parties can be identified as values in a meta-frame, which is not the frame of one party only. When reasoning in terms of this and the other three principles it will appear that positive outcomes can often be reached for all parties involved. Apart from the fact that 'all win', this method has the advantage of leaving the ground open for possible future contact.

I think everybody will agree that the principles are sound and the results may be superior, certainly when negotiators have to confront each other on a more regular basis. Since we are all living on the one planet earth, this prospect of repeated or even regular negotiation between parties is rather the rule than the exception in a multicultural world. The problem that remains is whether the Fisher-Ury model can be used easily and efficiently in the multicultural world I projected. When do we know a negotiation is 'good' or 'improves' the relationship between the parties? How can we judge efficiency in negotiation, except from the standpoint a particular culture's values (in this case the North American or maybe Western values)? In all fairness, Fisher and Ury do not explicitly claim to address the problem of multicultural negotiation. But of course, I do. I propose that, what we miss in the model is a comparative perspective on values and 'truth s' (or reasons) of cultural groups. The analysis of intercultural negotiation will make clear what is meant here.

b) intercultural negotiation

If my projection of the future world as a multicultural conglomerate of several culturally defined blocks, then a series of important negotiation situations will emerge which are inherently intercultural. That is to say, the European Union will undoubtedly have internal negotiating parties (regions, countries, eventually southern versus northern coalitions, and so on), but the values, common institutions and explicit policies they share will be outnumbering by far the differences they may have. Even in the past the difficulties we have seen arising between the United kingdom and the rest of the E.U. have never jeopardized the concept or the actual institution of the E.U.; they only slowed down progress in the eyes of the majority. 'Against' the rest of the world, E.U. unity (based in common economic interests) has been a greater common value than the separate demands of each of the members. The common interests have allowed for temporary or issue-centered coalitions and oppositions with several other 'blocks' over the past twenty year s: with the USA, with Arab countries, with Eastern European countries, and so on. The emphasis in this short history of the E.U. seems to be on the priority of economic dominance and of security. Over the past few years (and probably aggravated by internal economic problems and by the external policy leading to the Gulf War) the North African and Arab countries seem to be progressing toward an Islamic model that unites a series of Islamic interests and identifies itself against Western political, cultural and economic dominance. The so-called Islamists (be they Iran- or Saoudi-oriented) profess a turning away from Western models and a repletion of Muslims on their own tradition of values and habits. Those governments that are seen as Western-oriented come under the attack of the Islamists (in Algeria, and possibly in Egypt, but certainly in Senegal, Tanzania, and other places) and the old political views of the prophet Mohamed are heavily discussed anew (see Vermeulen, 1993). In the former Soviet Union a similar emergence of one or two blocks can be witnessed. Negotiations between these emerging blocks can not be carried out on any value-free or neutral basis. Neither can it take for granted that European (or North American) values are THE human values. Not only does such an attitude implicitly install a new colonial dominance in any negotiation process (explicitly rejected by more and more Islamic countries to begin with, followed by other Third World countries), but moreover does the death of ideologies in the West forego such a choice in the Western blocks themselves. Finally, as Blondel shows us in his comparative study of governments, the history of value systems contradicts the simple unilinear political thought that has been dominant in international negotiations of the West with other parts of the world: Blondel (1990) points to a basic trend in governmental types: with the lack or diminution of (material) wealth a worldwide emphasis on linguistic, ethnic or religious identity (or division) can be witnessed. With the growth of wealth these divisions seem to diminish in power and appeal (1990, 74). In the present era the decline of generally and equally spread wealth (because of different reasons: international guilt, overpopulation, ecological threat, and so on) seems to lead us to a world divided by cultural differences, rather than a world united by common interests. Hence, negotiations in the coming decades may well be between blocks with different, viz. opposed value systems, where the common interest is far from clear in the eyes of the negotiators.

Blondel mentions in passing that it may be appreciated as an oddity that only since the 80s a growing interest in the status and impact of the 'cultural factor' can be witnessed in the research in this domain. Along my hypothesis the analysis of the value systems, the habits and beliefs of cultural communities is what we should be thoroughly engaged in in order to conduct 'efficient', 'good' or peace enhancing negotiations in the world of the next decades. A major problem of analysis (in the sense of Raiffa) then becomes: how would we gain knowledge about and evaluate the values of each 'block' in the negotiation process in order to allow for fruit ful negotiations and to avoid needless and bloody confrontation in a multicultural world? The work of Hofstede (1991) offers a basic frame here.

Hofstede came in possession of the data of an empirical research in IBM, giving details on the size and shape of 'culture' in fifty different countries (where IBM has plants or offices). On the basis of this material he develops a frame of analysis that enables him to characterize 'cultural differences', which is, for Hofstede, what the world of human beings is largely made of. His notion of culture is rudimentary but sufficient for his purpose: culture is understood roughly like in anthropology as the

'mental programming of groups or communities'. The deepest of this programming is that of values, and the outer levels are filled in by different layers of practices (symbols, idols or heroes or exemplars, and rituals). Individuals get socialized in a culture in families first and most deeply (more values, less practices), in school or other education systems (less values, more practices) and in the professional circle (still less values and more practices). Moreover, on Hofstede's model, nationalities are identified first and foremost in terms of values shared by a group and less in terms of practices, while organizations (such as businesses, political parties, and so on) have a smaller investment in values and a lar ger self-definition in terms of practices (see especially his 1991, Introduction and Part II). Within this elementary frame Hofstede can now characterize the 'culture' of nations, organizations or other social entities and compare these relative entities with correlates in other parts of the world. The most important of his work, however, has to do with his actual research on the differences and on the implied value and practice distinctions. In a painstaking analysis he tracks down the differences according on five dimensions:
– power distance: in the fifty countries (and IBM organizations) one can measure the degree to which less powerful institutions and organizations expect and accept power inequality. Thus Swedish subjects have a low power distance index, whereas Malaysia or Panama have a very high index (times 10). Less educated people tend to have a high index, versus highly educated individuals. Examples and implications are given for all major social institutions such as family, school, job situation, state and ideology.
– individualism-collectivism dimension: this dimension measures the way individualistic values (such as making private time, asking for freedom of decision in a job, seeing work as a challenge and a personal satisfaction) are opposed to or combined with collectivistic values (such as high emphasis on training, high demands in terms of quality of the work situation, or optimal use of everybody's talents). Again countries, types of families and different formats or organizations coincide with different measures on this dimension. Typically capitalist (or rather protestant) countries are much more 'individualistic' than e.g., Islamic countries.
– masculinity-femininity dimension: cultures are highly masculine if they stress sex differences and assertivity and have a high esteem for material success. Japan ranks first here. Cultures have a more feminine tendency

if sex roles are overlapping and the priority is on the quality of life rather than the quantity of production. Sweden ranks highest.
– avoidance of insecurity: this dimension measures ethnocentrism, openness or closedness for other views, other traditions. Typical forms of high avoidance are programs of protectionism and xenophobia. Typical vehicles to that end are religious systems and (exclusive) ideologies.
– long term versus short term attitude: some cultural traditions tend to stress one of these polar extremes nearly exclusively (e.g., China is very long term minded, and Germany is very short term minded), while most cultures score some where in between the two polar extremes.

Hofstede then shows how the different values on some or all of these five dimensions allow for a fuller picture of the concrete cultures of countries and of organizations. For example, a low power distance and a small avoidance of insecurity rate are typical of the 'village market' type, where bureaucracy within the organization is fought against and control is optimized and accepted. A high index of power distance and a strong avoidance of insecurity leads to pyramidal structures (with Japan as a typical example). And so on. Since Hofstede believes, like me, that the world is becoming more and more a multicultural world he draws consequences from his study for the future. He predicts that collaboration will be possible or even likely between some types of cultures and next to impossible or very cumbersome between others. E.g., high indexes of power distance will make intercultural collaboration cumbersome, whereas long term oriented cultures which differ on all other dimensions will find collaboration easier.

The relevance of this study for my purposes is that Hofstede offers at least one possible way to analyse the value structure of the parties involved in intercultural or multicultural negotiation. The emphasis on 'culture' is shown to be a valid one. In that sense Hofstede realizes a break through. The fact that he comes from a 'non-suspicious' background in this regard (he was an international manager and does not belong to the tribe of anthropologists) only adds to the importance of this endeavor.

In order to make this research fully satisfactory, I claim that the critiques of the reflexive anthropologists (or the post-modernists one might say) should be taken to heart, as indicated in the first part of this book. In anthropology we are gradually becoming aware of the ethnocentrism or culture- and theory-ladenness of our methods and data. Hence, the description and 'measurement' of cultural groups (nations, organization, and so on) by means of one common grid of categories and values, is considered by many now to positivistic and hence inadequate, because this kind of approach disregards the values, concepts and traditions of the cultures described and inadvertently universalizes (merely) Western correlates of them. The use of sociological questionnaires as a basic methodology in Hofstede's study (or rather in the IBM research he bases his analysis on) is a major handicap here. The method bypasses the cultural differences in the actual experience and transfer of the values pointed at. Hence, only rough and sometimes oversimplified pictures emerge. Comparison, then, again comes down to comparing 'images of Others in the categories of the Westerner' rather than 'comparing images of the Other in the categories of the Other'. The method of comparison I pro posed (Part I of this book) overcomes this shortcoming. One striking example in Hofstede's work may illuminate this point even more: 'femininity' and 'masculinity' are predefined as potential poles on a universal dimension in terms of the values associated with the terms in the Western tradition. Any anthropologist will object that in her or his ethnography these categories do not obtain in exactly the same sense, or not at all. E.g., Navajo Indians hold that any individual person has male and female features, as a person (both physically and psychologically). The balance depends on the mixture you have in your 'programming'. According to that view it is impossible to say of a group or society that it is more masculine or feminine: this would be a category mistake along the Navajo criteria. The problem then arises: can we say that the Navajo tradition is mistaken in its judgment on these values or not? The answer depends on whether we can identify (by any means that are transcultural or otherwise culture-free) an objective level of universal values. Although this question surpasses the scope of this book (see e.g. Claes, 1991) I want to show I am conscious of it. One answer I can readily and safely give is that it is very un like ly that the concepts and values we use in contemporary social sciences, –such as the ones Hofstede uses as categories of interpretation and comparison–, have this objective status. They rather are Western categories (Herbert, 1991; Pinxten et al., 1988). Hence they are inadequate to serve or pose as universal features against which correlate phenomena in other cultures could be measured. The only way comparison can be engaged in is by analyzing concepts and values in the native categories as far as possible (see Part II of the present study) and see from there what form and contents of comparability can be reach ed. It is my contention that such a method of comparison should be at the basis of genuine intercultural negotiation. In order to live together in the world of the future, we will have to accept (in the West as elsewhere) that different value systems obtain and should be taken for granted by all. In my futuristic projection these value systems will be more or less dominant or even monolythic in the political formations I called 'blocks'. Hence between these blocks either war or negotiation will be the rule rather than the exception, certainly for common or global problems (overpopulation, starvation, ecological disaster, etc.). The only way to enter into negotiation in an efficient or at least non-destructive way, is by analysing the interests and values of each other and the question or case at hand in a competent and adequate way (remember Raiffa's basic message). The only vehicle I see in order to perform such an analysis is that of comparative research in the sense indicated in this book. However modest or scarce the outcome of this comparison may prove to be (in contrast to the sensational, systematic, overarching comparisons one finds in structuralist –Lévi-Strauss's– or empiricist –Hofstede's– research) it is this sort of comparison I would call 'scientific', because it reaches universal truths but does not universalize local knowledge to that end.

    With this paragraph I have come full circle: I have discussed the debate on the contemporary anthropological scene and found that the strive for a decolonized science going beyond naive positivism is a valid one (Part I). Meanwhile anthropology should not loose sight of the comparative nature of the discipline if it wants to surpass the mere descriptive level. I have developed some examples of what a genuine comparison should be according to me. Finally, I have sketched my view on the political-cultural situation of the world in this very tumultuous era and concluded that intercultural negotiation will have to supplant the direct or indirect northern dominance of values and norms we have known for the past centuries. The only vehicle I see at our disposal in order to engage in intercultural negotiation is an updated and critical version of the sort of comparative study anthropologists have been working on.

CHAPTER 10
A Parable about the Past?

I had a dream tonight. I dreamt that I was walking through a big plant, with hundreds of people working here. On a platform they were putting together a mirror. Piece after piece of the mirror was brought forward and matched into the frame. The work was not well coordinated: some workers walked in the wrong direction with pieces, threatening to leave the plant; some were sitting down and looking intently at their own mirror image in the piece they held; some were wandering endlessly and did not seem to find the way to the platform. Still, the mirror took shape gradually, because a lot of the workers followed the instructions which were shouted at them by a few foremen. Whenever the mirror had a clear form, some younger worker climbed on the platform and challenged the foremen about a particular piece or a specific image in the mirror. As a result the mirror broke down. Immediately workers began gathering the pieces again and initiated a new reconstruction of the mirror.

In the focal point of the mirror a variety of phenomena were recognizable: people, the sun, heaven, the atom, nature, the object, religion, the theoretical term, the prime number and even the verification principle were among them. However, my astonishment was great: whenever I looked in the mirror and whatever construction and deconstruction I witnessed, I always missed something in the mirror image. In each every construction some of the phenomena were more prominent than others, but in the image of humankind I invariably and exclusively saw the reflection of white people.

I asked my fellow bystanders what was going on here. With care and patience they explained to me that the workers were known to everyone as the transatlantic philosophers. The mirror they called 'Philosophy'.

General bibliography

Adams, R.N.
1988   Energy and the Regulation of Nation States. *Cultural Dynamics*, 1, 46-61.
1991   *The Eighth Day?* Austin, Texas: University of Texas Press.

Anderson, B.
1983   *Imagined Worlds. Reflections on the Origin and Spread of Nationalism.* London: Verso.

Apostel, L., D. Batens, E. Breusegem, J. de Coninck, D. De Waele, R. Pinxten, J. Swings, J.P. Van Bendegem & F. Vandamme.
1979   An Empirical Investigation on Scientific Observation. Callebaut, W., M. De Mey, R. Pinxten & F. Vandamme (Eds.). *Theory of Knowledge and Science Policy*. Gent: Commnucation and Cognition, 33-36.

Ascher, M.
1991   *Ethnomathematics*. New York: Harper.

Atran, S.
1990   *Cognitive Foundations of Natural History. Towards an Anthropology of Science.* Cambridge: Cambridge University Press.

Balagangadhara, S.N.
1994   *"The Heathen in his Blindness..."* Leiden: Brill Publishers.

Barnes, B.
1974   *Scientific Knowledge and Sociological Theory.* London: Routledge.

Bateson, G.
1972   Minimal Requirements for a Theory of Schizophrenia. In Bateson, G.: *Steps to an Ecology of Mind.* New York: Random House, p. 244-270.

Berkhofer, R.
1971   *A Behavioral Approach to Historical Analysis.* New York: The Free Press.

Berlin, B. & P. Kay
1969   *Basic Color Terms.* Berkeley: University of California Press.

Bernabé, J.
1974   Temps et Conception du Monde. In Bernabé & R. Pinxten (Eds.), 335-350.
1980   *Le Symbolisme de la Mort.* Gent: Communication & Communcation Books.

Bernabé, J. & R. Pinxten (Eds.)
1974   Diversifications within Cognitive Anthropology. *Communication & Cognition*, 7, 289-435.

Bernard, R.
1994   *Methods in Anthropology.* London: Sage Publications.

Bishop, A.J. (Ed.)
1988a   Education, Mathematics and Culture. *Cultural Dynamics*, 1(2) (special issue).
1988b   The Interactions of Mathematics Education with Culture. *Cultural Dynamics*, 1(2), 145-157.
1988c   *Mathematical Enculturation. A Cultural Perspective on Mathematics Education.* Dordrecht: Reidel Publishers.

Blondel, J.
1990   *Comparative Government.* New York: Allen.

Boas, F.
1911   *Introduction to North American Indian Languages.* Washington: Bureau of American Ethnology.

Bourdieu, P.
1971   *Esquise d'une Theorie de la Pratique.* Genève: Droz.
1980   *Le Sens Pratique.* Paris: Edition Minuit.
1981   *La Distinction.* Paris: Edition Minuit (translated as Distinction, Harvard University Press: Cambridge U.P., 1989).

Boyd, R. & P. Richerson
1983   *An Evolutionary Theory of Culture*. Chicago: Chicago University Press.

Callebaut, W. & R. Pinxten (Eds.)
1987   *Evolutionary Epistemology*. Dordrecht: Reidel Publishers.

Campbell, D.T.
1964   Distinguishing Differences of Perception from Failures of Communica-
        tion in Cross-cultural Studies. In Northrop F.S.C. & Livingstone, H.H.
        (Eds.): *Cross-cultural Understanding*, 308-336. New York: Harper &
        Row.
1973   Ostensive Instances and Entitativity in Language Learning. In Gray, W.
        & N.D. Rizzo (Eds.): *Unity through Diversity.*, 1043-1057. New York:
        Gordon & Breach.
1974   Evolutionary Epistemology. In P.A. Schilpp (Ed.), *The Philosophy of Karl
        Popper*, 413-463. LaSalle: Open Court.
1977   *Descriptive Epistemology: Psychological, Sociological, and Evolutionary.
        William James Lectures*. Harvard University. Mimeo (partially published
        in Campbell 1989).
1979   A Tribal Model of the Social System Vehicle Carrying Scientific
        Knowledge. In *Knowledge: Creation, Diffusion, Utilization.*, 1, 181-201.
1987   Selection theory and the sociology of scientific validity. In Callebaut, W.
        & R. Pinxten (Eds.), 139-158.
1989a   Descriptive Epistemology: Psychological, Sociological, and Evolution-
        ary. In Campbell, D.T., (1989b), 435-486.
1989b   *Methodology and Epistemology for Social Sciences. Selected Papers.* Chicago;
        Chicago University Press.

Campbell, D.T., M. Segall & M. Herskovitz
1966   *The Influence of Culture on Visual Perecption.* Indianapolis: Bobbs-
        Merrill.

Cazden, C., D. Hymes & V. John (Eds.)
1972   *Functions of Language in Classroom.* New York: Teachers College Press.

Chapple, E.D. & Spicer, E.H.
1979   Method in Cultural Anthropology: the Crucible of the Field. In
        Newsletter AAA, 20, 2, 9-11.

Chisholm, J.
1980   *Navajo Infancy.* Albuquerque: University of New Mexico Press.

Claes, T.
1991   *Moraalfilosofie en Antropologie (Moral Philosophy and Anthropology).* Unpublished doctoral dissertation: Universiteit Gent.

Clifford, J.
1986   Introduction: Partial Truths. In Clifford, J. & G.E. Marcus (Eds.), (1986), 1-10.

Clifford, J. & G.E. Marcus
1986   *Writing Culture: The Poetics and Politics of Ethnography.* Berkeley: University of California Press.

Cohen, R. & R. Naroll
1970   *A Handbook of Method in Cultural Anthropology.* In Naroll, R & Cohen, R. (Eds.), (1970), 3-24.

Cole, M. & S. Cole
1989   *Children in Development.* New York: Freeman Press.

Cole, M., Glick, J., Gay, J. & Sharp, N.
1971   *The Cultural Context of Learning and Thinking.* London: Methuen.

Conklin, H.C.
1973   Color Categorization. In *American Anthropologist*, 75, 931-942.
1981   *An Ethnographic Atlas of Ifugao.* New Haven: Yale University Press.

Davis, P.J.
1989   Applied Mathematics as Social Contract. In Keitel C. et al. (Eds.), (1989), 24-28.

Davis, P.J. & R. Hersch
1981   *The Mathematical Experience.* Boston: Birkhäuser.
1986   *Descartes' Dream: The World According to Mathematics.* San Diego: Harcourt Brace Jovanovich.

Dawe, L.
1988   The Impact of Culture in the Mathematics Classrooms of Multicultural
        Australia. In *Cultural Dynamics*, 1, 196-209.

De Mey, M.
1984   *The Cognitive Paradigm*. Dordrecht: Reidel.

Derrida, J.
1976   *Of Grammatology*. Baltimore, M.D.: John Hopkins University Press.

de Ruijter, A.
1995   Cultural Pluralism and Citizenship. *Cultural Dynamics*, 7, 215-231.

Devereux, G.
1967   *From Anxiety to Method*. The Hague: Mouton.

Dine Philosophy of Learning/Dine Bi'ohoo'aah Bindii'a'
1989   Faculty Implimentation Handbook. N.C.C. Tsaile (Arizona): Mimeo.

Dingler, H.
1933   *Einführung in die Geometrie*. Freiburg: Schmitt.

Elkana, Y.
1981   Anthropology of Science. In Whitley D. & Knorr K. (Eds.), (1981), 1-75.

Elzinga, A. & A. Jamison
1981   Cultural Components in the Scientific Attitude to Nature: Eastern and
        Western Modes? In *Discussion Paper*, 149, Götenborg: Götenborg
        University Press.

Erkens, F. & Balagangadhara
1990   Het Migrantenvraagstuk: Probleem of Oplossing? (The Immigrant
        Problem: Problem or Solution?). In *PMS-Leven*, 90, 1, 44-62.

Evans-Pritchard, E.E.
1937   *Witchcraft, Oracles and Magic among the Azande*. Oxford: Oxford
        University Press.

Fabian, J.
1971   Language, History and Anthropology. *Philosophy of the Social Sciences*, 1, 19-47.
1979a   Rule and Process: Thoughts on Ethnography as Communication. *Philosophy of the Social Sciences*, 9, 1-26.
1979b   Interview. In: Pinxten, R. (Ed.), *Beyond Kinship, Sex and the Tribe*. Gent: Story.
1984   *Time and the Other*. New York: Columbia University Press.

Farella, J.
1984   *The Main Stalk. A Synthesis of Navajo Philosophy*. Tucson: Arizona University Press.

Farrer, C. R.
1991a   *Living Life's Circle: Mescalero Apache Cosmovision*. Albuquerque: University of New Mexico Press.
1991b   *Playing with Tradition among the Mescalero Apaches*. New York: Garland Press.

Farrer, C. R. and Second, B.
1981   Living The Sky: Aspects of Mescalero Apache Ethnoastronomy. In Ray A. Williamson (Ed.) *Archaeoastronomy in the Americas*, 137-150. California: Ballena Press.

Featherstone, M. (Ed.)
1990   *Global Culture*. Los Angeles: Sage Publications.

Fernandez, J.
1974   The Mission of Metaphor in Expressive Culture. *Current Anthropology*, 15, 119-145.

Festinger, L.
1957   *A Theory of Cognitive Dissonance*. New York: Row Peterson.

Feyerabend, P.
1968   *Against Method*. London: New List Books.
1987   *Farewell to Reason*. London: Verso.

Fisher, R. & Ury, W.
1981   *On Getting Yes. The Harvard Negotiation Project*. London: Penguin.

213

Fishman, J.
1979   Interview. In Pinxten (Ed.), (1979),127-144.

Foster, M.L.
1991   Anthropology of Peace, In Rubinstein, R. & M.L. Foster (Eds.), *Peace and War.* Boulder: Westview Press

Frake, C.
1980   *Language and Cultural Description.* Stanford: Stanford University Press.

Frankenstein, M.
1989   *Relearning Mathematics. A Different Third R-Radical Maths.* London: Free Association Books.

Freudenthal, H.
1970   *Mathematics as an Educational Task.* Dordrecht: Reidel Publishers.
1979   Struktuur der Wiskunde en Wiskundige Strukturen: een Onderwijskundige Analyse. *Pedagogische Studiën,* 56, 51-60.

Frisbie, Ch.
1987   *Jish, or the Navajo Medicine Bundle.* Albuquerque: University of New Mexico Press.

Garisson, E.
1975   *Polytheism, Monotheism, and Henotheism in Navajo Religion.* Harvard University: Mimeo.

Geertz, C.
1973   *The Interpretation of Cultures.* New York: Basic Books.
1977   From the Native's Point of View. In J. Dolgin et al. (Eds.), *Symbolic Anthropology,* Chicago: Chicago University Press, 480-492.
1979   *Meaning and Order in Moroccan Society.* New York: Cambridge University Press (with H. Geertz & S. Rosen)
1983   *Local Knowledge. Further Essays in Interpretive Anthropology.* New York: Basic Books.
1984   Anti Anti-Relativism. *American Anthropologist,* 86, 2, 263-278.
1988   *Lives and Works.* New York: Basic Books.

Giddens, A.
1984   *The Constitution of Society.* Oxford: Polity Press.

214

Gill, S.
1987   *Mother Earth.* Chicago: University of Chicago Press.

Gilliéron, C.
1987   Is Piaget's "Genetic Epistemology" Evolutionary? In W. Callebaut &
        Pinxten, R. (Eds.), (1987), 247-266.

Goodenough, W.H.
1970   *Description and Comparison in Cultural Anthropology.* Chicago: Aldine.

Goodman, N.
1989   *Reconsiderations in Philosophy, Science and Art.* Boston: Hackett
        Publications.

Gould, P.R. & R. White
1974   *Mental Maps.* London: Penguin.

Griaule, M. & G. Dieterlen
1965   *Le Renard Pâle.* Paris: Institut d'Ethnologie.

Habermas, J.
1984   *A Theory of Communicative Practice.* New York: Beacon

Haile, R.
1943   Soul Concepts of the Navaho. *Annali Lateranensi,* VIII.
1945   *Navaho War Dance, Squaw Dance.* Arizona: St. Michaels Press.
1948   *Navaho Property Concepts.* Arizona: St. Michaels Press.

Harris, M.
1964   *The Nature of Cultural Things.* New York: Random House.
1968   *The Rise of Anthropological Theory.* New York: Columbia University
        Press.

Harvey, F.
1979   Interview. In R.Pinxten (Ed.), (1979), 145-150.

Hatcher, E. Payne
1974   *Visual Metaphors.* Albuquerque: University of New Mexico Press.

Herbert, C.
1991   *Culture and Anomie.* New Jersey: Princeton University Press.

Hesse, M.
1970   Is there an Independent Observation Language? In R. Colodny (Ed.), *The Nature and Function of Scientific Theories.* Pittsburg: University of Pittsburg Press.

Hobart, M.
1987   Summer's Days and Salad Days: The Coming of Age of Anthropology? In L. Holy (Ed.), (1987), Oxford: Blackwell, 22-51.

Hofstede, G.
1991   *Allemaal Andersdenkenden (People Thinking Differently).* Amsterdam: Contact.

Holland, D. & N. Quinn (Eds.)
1988   *Cultural Models in Language and Thought.* Berkeley: University of California Press.

Holy, L.
1987a   (Ed.) *Comparative Anthropology.* Oxford: Blackwell.
1987b   Introduction. Description, Generalization and Comparison: Two Paradigms. In L. Holy (Ed.), *Comparative Anthropology*, 1-21. Oxford: Blackwell.

Horton, R.
1967   African Traditional Thought and Western Science. *Africa*, XXXVII, 50-71 & 155-187.
1991   *African Systems of Thought.* Oxford: Oxford University Press.

Hsu, F.L.K.
1979   The Cultural Problem of the Cultural Anthropologist. *American Anthropologist*, 81, 517-532.

Huntington, S.
1996   *The Clash of Civilazations and the Remaking of Word Order.* New York: Simon & Schuster.

216

Hymes, D.
1981   *"In Vain I Tried To Tell You."* Philadelphia: University of Pennsylvania
        Press.

Illich, Y.
1970   *Deschooling Society.* London: Penguin.

Ingold, T.
1986   *Evolution and Social Life.* Cambridge: Cambriduge University Press.

I.O.W.O.
1978   Five Years of I.O.W.O. *Educational Studies in Mathematics, 7, 3.*

Joseph, G. G.
1989   Eurocentrism in Mathematics: The Historical Dimensions. In Keitel, C.
        et al. (Eds.). *Mathematics, Education, and Society,* 32-35.

Jurdak, M.
1989   Religion and Language as Cultural Carriers and Barriers in Mathematics
        Education. In Keitel C. et al. (Eds.), (1989), 12-14.

Karnoouh, C.
1981   L'observation Ethnographique ou les Vertus du Paradox. In Pinxten, R.
        & C. Karnoouh (Eds.), Observation in Anthropology, (1981), 14, 39-56.
1989   *L'Invention d'un Peuple. Chroniques de Roumanie.* Paris: Arcantère.

Kay, P.
1979   Interview. In R. Pinxten (Ed.), 29-38.

Kearney, M.
1984   *World View.* Novato (California): Chandler & Sharp Publishers Inc.

Keitel, C., P. Damerow, A. Bishop & P. Gerdes (eds.)
1989   *Mathematics, Education and Society. Science and Technology Education
        Documents,* 35, Paris: Unesco.

Keyes, R.
1987   Notes on the Language of Processual Analysis. In Dolgin, J. et al. (Eds.):
        Symbolic Anthropology. Chicago: Chicago University Press, 126-138.

King, U.
1984   Historical and Phenomenological Approaches. In F.Whaling (Ed.), 29-164.

Kissinger, H.
1994   *Diplomacy.* New York: Basic Books.

Kitcher, P.
1984   *The Nature of Mathematics.* Oxford: Oxford University Press.

Kluckhohn, C.
1944   *Navajo Witchcraft.* Cambridge (Mass.): Peadbody Museum.

Kluckhohn, C. & D. Leighton
1946   *The Navahos.* Cambridge (Mass.): Harvard University Press.

Knorr, K.
1981   *The Manufacture of Knowledge.* London: Pergamon Press.

Koyré, A.
1957   *From the Closed World to the Infinite Universe.* Chicago: University of Chicago Press.

Krewer, B.
1990   Psyche and Culture - Can a Culture - Free Psychology Take into Account the Essential Features of the Species "Homo Sapiens"? *The Quarterly Newsletter of the LCHC*, 12, 24-36.

Kuhn, T.
1970   *The structure of Scientific Revolutions.* Chicago: Chicago University Press.

Lakoff, G.
1986   *Women, Fires and Dangerous Things.* Chicago: Chicago University Press.

Latour, B. & S. Woolgar
1979   *Laboratory Life.* Los Angeles: Sage Publications.

Lave, J.
1988   *Cognition in Practice: Mind, Mathematics, and Culture in Everyday Life.* Cambridge: Cambridge University Press.

218

LCHC (Laboratory of Comparative Human Cognition)
1978   Cognition as a Residual Category of Anthropology. *Annual Review of Anthropology*, 7, 51-79.

Laughlin, C.D. & E. d'Aquili
1974   *Biogenetic Structuralism*. New York: Columbia University Press.

LeVine, R.
1970   Research Design in Anthropological Fieldwork. In Naroll, R. & R.Cohen (Eds.), (1970), 246-265.

LeVine, R. & D.T. Campbell
1972   *Ethnocentrism: Theories of Conflict, Ethnic Attitudes and Group Behaviour*. New York: Wiley.

Lévi-Strauss, C.
1958   *Anthropologie Structurale*. Paris: Plon.
1962a   *La Pensée Sauvage*. Paris: Plon.
1962b   *Le Totémisme Aujourd'hui*. Paris: Plon.
1973   *Anthropologie Structurale Deux*. Paris: Plon.
1987   Racisme. In C. Lévi-Strauss, *Le Regard Eloigné*, p. 1-28. Paris: Plon.

Lukes, S.
1973   On the Social Determination of Truth. In Horton, R. & R. Finnegan (Eds.). *Modes of Thought. Essays on Thinking in Western and non-Western Societies*. London: Macmillan.
1982   Relativism in its Place. In Hollis, M. & S. Lukes (Eds.), *Rationality and Relativism*. Oxford: Blackwell.

Lynch, K.
1960   *The Image of the City*. New York: Wiley.

Lyotard, J.F.
1984   *The Post-Modern Condition: A Report on Knowledge*. Manchester: University of Manchester Press.

Malinowski, B.
1976   *A Diary in the Strict Sense of the Term*. Oxford: Blackwell.

219

Mead, M.
1970   The Art and Technology of Fieldwork. In Naroll, R. & R.Cohen (Eds.),
        (1970), 246-265.

Merton, R.
1974   The Institutional Imperatives of Science. In Barnes, B. (Ed.), *Sociology of
        Science.* London: Penguin, 172-186.

Middleton, J.
1970   Entree into the Field. Africa. In Naroll, R. & R. Cohen (Eds.), (1970),
        225-229.

Mumford, L.
1965   *American Cities.* New York: Doubleday.

Naroll, R. & Cohen, R. (Eds.)
1970   *A Handbook of Method in Cultural Anthropology.* New York: Columbia
        University Press.

Needham, J.
1965   *Science and Civilization in China.* Cambridge: University of Cambridge
        Press.
1969   *The Grand Tradition.* London: George Allen & Unwin.
1972   Mathematics and Science in China and the West. In Barnes, B. (Ed.)
        Sociology of Science. London: Penguin, 70-84.

Nordenskiöld, T.
1938   *Comparative Ethnology.* Turku: Finland.

Northrop, F.S.C. & H.H. Livingstone (eds.)
1964   *Cross-cultural Understanding, Epistemology and Anthropology.* New York:
        Harper & Row.

Owusu, M.
1978   The Usefulness of the Useless: Ethnography of Africa. *American
        Anthropologist*, 80, 310-334.
Parkin, D.
1983   *The Anthropology of Evil.* London: Tavistock.
1987   Comparison as the Search for Continuity, In Holy, L. (Ed.). (1987), 52-
        69.

220

Pelto, P. & G. Pelto
1978   *Anthropological Research.* New York: Cambridge University Press.

Perelman, C. & S. Olbrechts-Tyteca
1957   *Traité d'Argumentation. La Nouvelle Rrhétorique.* Paris: P.U.F.

Philips, S.
1972   Participant Structures and Communicative Competence: Warm Springs Children in Community and Classroom. In Cazden, C. et al. (Eds.), (1972), 110-124..

Piaget, J.
1937   *The Child's Construction of Reality.* London: Routledge & Kegan Paul.
1970   *L'Epistémologie Génétique.* Paris: P.U.F.

Piaget, J. & Inhelder, B.
1947   *La Conception de l'Espace chez l'Enfant.* Paris: P.U.F.

Pinxten, R.
1975   *Bijdrage tot een Studie van het Wereldbeeld van de Mens (Contributions to a Study of the Human Worldview).* Gent: PhD.
1976   (Ed.) *Universalism versus Relativism in Language and Thought.* The Hague: Mouton.
1976   Epistemic universals. A Contribution to Cognitive Anthropology. In Pinxten (Ed.), (1976), 117-176.
1977   Descriptive Semantics and Cognitive Anthropology. *Communication & Cognition,* 10, 89-106.
1979a Morality and Knowledge. Teachings from a Navajo Experience. *Philosophica,* 23, 177-199.
1979b *On going beyond kinship, sex and the tribe.* Gent: Story Scientia.
1980   Dimensions of science and science policy. In *Theory of Science and Science Policy,* II, 127-133. (Communication and Cognition Books).
1981   Atheism and its Cultural Anthropological Context, In *Religious Atheism,* Gent: Story, 103-124
1983   Taxonomy versus Constitution. In A. De Ruijter & J. Oosten: *The Future of Structuralism.* Göttingen: Herodot.
1987   Science and Science Policy: the Need for a Reorientation. In Gosselin, M. & L. Demeyere (Eds.). *Science and Society,* 55-68. Brussel: VUB press.
1990   An Appraisal of the Diné Philosophy of Learning. Expert Report, Tsaile (Arizona): Navajo Community College, mimeo.

1994a   *Culturen Serven Langzaam.* Antwerpen: Hadewych.
1994b   Anthropology in the Mathematics Classroom? In Lerman, S. (Ed.), (1994) *Cultural Perspectives on the Mathematics Classroom.* Dordrecht: Reidel, 85-97.

Pinxten, R., Balu, E. Soberon, D. Verboven & K. Snoeck
1988   Cultural Dynamics: A Vision and a Perspective. *Cultural Dynamics*, I, 1-28.

Pinxten, R. & Balagangadhara
1989   Rhetorics and Comparative Anthropology. In Maier, R. (Ed.). *Norms in Argumentation*, 80-93, Leiden: Foris.

Pinxten, R. & C. Farrer
1993   A Comparative View on Learning. In de Graaf, W. & R. Maier (Eds.), (1993). *Sociogenesis.* New York: Springer.

Pinxten, R. & C. Karnoouh (Eds.)
1981   *Observation in Anthropology.* Gent: Communication & Cognition Books.

Pinxten, R. & I. van Dooren & F. Harvey
1983   *Anthropology of Space. Explorations into the Natural Philosophy and Semantics of the Navajo.* Philadelphia: University of Pennsylvania Press.

Pinxten, R., I. van Dooren & E. Soberon
1987   *Towards a Navajo Indian Geometry.* Gent: KKI Books.

Priest, G.
1987   *In Contradiction.* Dordrecht: Nijhoff Publishers.

Prigogine, I
1969   La fin de l'Atomisme. *Académie Royale Belge, Bulletin 12*, LV, 1110-1117.
1981   *From Being to Becoming.* San Francisco: Freeman Press.

Prigogine, I. & I. Stengers
1984   *Order out of Chaos.* New York: Interwiley. (orig.1979: La Nouvelle Alliance)

222

Quine, W.V.O.
1960   *Word and Object.* Cambridge: MIT Press.
1969   *Ontological Relativity.* Cambridge: MIT Press.

Raiffa, N.
1982   *The Art and Science of Negotiation.* Cambridge (Mass.): Harvard University Press.

Raven, D., L. Van Vucht-Tijssen & J. de Wolf (Eds.)
1992   *Cognitive Relativism and Social Science.* Brunswick: Transaction Books.

Restivo, S.
1981   Multiple Realities, Scientific Objectivity and the Sociology of Knowledge. *Reflection*, 16, 61-76.

Roberston, C
1990   *Globalization.* Los Angeles: Sage Publication.

Rogoff, B.
1990   *Apprenticeship in Thinking.* Oxford: Oxford University Press.

Rogoff, B. & J. Lave (eds.)
1984   *Everyday Cognition: Its Development in Social Context.* Cambridge (Mass.): Harvard University Press.

Rothenberg, J.
1972   Total Translation. In J. Rothenberg (Ed.), (1972), *American Indian Literature.* New York: Harper Torchbooks.

Routley, R.
1989   Nihilism and Nihilist Logics. In Vandamme, F. & R. Pinxten (Eds.), (1989),. *The Philosophy of Leo Apostel*, vol. II, 407-452. Gent: Communication & Cognition Books.

Rubinstein, R.A.
1993   Culture and Negotiation. In Warnock F. & M.E. Hocking (Eds.), (1993), *The Struggle for Peace: Israelis and Palestinians*, 116-129. Austin, Texas: University of Texas Press.

Rubinstein, R.A. et al.
1984   *Science as Cognitive Process: A Biosocial View.* Philadelphia: University of Philadelphia Press.

Ruby, J.
1982   *A Crack in the Mirror.* Philadelphia: University of Philadelphia Press.

Salamone, F.
1979   Epistemological Implications of Fieldwork. *American Anthropologist*, 81, 46-60.

Schlesinger, A.
1991   *Disuniting America.* New York: Random House.

Schultz, D.
1989   PRIMITE-Project in Real-Life Integrated Mathematics in Teacher Education. In Keitel C. et al. (Eds.). (1989), 91-94.

Scribner, S. & M. Cole
1981   *The Psychology of Literacy.* Cambridge (Mass.): Harvard University Press.

Service, E.
1989   *A Century of Controversy.* New York: Wiley.

Shaner, D.D. & S. Nagatoma & Yuasa Yasuo
1991   *Science and Comparative Philosophy.* Leiden: E.J. Brill.

Sherzer, J. & A.C. Woodbury (eds.)
1987   *Native American Discourse.* Cambridge: Cambridge University Press.

Shweder, R.
1990   Cultural Psychology – What is it? In Stigler, J. W. et al. (Eds.), (1990), 1-43.

Sivin, N.
1984   Why the Scientific Revolution did not take Place in China or didn't it? In Mendelsohn, E. (Ed.), (1984), *Transformation and Tradition in the Sciences.* Cambridge: Cambridge University Press.

Smith, W.C.
1964   *The Meaning and End of Religion*. New York: New American Library, Mentor.

Sperber, D. & R. Wilson
1987   *On Relevance*. Oxford: Basil Blackwell.

Spradley, J.
1979   *The Ethnographic Interview*. New York: Holt, Rhinehart & Winston.

Steiner, G.
1973   *After Babel*. Oxford: Oxford University Press.

Stigler, J.W., R. Shweder & G. Herdt (eds.)
1990   *Cultural Psychology. Essays on Comparative Human Development*. Cambridge: Cambridge University Press.

Suppe, F.
1977   *The structure of scientific theories*. Chicago: University of Illinois Press.

Symposium
1977   Symposium on the Summer Healing Ceremony. Tsaile (Arizona): Navajo Community College.

Talal Asad, M.
1974   *Anthropology and the Colonial Encounter*. Edinburgh: Edinburgh University Press.

Tax, S.
1945   Anthropology and Administration. *America Indigena*, V, 21-33.

Turner, V.
1969   *The Ritual Process*. Chicago: Aldine Press.
1978   *Image and Pilgrimage in Christian Culture*. Oxford: Basil Blackwell.

Uchendu, V.
1970   Entree into the Field. A Navajo Community. In Naroll, C. & C.Cohen (Eds.), (1970), 230-236.

Van den Berghe, P.L.
1981   *The Ethnic Phenomenon.* New York: Elsevier.

Van der Veer, R. & J. Valsiner
1991   *Understanding Vygotsky.* Oxford: Basil Blackwell.

Van Dijk, T.
1984   *Handbook of Discourse Analysis.* New York: Academic Press.

van Dooren, I.
1989   Navajo Hooghan and Navajo Cosmos. Amerindian Cosmology. *Cosmos & The Canadian Journal of Native studies*, 3, 259-266.

Vermeulen, V.
1993   Umma en Kalifaat: enkele Aspecten van de Klassieke Soennietische Islam (Umma and Kalifath: some Aspects of Classical Suni Islam). In Pinxten, R. (Ed.), (1993), *Geef aan de Keizer...* Leuven: Kritak, 173-183.

Watson, J.D.
1968   *The Double Helix.* Cambridge: Cambridge University Press.

Weinert, F.
1984   Contra Res Sempiternas. *The Monist*, 67, 376-394.

Werner, O.
1979   Interview. in: Pinxten, R., 39-56.
1981   *Ethnographic Fieldwork in Ethnoscience.* Hungary Academy of Sciences, Folklore Institute: Mimeo.

Werner, O. & M. Schoepfle
1987   *Systematic Fieldwork*, 2 vol. Los Angeles: Sage Publications.

Whaling, F. (Ed.)
1984a   *Contemporary Approaches to the Study of Religion*, 2 vol. The Hague: Mouton.
1984b   Introduction. The Contrast between the Classical and Contemporary Periods in the Study of Religion. In Whaling, F. (Ed.), (1984), I, 1-28.
1984c   The Study of Religion in a Global Context. In: Whaling, F. (Ed.), (1984), I, 391-454.

Whitley, B. & K. Knorr (Eds.)
1981   *Science and Culture.* Dordrecht: Reidel Publishers.

Whorf, B.L.
1956   *Selected Essays by B.L. Whorf.* (Ed. by B. Carroll). Cambridge (Mass.): MIT Press.

Wilson, B. (Ed.)
1970   *Rationality.* New York: Harper Torchbooks.

Witherspoon, G.
1977   *Language and Art in the Navajo Universe.* Ann Harbor: University of Michigan Press.

Wittgenstein, L.
1956   *Remarks on the Foundations of Mathematics.* Oxford: Basil Blackwell.

Wolf, E.
1981   *Europe and the People without History.* New Haven: Yale University Press.

Wyman, L.C.
1970   *Blessingway.* Flagstaff: University of Arizona Press.

Wyman, Leland C.
1983a   Navajo Ceremonial System. In Sturtevant, W. (Ed.), (1983), *Handbook of North American Indians,* vol. 10, p. 536-557.
1983b   *Southwest Indian Drypainting.* Santa Fe: School of American Research.

Young, R. & W. Morgan
1980   *The Navajo Language.* Albuquerque: University of New Mexico Press.

Zaslavsky, C.
1973   *Africa Counts.* Boston: Prindle, Weber & Schmidt.
1989   Integrating Mathematics with the Study of Cultural Traditions. In Keitel C. et al. (Eds.), (1989), 14-16.